ROBOTS

ISAAC ASIMOV and KAREN A. FRENKEL

Machines in Man's Image

Harmony Books / New York

Published by Harmony Books, a division of Crown Publishers, Inc.,
One Park Avenue, New York, New York 10016 and
simultaneously in Canada by General Publishing Company Limited

HARMONY and colophon are trademarks of Crown Publishers, Inc.

Manufactured in the United States of America

Book design and display typeface by Peter A. Davis

Library of Congress Cataloging in Publication Data

Asimov, Isaac, 1920–
    Robots, Machines in Man's Image

    Bibliography: p.
    Includes index.
    1. Robotics—History. I. Frenkel, Karen A. II. Title.
TJ211.A83 1985   629.8'92   84-22758
ISBN 0-517-55110-1

10 9 8 7 6 5 4 3 2 1

First Edition

*This book is dedicated to Ms. Frenkel's father, the late
Dr. David A. Frenkel, who always encouraged her to be a
writer.*

Isaac Asimov and Karen A. Frenkel

ACKNOWLEDGMENTS

Many people generously gave us their time, assistance, and support as we researched and wrote *Robots*. We thank all robot industry members and robotics and artificial intelligence researchers for their guidance. We especially appreciate the help of George C. Devol, Jr., Joseph F. Engelberger, and Marvin L. Minsky. Without them there would have been a lesser story to tell.

   Ms. Frenkel wishes to thank Professors Robert C. Birney, John R. Boettiger, Kirtland H. Olson, and Caryl Rivers for their excellent tutelage. Special thanks go to our colleagues and friends Stephen Kindel, Jeanne McDermott, and Kristin White for sharing information and offering journalistic insight. We express heartfelt thanks to Irene G. Frenkel, Michelle D. Sidrane, and Ivy T. Frenkel, and also to Jean Fine, Gary Fishman, Roger Mummert, Marta Osnos, Jeanette Paschall, Ellen Rosenbush, Vivien Sherry, Gary Torres, and Livia Yanowicz.

CONTENTS

Color insert A follows page 54

Color insert B follows page 118

Color insert C follows page 182

THE ORIGIN OF ROBOTS: MYTH AND REALITY

EARLY HISTORY

In 1816, the great English poet Lord Byron was in self-imposed exile in Switzerland. With him one summer day was the equally great poet Percy Bysshe Shelley. They were joined by Byron's physician, Dr. Polidori, and Shelley's nineteen-year-old mistress, Mary, who later married him.

In the course of an animated conversation, they made a pact that each would write a tale of the supernatural. The results were a narrative about a vampire, which Byron never finished; a complete story called "The Vampyre" that is often attributed to Byron but which Polidori wrote, and Mary Shelley's great novel *Frankenstein*.

Mary Shelley's book was published in 1818, and although its style reflects the author's extreme youth and is overly melodramatic by today's standards, it has retained its popularity through nearly two centuries.

Indeed, there are good reasons for considering *Frankenstein* the first true science-fiction novel. It deals with the creation of life, and Mary Shelley subtitled the book *The Modern Prometheus*, after the Titan, in Greek mythology, who fashioned the first human beings out of clay. Prometheus, however, was a god and possessed divine powers. Victor Frankenstein was merely a human being who made use of new scientific discoveries (not specified in the book) to achieve the goal of creating life.

René Descartes (1596–1650), the philosopher and inventor of analytic geometry, was a mechanist who believed that the bodies of humans and animals are complex automata. In his treatise Discourse on Method, *Descartes discusses how humans, who have the power of reason, and animals, which cannot reason, can be distinguished from one another and machines. Descartes was said to have built a female automaton, which he fondly called "Ma fille Francine," c. 1640. She accompanied him on a voyage, but the captain cast her overboard, thinking her the work of Satan.*

This 1350 Italian fresco depicts Albertus Magnus (1204–82), a Bavarian bishop said to have held a banquet in honor of William, count of Holland, at which guests were served by metal attendants. Also according to legend, Albertus spent thirty years building a mobile robot that could answer questions and solve problems. When the philosopher Saint Thomas Aquinas saw it, however, he smashed it to bits, calling its inventor a sorcerer.

The book appeared at an appropriate time. Great Britain was undergoing the birth-throes of the Industrial Revolution and science and technology were making great strides. For the first time in history, wonder concerning the future path society might take became inescapable.

Frankenstein depicted the "Monster" (who had no other name) as suffering because of the callous neglect of its creator and as taking a horrible and bloody revenge. Whether Mary Shelley intended this or not, the result portrayed technological advance as dangerous, and this, too, fit in with the social preoccupations of the time—just as robots, which in some ways, are the man-made analog of Frankenstein's handiwork, rouse fears in some people that grow out of our own present social preoccupations.

While Mary Shelley was writing her book, Great Britain was in the depths of an economic depression. Workers, fearful of losing their jobs, were rioting and destroying new industrial machinery. Undoubtedly, the book reflected this wild, though, to some extent, reasonable, opposition to advances in technology. And the history of technological advance in the manufacture of artificial life and intelligence has ever since reflected this ambivalence—admiration of the ingenuity involved and fear of the possible consequences.

Fascination with the creation of intelligent life, even in the pre-*Frankenstein* era, is evident in many myths and legends. We can omit the numerous tales of the creation of actual intelligent life (ourselves), but there are myths that help describe the origin of the *concept* of robots, and it is the concept that often directs the labors of scientists and inventors in later times. What, then, of the formation of nonhuman intelligent life—objects that would someday be thought of as robots?

One of the earliest myths is of Hephaestus, the divine smith who was the Greek god of fire. He is described in *The Iliad* as having fashioned girls out of gold—no inferior substance would do. These golden girls could move, speak, and think, and helped him in his work. He also fashioned twenty three-legged tables that could move about automatically without outside guidance.

Hephaestus made his work available to human beings, too, for he was said to have fashioned and animated a bronze statue for King Minos of Crete. This living statue tirelessly circled the island, guarding it against invasion. On a more romantic note, Pygmalion, king of Cyprus, fashioned a statue of a woman of surpassing loveliness and fell in love with her, according to Greek myths. His ardent prayers to Aphrodite, goddess of love, brought relief, for the goddess consented to bring the statue to life. Pygmalion married the newly living woman and lived with her happily ever after.

Such creations were authorized, so to speak, in that they were the work of true deities. Presumably they could exist only with the general consent of divine powers.

What if life were created without such consent? Myths and legends show that people felt this was impermissible, that it was "playing God" and that there was bound to be punishment from offended deities as a result. And, to be sure, this queasy feeling due to dealing with forces we may not be able to handle still animates some people in a less theological fashion.

The case of Prometheus is an example. He was a Titan, one of the gods who had been defeated by Zeus and his allies. It was Zeus, not Prometheus, who now ruled. Prometheus' creation of human beings, without prior consultation with Zeus, was not viewed kindly. When Prometheus went on to bestow upon his intelligent creations the gifts of fire and technology, Zeus found it intolerable. Prometheus was immortal and could not be killed, so, as a punishment, he was bound to a mountainside in the distant Caucasus. Every day an eagle swooped down to gnaw at his liver, which grew back every night, to be ready for the next day's agony.

Undoubtedly, in speaking of Dr. Frankenstein as the modern Prometheus, Mary Shelley had in mind Prometheus' punishment, as well as his feat of creation.

From late antiquity through the Middle Ages, the aura of blasphemy that hovered about the nondivine creation of life intensified. The Judeo-Christian idea of God was exalted far beyond the ancient concepts of numerous, sometimes competing, and usually all-too-human gods. Rebellion against God, even to the extent of unauthorized imitation, was correspondingly more sinful.

There were legends of the creation of *homunculi* ("little men") around A.D. 250, by Gnostics and others who apparently diluted Christian teaching with various forms of mysticism and magic. In the same way, Jewish mystics created artificial human beings out of clay through the use of magical rites involving the secret name of God. The Jewish homunculus was referred to as a *golem* from a Hebrew word meaning "an unformed substance"—referring to the clay out of which the artificial life was formed. The best-known

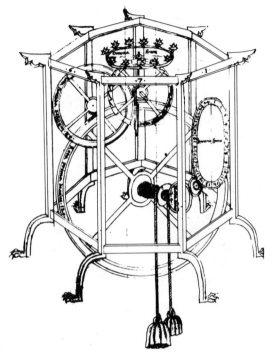

A medieval clock—no pendulum, no accuracy, but the beginning of clockwork.

ROGERIVS BACO,
Monachus in Anglia
Astrologiæ Chemiæ et Mathe,
seos peritissimus.
Nat. A. 1206.   Den. A 1284.
Ex collectione Friderici Roth-Scholtzii Nor

The English friar Roger Bacon (1214–94) described such automata as a mechanical chariot, a diving bell, a mechanical bird, and a flying machine in a chapter called "Admirable Artificial Instruments" in his book Discovery of the Miracles of Art and Nature. Bacon was also supposed to have built a brass talking head with the help of a conjurer. The team wanted to surround England with a brass wall, but first they spent seven years constructing the head because it was supposed to teach them how to complete the larger task. When the head was finally ready, it could not speak. A spirit told them that it eventually would speak, but that if they failed to hear it, all their labor would be in vain. After attending the head night and day, the friars asked a guard to watch while they slept. The head uttered the words "Time is," but the guard deemed this too trivial a statement to interrupt the friars' slumber. Half an hour later, the head said, "Time was," but again was ignored. At the end of the hour it cried, "Time is past," and collapsed.

golem is that of Rabbi Loew in sixteenth-century Prague, who formed one to protect the Jews against the accusations of ritual murder of Christian children.

Even when such examples of artificial life were formed with due invocations of the powers of God and for laudable purposes, there was always a certain uneasiness about the usurpation of God's role. All homunculi, all golems, were forced into quick destruction. Unlike the case of Pygmalion's statue, there was simply no room for such quasi-human creations in the Universe.

But these were legends. In actual fact, ingenious human inventors in ancient and medieval times were creating not artificial intelligence but devices that automatically performed the kinds of acts ordinarily associated with intelligence. In other words, they were forming not Hephaestus' golden girls but his self-moving three-legged tables, a direction of inventive energy that would eventually lead to robots.

In Western lands (perhaps in the first century A.D.) Hero of Alexandria, and, later, Ctesibius, constructed automatic devices powered by steam, moving fluids, and compressed air. Hero is supposed to have created one device that delivered holy water when a coin was placed in a slot, another shaped like a head that seemed to drink water, a trumpet that sounded through the agency of compressed air, and so on. These, and later similar devices (sometimes exaggerated in the telling), both in the West and in China, were essentially toys and wonder-gadgets of no real use.

The first truly useful devices were clocks—automatic time-telling gadgets. Hero and Ctesibius worked out "water clocks," in which a float was slowly lifted by water dripping into a reservoir, while a pointer attached to the float indicated the time as it slowly moved upward.

Mechanical clocks were invented during the Middle Ages. The motive power was that of gravity pulling on weights. Escapements were added that made it possible for the weights to force wheels to turn in regular, interrupted fashion. A hand attached to one wheel indicated the time on a dial. These clocks were not very accurate, but they were the most advanced. About A.D. 1000, the churchman Gerbert (later to be Pope Sylvester II) was supposed, in legend, to have created a talking head that could predict the future; and, in actual fact, to have constructed a clock.

Later scientists such as Roger Bacon, who devised spectacles and may have worked on gunpowder, and Albertus Magnus, who discovered arsenic, were also thought to have devised talking heads. In part, this resulted in an inability to see how wise men could be truly wise without magical help. It also expressed the continuing fear of the uses to which advancing technology could be put. There remained something blasphemous about this urge to probe the secrets of the Universe, secrets that should belong to God alone.

As clocks advanced in complexity, clockwork, the use of intricately related wheels that would cause a device to perform certain motions in the right order and at appropriate times, made it possible to manufacture objects that mimicked the actions associated with life more closely than ever. These objects that moved automatically were called "automatons."

In fact, as knowledge of the human body increased, the view arose that actual living organisms, even human beings, were themselves complex automata as far as their physical structures were involved. The human mind and soul were something else. This view was strongly argued by the seventeenth-century French philosopher René Descartes. As technology continued to advance, with the coming of such amazing devices as the telescope, the microscope, and the pendulum clock, this view made it possible to envisage improved automata that would be truly lifelike. On the other hand, it also increased fears, for the automata would have to be mindless and soulless. Therefore, if they went out of control, they could wreak much havoc. And this, too, influenced *Frankenstein*, and it influences those who fear robots today.

In the eighteenth century, as a result of the miniaturization of clocks and advancing clockmaking techniques, animated dolls developed and became the rage. Louis XIV of France requested that a German named Gottfried Hautsch build automatic toy soldiers for the dauphin's amusement. A Frenchman, Father Truchet, made a mechanical opera for the king.

In India, a ruler, Tipu Sahib, owned a six-foot mechanical tiger that mauled a toy English soldier, and in Europe and the United States, tiny figures that moved on rails set in a stage remained popular until the end of the nineteenth century. The figures performed dramas in pantomime or with voices supplied by human beings.

The most celebrated automata of the day were Jacques de Vaucanson's mechanical duck (1738), and Pierre Jacquet-Droz's automatic scribe (1774). The duck was con-

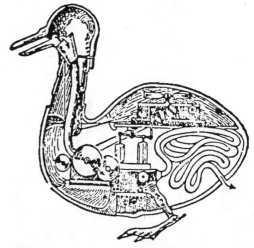

Jacques de Vaucanson's mechanical duck enjoyed greater success as an entertainer than most human performers. Built in 1738, the duck's purpose was to tour and raise money to fund experiments so that its inventor could learn to create life artificially. The copper duck quacked, bathed, drank water, ate grain, digested it, and voided. Indeed, after seeing the duck, Voltaire dubbed Vaucanson "Prometheus' rival" in his Discourse on the Nature of Man. *Vaucanson eventually sold the duck and after a series of owners, it came into the hands of an eccentric German doctor, Godfrey Christopher Beireis, of Helmstedt. In 1805, a disappointed Goethe saw what was left of the duck in the doctor's house and wrote in his diary, "the duck still ate his oats heartily, but no longer digested them."*

For thirty-five years the duck could not be found. Then a Swiss named Johann Bartholomew Reichsteiner, who operated a traveling museum of automata, found it in a Berlin clockmaker's shop. Reichsteiner repaired it—no small task since the metal creature contained over 4,000 parts, and took three and a half years at a cost of about $3,350. The refurbished animal made its debut at Milan's famous opera house, La Scala, in 1844. The duck was an immediate hit, and Reichsteiner spent another three years making a facsimile. But eventually Reichsteiner went broke due to litigation over another invention and the duck's whereabouts remain a mystery.

Invented in 1801, Jacquard looms wove patterns according to information on punched paper cards. Here an 1856 Jacquard loom and punch cards hanging above is used to weave silk tapestry. The loom and the intricate and beautiful designs that resulted offered the first glimpse of a seemingly intelligent machine.

Blaise Pascal (1623–1662) is credited with the first adding machine, pictured here. It is just one of many devices that influenced the design of Babbage's machines.

structed as a commercial venture. Made of copper, it quacked, bathed, drank water, ate grain, seemed to digest it, and voided. It was exhibited all over Europe for decades with great success and was seen and described by both Voltaire and Goethe.

The duck has been lost, but Droz's automatic scribe still survives and can be seen in the Swiss Musée d'Art et d'Histoire in Neuchâtel. The boy dips his pen in an inkwell and writes a letter.

Three years after building his duck, Vaucanson tired of it and sold it. He applied his mind to more practical matters and invented the first automatic weaving loom in 1745. The loom's control system was the precursor of today's punch cards and tapes. It is computerization that turns an ordinary machine into a robot. Such systems represented a great advance in machine-control history. With such devices a program could be imposed on a machine. The program on one hand was long and complex, and on the other could be easily altered or replaced by something perhaps just as long and complex, but entirely different.

The idea was improved by Joseph Marie Jacquard (1752–1834). He devised the "Jacquard loom" in 1801. In such a loom, needles ordinarily move through holes set up in a block of wood. Suppose a punched card is interposed between the needles and the holes. Holes in the card here and there allow needles to pass through and enter the wood as before. In places where holes are *not* punched through the card, the needles are stopped. By using different cards in a particular order, needles move through the wood and engage the yarn in a particular series of arrangements. Any intricate pattern can be imposed upon cloth quite automatically. These Jacquard looms, and even Jacquard himself, met with worker hostility, but it wasn't long before the obvious advantages of the looms forced their acceptance. By 1812 there were 11,000 of these looms in France and Jacquard was honored with medals and decorations. After the Napoleonic wars, the looms spread to Great Britain.

A punched or unpunched hole is "yes-no" information, and this concept was developed by George Boole (1815–64) into "Boolean algebra," which could be used as an analog of the rules of logic. Yes-no was the equivalent of 1 and 0 in the binary system, which in turn could be made equivalent to electrical switching devices that are either "on" (1) or "off" (0). This concept became the basis of digital computers today.

The first digital calculating machine was designed in 1823 by Charles Babbage for the British Post Office. Babbage had no electrical switches to mimic Boolean algebra. He was forced to rely on enormously slower and clumsier mechanical switches. He worked on two prototypes, a "Difference Engine" and an "Analytical Engine" (1836) but completed neither. In theory, his notions were completely correct. He planned to have arithmetical operations carried out automatically by the use of punch cards and then to have the results either printed out or punched out on blank cards. He also planned to give the machine a memory by enabling it to store cards that had been properly punched out, and then making use of them at later times when called upon to do so. The engine's physical movements were to be performed by rods, cylinders, gear racks, and geared wheels cut in accordance with the ten-digit decimal system. Bells would tell attendants to feed in certain cards and louder bells would tell them if they had inserted a wrong card.

Besides having their roots in the Jacquard loom, Babbage's machines had as their precursors various seventeenth-century mechanical calculators. Blaise Pascal (1623–62) invented the first device that could add and subtract mechanically, while Gottfried Wilhelm von Leibnitz (1646–1716) constructed a calculator that could multiply as well. These eventually gave rise to the mechanical cash registers that were features of stores before World War II, and to mechanical desk calculators. Multiplication and division of numbers could be converted into addition and subtraction, respectively, by making use of the logarithms of those numbers. The concept of logarithms was first worked out in 1614 by John Napier (1550–1617), and their use was mechanized in 1622, when William Oughtred (1575–1660) invented the slide rule, a very primitive forerunner of analog computers.

Babbage's devices would have replaced all these various calculators and slide rules had mere theory been all that counted. Unfortunately, Babbage, a hot-tempered and eccentric person, periodically tore his machines apart to rebuild them in a more complex fashion as new ideas came to him, and he ran out of money. Even more important was the fact that the mechanical wheels and levers on which he had to depend were simply not up to the demands he put upon them. A Babbage machine could not be made to work in any practical sense without electricity and, eventually, electronics—which was for the future.

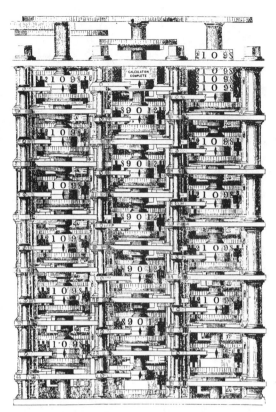

In 1812, while a student at Trinity College, Cambridge University, Charles Babbage had a daydream that machinery could compile tables of logarithms. Although neither of his two machines were completed, Babbage is credited with designing the first digital calculating machines. An eccentric mathematician far ahead of his time, Babbage moved in privileged circles, entertaining Charles Darwin, Charles Dickens, Pierre Simon de Laplace, and Alfred, Lord Tennyson. He was also capable of extreme antagonism and feuded with organ grinders because their music disturbed his work. When he tried to have them prosecuted, neighborhood children followed him through the streets, jeering and playing fifes and drums.

In 1930, Vannevar Bush completed his Differential Analyzer, which he had designed in order to compute complex differential equations that had stymied him in his study of electric power failures.

René Grillet, clockmaker to Louis XIV, created this pocket calculator in an effort to mechanize Napier's bones. The upper part of the calculator was a set of "accumulator dials"—digits were on the perimeters of the disks. The lower part of the calculator was a set of Napier's bones.

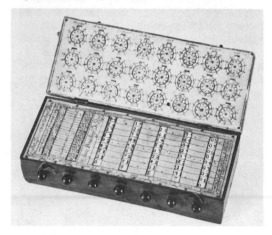

For these reasons, Babbage's work petered out and was forgotten for a century. When calculating machines of the Babbage type were eventually constructed successfully, it was because Babbage's principles were independently rediscovered.

A more successful application of punch cards to the task of automatic calculations was carried through by Herman Hollerith (1860–1929), a statistician with the U.S. Census Bureau. During the 1880s he worked out a way of recording statistics by a system that mechanically formed holes in appropriate positions in cards. The cards themselves were nonconductors, but electrical currents could pass along contacts made through the holes. In this way, counting and other operations could be carried through automatically by electrical currents, an important advance on Babbage's purely mechanical devices.

Hollerith's electromechanical tabulating machine was successfully used in the U.S. censuses of 1890 and 1900. The 1890 census of 65 million people took two and a half years to tabulate even with the Hollerith device. By 1900, Hollerith had improved his machine so that cards could be automatically fed through brushes for reading, and although the 1900 census contained still more information than the earlier one had, the count was completed in a little over one and a half years. It was estimated that hand tabulation of merely three factors, such as sex, nativity, and occupation, would have taken one hundred clerks over seven years to complete.

Hollerith founded a firm that later became IBM. The new company, and Remington Rand (under the leadership of Hollerith's assistant, John Powers), steadily improved the system of electromechanical computations over the next thirty years.

MINIATURIZATION

It was clear that the quantity of information required for industry and government to work with some semblance of efficiency was increasing so quickly that human beings would soon be unable to handle it unaided. An advancing technological society might then collapse under the weight of the inability to know what had to be known. The Hollerith device did help, but the need to know would inevitably outrun its capabilities.

It was this sort of unforgiving pressure, of *having* to handle increasing quantities of information, that drove society forward toward the invention of successively more subtle, variegated, and capacious computing devices throughout the twentieth century.

Electromechanical calculating machines became faster and were used through World War II. But their speed and reliability were limited as long as they depended on moving parts like switching relays and electromagnets, which controlled counting wheels. At first, devices that brought calculating machines closer to today's electronic computers often solved one problem but introduced others. Speed would be improved, for example, while reliability

The first mechanical multiplier was created by Gottfried Leibnitz (1646–1716), who invented the calculus simultaneously but independently of Sir Isaac Newton.

Harold L. Hazen, a student of Vannevar Bush, built this room-size computer, Network Analyzer, for representing an entire power system on a scale model. In 1934 Hazen wrote a classic paper on servomechanisms, the devices now so important to the movement of robotic arms.

remained the same and cost and size increased. It was only when transistors arrived (1948) and microchips followed that trade-offs between speed, size, and cost were no longer necessary. Speed and cheap miniaturization made possible the computer-controlled robots we have today.

In 1930, Vannevar Bush (1890–1974) and his associates at the Massachusetts Institute of Technology made the first analog computer, the first fully automatic calculator ever, the Differential Analyzer. And in 1937, Howard Aiken, a Harvard professor working with IBM, designed a calculating machine for scientific applications. This machine, the IBM Automatic Sequence Controlled Calculator, known at Harvard as Mark I, was completed in 1944. It incorporated principles similar to those of Babbage and Hollerith, with

The first automatic, general-purpose digital calculator was the Harvard Mark I, or the Automatic Sequence Controlled Calculator. Completed in 1944, it solved ballistics problems for the navy.

important improvements, and could perform mathematical operations involving up to twenty-three decimal places. Two eleven-digit numbers could be multiplied, correctly, in three seconds. Punch cards were still used, but so were electrical switches. Mark I was still electromechanical, and not electronic, and it was very large and slow by today's standards. But it was the first digital computer.

The first electronic computer was ENIAC, a digital device that came into use in 1946. Designed by John William Mauchly and John Presper Eckert, Jr., at the University of Pennsylvania, ENIAC made use of vacuum tubes. The vast numbers required for computers, however, forced ENIAC and other such devices to be very large and comparatively slow, while using inordinate quantities of energy.

The 1951 Harvard computer, Mark IV, was the size of a room. It employed vacuum tubes, the forerunner of transistors and chips.

The co-inventors of the Mark I were, from the left, Francis Hamilton and Clair D. Lake of IBM, Howard Aiken of Harvard University, and Benjamin M. Durfee of IBM. The idea for the machine was Aiken's—one he had thought up in 1937 while still a Harvard graduate student. His professor suggested that he present it to IBM.

In 1948, the transistor was invented by William Bradford Shockley and his collaborators at Bell Telephone Laboratories. It did not make use of a vacuum, but was solid throughout, and was therefore a "solid-state device." Transistors were smaller than vacuum tubes, sturdier, and required no warm-up period. They were superior in every way.

The computers that came into use after World War II already seemed to be "thinking machines" to the general public, so that both scientists and laypeople began to consider the possibilities, and consequences, of "artificial intelligence." If a computer of the proper sort could somehow be inserted into a structure resembling the human body, might we not have a true automaton—not like the toys of the seventeenth century, but more like Frankenstein's "Monster"?

Science-fiction writers had been considering this possibility all along. In 1920, Karel Capek (1890–1938) wrote *R.U.R.*, a play in which automata were mass-produced by an Englishman named Rossum. The automata were meant to do the world's work and to make a better life for human beings, but in the end they rebelled, wiped out humanity, and started a new race of intelligent life themselves. It was the theme of *Frankenstein* expanded to a much larger scale.

R.U.R. stood for "Rossum's Universal Robots." Rossum came from a Czech word *rozum*, meaning "reason," and *robot* is a Czech word for "worker," with the implication of involuntary servitude, so that it might be translated as "serf" or "slave." The popularity of the play threw the old term *automaton* out of use. *Robot* replaced it in every language, so that now a robot is commonly thought of as any artificial device (often pictured in at least vaguely human form) that will perform functions ordinarily thought to be appropriate for human beings.

The popularity of science fiction grew during the 1920s and 1930s, particularly in the United States, and especially after the establishment, in 1926, of the first magazine (*Amazing Stories*) to be devoted exclusively to that type of story. Stories dealing with robots soon became a staple of science fiction. In most cases, however, robots were viewed as dangerous. Their construction was, by declaration or implication, still held to be an example of human arrogance, invading the province of the Creator. It was the tale of the forbidden fruit, of the Tower of Babel, and of Frankenstein, told over and over again. Occasionally, though, science-fiction stories were written that viewed robots sympathetically. Notable among these was "Helen O'Loy" by Lester del Rey, in which a robot, marvelously humaniform and female in appearance, proved to be a perfect wife.

In 1939, Isaac Asimov (only nineteen at the time), tiring of robots that were either unrealistically wicked or unrealistically noble, began to write science-fiction tales in which robots were viewed merely as machines, built, as all machines are, with an attempt at adequate safeguards. Throughout the 1940s, he published stories of this sort in *Astounding Science Fiction* and, in 1950, nine of them were collected into a book entitled *I, Robot*.

Asimov's safeguards were formalized (in consultation with John W. Campbell, Jr., the editor of *Astounding*) in his story "Runaround," which appeared in the March 1942 issue of the magazine. There, one of the characters says, "Now, look, let's start with the three fundamental Rules of Robotics." This, as it turns out, was the very first known use of the word *robotics*, the now-accepted term for the science and technology of the construction, maintenance, and use of robots.

The "rules" referred to in that story are now usually known as Asimov's Three Laws of Robotics. They are:

1. A robot may not injure a human being, or, through inaction, allow a human being to come to harm.

2. A robot must obey the orders given it by human beings except where such orders would conflict with the First Law.

3. A robot must protect its own existence as long as such protection does not conflict with the First or Second Law.

These "SCOOPS" covers depict raw robot rigor. On the April 1934 cover above, metal muscles flex themselves above a dwarfed city. Below, the first issue, February 1934, a robot stalks away with human booty.

 # FEEDBACK

ttempts at controlling automatic devices in the real world with something less than these imaginary "rules" date back to James Watt (1736–1819), the inventor of the first practical steam engine. In 1789, just a few years before the Jacquard control system was introduced, Watt developed the centrifugal governor to control the energy-output of his steam engine.

Norbert Weiner (1894–1964) coined the word cybernetics *in a 1948 book with that title. Two years later, in a second book,* The Human Use of Human Beings, *he warned readers about the effects of automation: "Let us remember that the automatic machine, whatever we think of any feelings it may or may not have, is the precise economic equivalent of slave labor. Any labor which competes with slave labor must accept the economic conditions of slave labor."*

The governor operated a "throttle" control, or valve, placed in the steam pipe. After being adjusted by hand, the throttle could control the flow of steam, and was, in turn, controlled by the flow itself. If the flow increased, the governor spun more quickly and the centrifugal effect upon it was such as to decrease the flow. If the flow decreased too much, the governor spun more slowly and the flow was allowed to increase. Thus, the flow, by way of the governor, controlled itself, and maintained a fairly uniform speed, and, therefore, energy output, in the working engine.

In 1868, James Clerk Maxwell presented an analysis of Watt's governor to the British Royal Society. He recognized the significance of Watt's design as a "feedback system." *Feedback* is the return to a system of information concerning its output, permitting self-regulation. A thermostat in a room, for example, provides feedback to a house heating system by measuring and comparing the room's temperature with the temperature setting. If the room is cooler than the setting, the thermostat behaves automatically in such a way as to switch on the heat. If the room is warmer than the setting, it switches off the heat. In this way the temperature of the room is fed back to the control and, through the control, acts to regulate itself.

It is precisely this sort of feedback that controls the body temperature of warm-blooded animals (including the human being), as well as muscular balance, hormonal balance, and any number of other factors that are absolutely required to keep the living system in efficient operation.

Feedback is basic to the theory of cybernetics (from a Greek word that is equivalent to the Latin-derived *governor*), which deals with control and communication processes as statistical information. In 1948, Norbert Weiner coined the word and expounded on the theory in his book *Cybernetics*, linking the fields of neurophysiology, information theory, computers, and the control of machine tools.

In his book *The Human Use of Human Beings* (1950), Weiner anticipated that computers would be adapted to a series of judgment situations that occur in manufacturing and distribution. He saw the automatic factory as possible within a decade and predicted economic turmoil. Though proper automation in Weiner's sense did not come as quickly as he thought it would, progress was steady.

In 1950, the United States Air Force, in conjunction with M.I.T., was just beginning to apply the first numerical control system to machines on a tape that was interpreted by a computer. The tape, either punch hole or magnetic, contained instructions encoded in a numeric syste n of four to eight digits. The computer read the tape—information was not just fed, as it was to a Jacquard loom. In that sense, the computer acted both as the machine's intelligence and as its automatic controller. Variations in tape instructions could result in variations in the task the machine was to perform. The task, however, remained essentially fixed—the machine still performed the same function, such as drilling—and so numerically controlled machines are considered "hard" automata.

The first patent for an industrial robot was developed in 1954 by George C. Devol, Jr. He called its control and computer memory system "universal automation" or "unimation" for short. Devol developed thirty to forty related patents, and sold the rights in 1961 to Consolidated Diesel Electric Corporation. A subsidiary, Unimation, Inc., which was in turn sold to Westinghouse in 1982, was formed, and, with the guidance of Joseph F. Engelberger, grew into the world leader in industrial robot manufacturing. As a result of the Devol-Engelberger team, the industrial robot field took off—other machinery manufacturers recognized a market potential too.

This early automaton of a monk is thought to have been built by a Spaniard, Juanelo Turriano or Giovanni Torriani, during the early sixteenth century for the Emperor Charles V. Driven by key-wound, spring-powered clockwork, it turns its head and bows, moves its eyes from side to side, opens and closes its lower jaw, and beats its chest with its right hand while the left hand moves up and down. Although the feet imitate a walking movement, the automaton actually rolls on three wheels. It was said to fetch bread from the archbishop's palace in Toledo and offer it to the monarch, who had abdicated and was living in the monastery of St. Just.

ETYMOLOGY OF THE WORD *ROBOT*

ust as technology changed man's ability to create devices in his own image, it filtered into definitions of those devices. The evolution of automaton definitions, for example, reflects changes in the ways "self-movement" could be achieved. Attitudes toward new technologies also permeated some definitions. The origin of the word *robot* was itself a comment on technology's role in society. Whereas automaton definitions reflected the technology of the day, robot definitions remained vague regarding the technology required to make them run. Forty years after *robot* entered the English language, a definition of *industrial robot* finally specified what was meant technically, but a

IBM's Pioneer Products — and

PIONEER PRODUCTS

The First Tabulating Machines

DAYTON MONEY-WEIGHT COMPUTING SCALES, in all capacities for all mercantile and industrial purposes — both cylinder and fan types. (More than 150 models to meet all requirements.)

INTERNATIONAL ELECTRIC TIME SYSTEMS, including the famous Electric Self-Regulating System. A few representative International Master and Secondary Clocks are shown in this panel. (Models to meet all requirements.)

INTERNATIONAL PROGRAM DEVICES, for signalling, scheduling, etc.

INTERNATIONAL JOB TIME AND COST RECORDERS. Spring driven or electrically operated. (Forty models to fill all requirements.)

INTERNATIONAL ELECTRIC TABULATING and ACCOUNTING MACHINES (Hollerith Patents), for all types of accounting and statistical work. Illustrated here are representative models of Electric and Hand

INDUSTRIAL — PORTABLE and DORMANT — SCALES. (Models to meet all requirements.)

IBM in its early pioneering days was a success, but there was not much indication yet of the super-giant it was to become.

the Great IBM Line of Today—

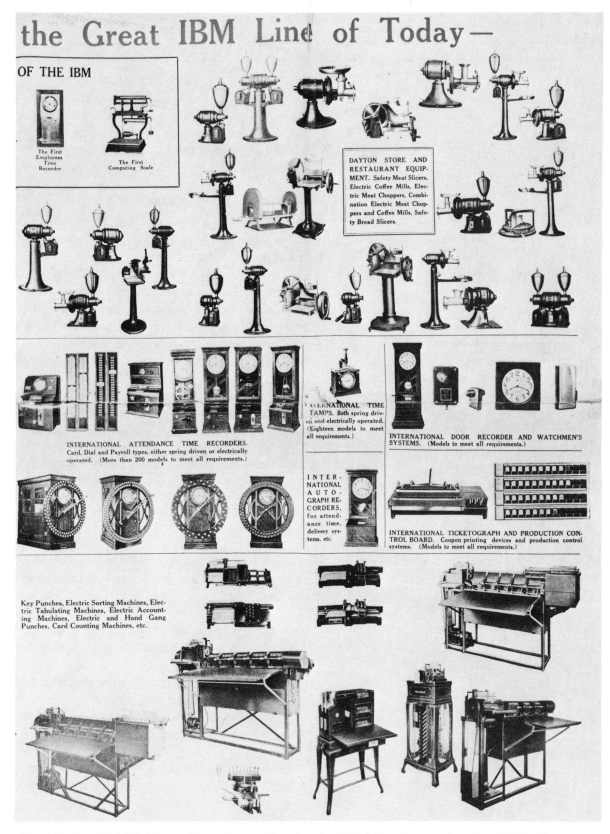

OF THE IBM

The First Employees Time Recorder

The First Computing Scale

DAYTON STORE AND RESTAURANT EQUIPMENT. Safety Meat Slicers, Electric Coffee Mills, Electric Meat Choppers, Combination Electric Meat Choppers and Coffee Mills, Safety Bread Slicers.

INTERNATIONAL ATTENDANCE TIME RECORDERS. Card, Dial and Payroll types, either spring driven or electrically operated. (More than 200 models to meet all requirements.)

INTERNATIONAL TIME STAMPS. Both spring driven and electrically operated. (Eighteen models to meet all requirements.)

INTERNATIONAL AUTOGRAPH RECORDERS, for attendance time, delivery systems, etc.

INTERNATIONAL DOOR RECORDER AND WATCHMEN'S SYSTEMS. (Models to meet all requirements.)

INTERNATIONAL TICKETOGRAPH AND PRODUCTION CONTROL BOARD. Coupon printing devices and production control systems. (Models to meet all requirements.)

Key Punches, Electric Sorting Machines, Electric Tabulating Machines, Electric Accounting Machines, Electric and Hand Gang Punches, Card Counting Machines, etc.

Top-of-the-line electric tabulating and accounting machines based on Hollerith's patents are shown in a 1920s catalogue.

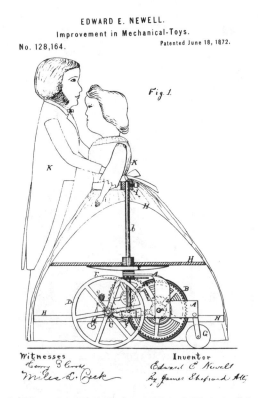

EDWARD E. NEWELL.
Improvement in Mechanical-Toys.
No. 128,164.　　　　　　　Patented June 18, 1872.

Fig. 1.

Witnesses　　　　　　　　Inventor

Fashions of the Civil War era facilitated the design of this 1872 mechanical toy. The voluminous skirt left considerable room for clockwork, perhaps keeping time so that this couple could waltz.

world consensus was not reached and definitions continue to vary from language to language.

Automaton is derived from the Greek words for self and move, but only a related word, *automatous*, appeared in a 1671 English dictionary as:

Automatous [Gk] having a motion within itself.[1]

Automaton did not appear in the first edition of the *Encyclopedia Britannica* of 1778 either, but did find its way into one of Noah Webster's first dictionaries.

Automaton, *n* [Gk, autómatos; autós, self, and man, moveo, motus. The Greek plural, *automata*, is sometimes used; but the regular English plural, *automatons*, is preferable.] A self-moving machine or one which moves by invisible springs.[2]

Here, self-movement was closely associated with springs, reflecting the significance of clockmaking in the history of automata. Definitions of *automatic* and *automatical* indicated that an automaton might "have the power of moving itself," but the action was not necessarily voluntary or willed. Since automata of the day were created to amuse the wealthy, there was no reference to automata that do work. Less than twenty-five years later, however, the influence of the Industrial Revolution crept into both *automatical* and *automaton* explanations.

automatic 1: Belonging to an automaton; *automatical*, having the power of moving itself; applied to machinery. 2. Not voluntary; not depending on the will; applied to animal motions.

The term *automatic* is now applied to self-acting machinery, or such as has within itself the power of regulating entirely its own movements, although the moving force is derived from without; and to what pertains to such machinery; as, *automatic* operations or improvements.

Automatic arts; such economic arts or manufactures as are carried on by self-acting machinery.

automaton *n* [Gk, autómatos; autós, self, and man, moveo, motus. The Greek plural, *automata*, is sometimes used; but the regular English plural, *automatons*, is preferable.] A self-moving machine, or one which has its moving power within itself. The moving power is usually a spring or weight, particularly the former. The term is generally applied to machines constructed so as to imitate the form and motions of men or animals.[3]

Here, automata were self-powered machines that *produced* and the technology to do so was referred to as *automatic art*. Power came from springs *or* weights, was not quite as invisible as before, and was to create animal-like movement.

The definition of *automatical* remained basically the same in an 1879 edition, but added that automatic machines made movements commonly made by the human hand. It is tempting to think that the editors foresaw today's robotic arms and grippers, but the example of automatic movement that followed was instead "the automatic dividing engine," probably a reference to Babbage's machine.

The word *spontaneous* filtered into the 1879 *automaton* definition, perhaps because notions of "spontaneous generation" were highly disputed during this time, even though the dispute was dispelled by microbe hunter Louis Pasteur during the 1860s and 1870s.

> **automaton** *n pl* **automata** or **automatons** A self-moving machine, or one which has its moving power within itself;—applied chiefly to machines which imitate the motions of men or animals. The term is sometimes applied to anything which has the power of spontaneous movement. "So great and admirable *automaton* as the world."[4]

It took over five years for *robot*, introduced by Karel Capek in his play *R.U.R.*, to appear in an English dictionary. In the 1934 Webster's it appeared as:

> **robot** *n* [Czech, fr. *robota* work, compulsory service; akin to Oslav *rabota* servitude, OE *earfothe* hardship, labor, OHG *arabeit* trouble, distress, ON *erfithi* toil, distress, Goth *arabaiths* labor, L *orbus* orphaned, bereft—more at ORPHAN] 1. In Karel Capek's play *R.U.R.* (Rossum's Universal Robots), one of a large number of artificially manufactured persons, mechanically efficient, but devoid of sensibility; hence, a brutal,

In 1805 a mechanician, Maillardet, also built an automaton that wrote. When a spring was released, the figure wrote a line and then returned to dot or stroke a letter. It was bilingual, writing in both French and English, and could also draw landscapes. After 1812, the mechanical doll was reincarnated and is shown here as a female automaton, known as The Philadelphia Doll. In "her" new "life," "she" draws a clipper ship with elaborate rigging.

Thomas Edison miniaturized and then integrated one of his inventions, the phonograph, with dolls in 1877. A child had only to turn the doll's crank to hear it recite "Mary had a little lamb." Five hundred talking dolls were turned out by an Orange, New Jersey, factory near Edison's home.

efficient insensitive person; an automaton. 2. Any automatic apparatus or device that performs functions ordinarily ascribed to human beings, or operates with what appears to be almost human intelligence; esp. such an apparatus that is started by means of radiant energy or sound waves.[5]

During the 1950s and 1960s, as computer technology advanced, the question arose as to whether computers, by virtue of their humanlike ability to memorize, were immobile robots. As computers became scaled down and were used to control machinery, the converse question arose—were robots merely mobile computers? Also debated was whether, in addition to duplicating human functions, a robot had to *look* like a human.

The debate continues today, among hobbyists who have built their own versions of what a robot should be, advertisers who have moved from traditional media to building robotlike facsimiles of products, manufacturers of personal robots that consumers can have in their homes, and manufacturers of industrial robots that toil in factories.

One hobby roboticist, Andy Reichelt, includes the human element in his definition: A robot is "an automated machine with the motor capabilities to duplicate some human motor functions or a shape that emulates the human shape."[6]

Promotional robot manufacturer J. W. Anderson, president of ShowAmerica Inc. in Elmhurst, Illinois, makes radio-controlled devices operated by behind-the-scene actors who supply voice and speech content. Says Anderson, "a promotional robot is mobile and can move among people while conversing with them and display various animated features and capabilities."

He distinguishes his robots from Disney World's audioanimatronic figures, like the Abraham Lincoln character, which speaks, turns, and nods, but does not walk.

While these definitions do not mention computers, personal robot manufacturers think of their devices as mobile extensions of personal computers. Some are also planning robots with computers on board. This group sees robots as both educational devices that present challenges to amateur programmers and as home entertainment. Their robots either look humanoid or are at least designed to suggest some personality.

Industrial robots do not have the humaniform appearance of their robotic brethren. They look more like small construction cranes, and are basically computerized arms. According to the Robotic Industries Association (RIA), which was formerly the Robot Institute of America, a trade association affiliated with the Society of Manufacturing Engineers, an industrial robot is a reprogrammable, multifunctional manipulator designed to move materials, parts, tools, or specialized devices through variable programmed motions to perform a variety of tasks.

The key word here is *reprogrammable*, because it refers to a built-in computer control system. This distinguishes robots from numerically controlled machine tools that cannot adapt to new tasks. The computer memorizes instructions "telling" the robot what motions are needed to complete a given task. Because it is reprogrammable, the robot can adapt by "learning" new motions when a task changes. For this reason, today's robots are sometimes called "flexible" or "soft" automata, in contrast to machine tools that can perform only one type of task, and so are called "hard" automata.

Most industrial robot definitions in Western countries match the RIA's, but the definition of the Japanese Industrial Robot Association (JIRA) encompasses a wider range of equipment. It includes two more classes of manipulators, those that are operated manually and those that repeat one task according to fixed sequences that cannot be easily changed. These would be considered hard automata in the United States, and so data on robots in use, by country, must be regarded with these different definitions in mind.

The RIA and JIRA industrial robot definitions are for robots that would work apart from other machinery and so are often called stand-alones. An industrial robot also often works with several machine tools in a group that is called a robot workcell. A machine tool might stamp parts before a robot welds them together, for example, and these activities would be coordinated by one computer. Similarly, a series of robots might work with machine tools on an assembly line.

A factory with robotic workcells, assembly lines, and robotic carts that carry parts to and from lines is called a "flexible manufacturing system," or FMS. One large computer integrates activities and controls production, and in some instances products are designed on that computer. This process, called Computer-Aided Design/Computer-Aided Manufacturing or CAD/CAM, allows information about a product to be stored in one data base from the product's inception to its completion.

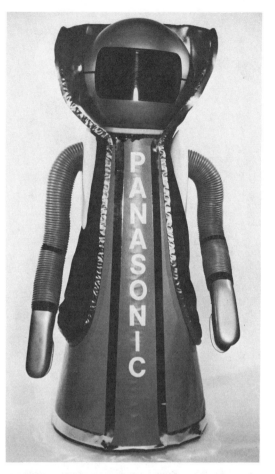

This 180-pound, 5 feet 2 inch entertainment robot was built in 1969 by Andy Reichelt for Quasar Industries, Inc., which is now defunct. The company called it a "Sales Promotional Android," but when its voice system malfunctioned, the robot repeated the word klatu, *a garbled version of the phrase "you talk," and that became its name.*

ANTENNA FOR
RADIO LINK

TELEVISION
CAMERA

RANGE
FINDER

ON-BOARD
LOGIC

CAMERA
CONTROL
UNIT

BUMP
DETECTOR

CASTER
WHEEL

DRIVE
MOTOR

DRIVE
WHEEL

This 1960s vintage robot was created under the direction of Charles Rosen at Stanford Research Institute International. Named "Shakey," because of its wobbly locomotion, this robot was linked with a computer in another room and could sense its environment.

THE DAWN OF ARTIFICIAL INTELLIGENCE RESEARCH

While industrial robots were making their market debuts, research computer scientists interested in cybernetics were busy making inroads that would contribute to the next generation of robots.

During the 1950s, British scientist W. Grey Walter created mechanical "tortoises" that could move toward light sources. These machines showed that simple combinations of electronic and mechanical parts could behave automatically yet seem to act like animals or insects.

In the 1960s, researchers' aims were to integrate perceptual and problem-solving capabilities into one system, using computers, TV cameras for vision, and touch sensors for robot grippers. Since the final objective was to determine what intellectual activities such systems could carry out, their discipline became known as artificial intelligence, or AI. John McCarthy coined the phrase in 1956, and with Marvin Minsky founded MIT's AI laboratory the following year. McCarthy went on to found the Stanford University AI lab in 1963, which he directs today. Other AI labs around the world were created in the early 1960s. At that time a creature known as the Hopkins' Beast prowled around Johns Hopkins University's corridors. Powered by batteries, the Beast was to keep its batteries charged and to demonstrate decision-making capabilities by sensing when to plug into a hallway outlet to "feed" itself. Once properly nourished, the Beast continued to roam, always alert for the next delectable outlet.

In 1969 and 1971, researchers at SRI International under Charles Rosen completed two versions of another mobile robot, known as Shakey, fondly named for its wobbly locomotion. Both versions were designed to roll around a room filled with large blocks. Each robot had a TV camera mounted on a radio-controlled cart and touch and distance sensors, but they differed in their computer systems and programming languages.

Shakey I demonstrated some perception and problem-solving abilities, but assembling it was really an exercise that revealed weaknesses in these capacities. Researchers also discovered that immense computing requirements were needed for Shakey I to perform the simplest tasks. There was no way for Shakey I to note the correctness of its progress during the execution of a task. This meant that a slight inaccuracy in task instructions (that is, an error in the software program or sequence of steps to accomplish that task) would bring about a useless result without chance of mid-course correction.

Shakey II had a better computing system and more sophisticated software that allowed the robot to apply special-purpose instructions to general problems. If Shakey II was told to move from room A to room B, for example, a program could instruct it to go to the door between the two rooms and then pass through the door. Without the ability to generalize the program, grouping many similar activities under blanket instructions, Shakey would not be able to go from room B back to room A even though doing so would only involve reversing instructions. To generalize a program, Shakey II had to recognize its environment or make a

This Westinghouse mechanical dog was a robot's best friend. Built in 1940, Sparko used his canine charms to keep promotional robot Electro company. The year before, Electro had to go it alone at the New York World's Fair, where ''he'' informed potential customers of Westinghouse's latest appliances.

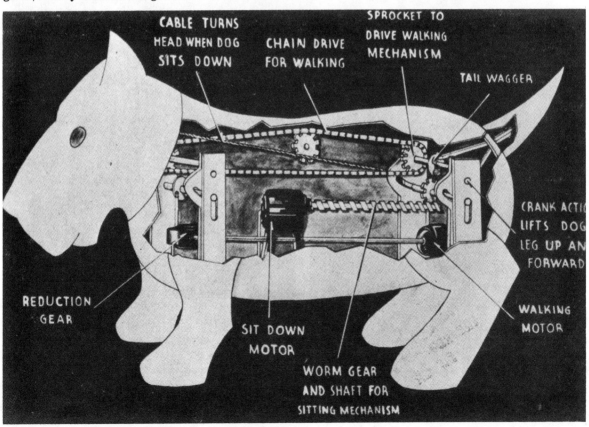

With clocks came ornamentation in the form of elaborate mechanical figures, known as Jacquemarts, to sound chimes on the hour or half-hour. The first Jacquemart was installed on the clock of Notre Dame de Dijon during the thirteenth century. Shakespeare referred to one as a Jack-of-the-Clock and a 1605 pamphlet declared that the Jack-of-the-Clock "goes upon screws and his office is to do nothing but strike."

judgment about "the current state of the world." This was done with a less specific instruction telling it to move from one room to another for *any* two adjacent rooms.

Besides moving between rooms and avoiding objects in those rooms, eventually Shakey II was able to stack wooden blocks according to spoken directions. It could pick up a block on its left, for example, and place it on top of another block. Its camera even looked to see if the blocks were properly aligned, and if not, it adjusted the stack. Shakey was once asked to push a box off a platform, but Shakey could not reach the box. The robot looked around, found a ramp, pushed the ramp up against the platform, rolled up the ramp, and then pushed the box onto the floor.

Putting together the toy automaton tradition of the last three centuries and the outcomes of artificial intelligence research labs and hobbyist activities has also resulted in mass-market "personal robots" introduced in late 1982. Some can navigate around the house with the help of ultrasonic or infrared sensors, some "talk" but can't "listen," and some serve drinks and deliver mail. Coming soon are personal robots that can vacuum.

Even though personal robots were designed and developed in the late seventies, these robots did not catch on immediately because their potential dealers turned to personal computers first. Now that personal computers have achieved wide acceptance in offices and households, high-technology industry watchers expect personal robots to follow suit.

Advanced computerization could lead to robots that "see," "hear," and "touch." These lifelike senses plus humanoid appearances—staples of the science-fiction robot—may even become a reality for personal robots. But industrial robots will probably continue to look like small cranes. They have computerized arms that weld, spray paint, assemble, inspect, and sort parts. New applications in space and ocean exploration are under way. Robotic arms will eventually have touch sensors in their grippers, and some already have vision as a result of digitized camera information. Improving the mechanics of these arms so that they can reach with greater speed and accuracy is also a priority. The race is on to create intelligent robots with the most accuracy and speed. The hope is that this combination will achieve the greatest productivity increases in factories.

THE CREATORS AND PIONEERS OF INDUSTRIAL ROBOTS: AN INTERVIEW WITH JOSEPH ENGELBERGER

Over and over, the advice was "Don't call it a robot. Call it a programmable manipulator. Call it a production terminal or a universal transfer device." The word is *robot* and it *should* be *robot*. I was building a robot, damn it, and I wasn't going to have any fun, in Asimov terms, unless it *was robot*. So I stuck to my guns.

> *Joseph F. Engelberger (interview 12/6/83),*
> *founder and past president of Unimation, Inc.*

For Joseph F. Engelberger, thirty years of building robots and founding a new industry have been both fun and a "big battle." Now known as the Father of Industrial Robotics, he speaks of "playing in the robotics business" in one breath, and of surmounting "institutional barriers" in another.

An independent, analytical thinker who knew how to find and use information, he again and again eschewed the advice of "experts." And once others caught on, he found himself in a competitive arena where secrets could not be safeguarded enough. Yet he managed to make an innovation succeed.

Engelberger is just as comfortable describing economic and marketing models as he is with servo theory, the

Joseph F. Engelberger, the "Father of Industrial Robots," was the first to recognize the potential of inventor George Devol's programmable machinery concept and obtain financial backing.

technology that piqued his interest when he was an engineering student. Clad in a suit and bow tie, an accessory that the fifty-nine-year-old Engelberger says saves time, he leans forward to draw an imaginary graph on a tabletop. His index finger zig-zags wildly across the polished wood surface, charting the course the robotics industry has taken. This engineer-turned-businessman also uses terms like "open or closed valves" and "positive or negative feedback" to convey how financial backers received his ideas.

Today the company he founded has close to eight thousand robots installed around the world and is the world's largest manufacturer of industrial robots. Unimation sold $43 million worth in 1983, about 17 percent of that year's $250 million market. Some industry experts expect the United

Joseph Engelberger with one of his Unimates.

States market to grow to $2 billion and the world market to reach $10 billion by 1990. But Unimation did not turn a profit until 1975, fourteen years after its first sale. Despite all the ups and downs, Engelberger never wavered. He was busy pushing through sound barriers with the "right stuff" that true entrepreneurs are made of.

Born in Brooklyn in July 1925, Engelberger grew up in Connecticut during the Depression. He recalls his mother telling him to "carry in his head most of the assets he would have the rest of his life," and, heeding her advice, he did well in high school. Then along with thirteen others selected from a nationwide pool, he attended Columbia University's special accelerated college and officer training program. After receiving his B.S. in physics in 1946, he served in the navy.

When World War II ended, Engelberger returned to Columbia, where he took the university's first course on servo theory. At that time, he also became "something of a science-fiction nut," and was delighted with Isaac Asimov's early robot stories. Engelberger says the stories and the Three Laws of Robotics set his subliminal gears in motion, preparing him for a chance meeting with inventor George C. Devol, Jr.

After graduate school, Engelberger joined Manning, Maxwell, and Moore, an old-line industrial firm in Stratford, Connecticut. As general manager of its aerospace division, he pursued his interest in servo controls, the leading edge in sophisticated aerospace technology at that time. Then, in 1956, he met George C. Devol, Jr., at a cocktail party.

Devol was a self-made engineer who at one time had considered enrolling in MIT. Instead, in 1932, he formed his own motion-picture sound-recording equipment company, United Cinephone Corporation. Next, he worked for Sperry Gyroscope Research Company for several years. He later organized a new company, General Electronics Industries, a diversified industrial electronics and radar test equipment firm. During the war his three-thousand-man firm specialized in electronic countermeasures and produced jamming devices for the navy. By the time the two men met, Devol had formed a third company, Devol Research Associates. He had developed a new form of magnetic recording, as well as a large-scale random access memory system, various control systems, sensors, and ultrahigh-speed printers.

So it is no wonder that Engelberger describes Devol as a "very ingenious chap." He watched and listened as Devol "waved his hands a lot and said 'You know, we ought to

George C. Devol, Jr., whose forty patents, including the 1954 one for "programmed article transfer," earned him the title "Grandfather of Industrial Robots."

realize that 50 percent of the people in factories are really putting and taking.' '' The two men asked themselves why machines were made to produce only specific items. How about approaching manufacturing the other way around, by designing machines that could put and take anything? That notion was the essence of a programmable manipulator, and in Engelberger's mind, a programmable manipulator was a robot. In the cold gray dawn that followed, hangover or not, Devol's idea still looked pretty good.

As early as 1946, Devol had developed a playback system for teaching machine tools to remember their motions. The idea had not looked good to many companies that Devol had approached. A patent was issued in 1950 and licensed to Remington Rand for use in computers. Although adequate for machine tools, Devol's magnetic recording system was not fast enough for computers and eventually Remington Rand returned the patents to Devol. The inventor began investigating other avenues for the control system, which culminated in approximately forty patents. The key patent, "Program Controlled Article Transfer," was issued in 1954. Devol showed his system to Thomas J. Watson, Sr., president of IBM. Although Watson was interested, he was unable to convince others who felt they were busy enough starting the mainframe computer business. On the one hand, Devol says IBM's decision was wise. "They had their hands full many times over and 'Why do we want to go off in another direction?' was the attitude," he says. And while today Devol thinks of a robot as a small part of the production process, "just as a catalyst in an oil refinery is a minor part," he still believes "it's the most important part because without the catalyst, you can't properly crank up the oil." So, on the other hand, he says, "I can't understand why it took so darned long for anybody to understand what I was talking about, but that's common too."

Engelberger not only understood, he felt that an entrepreneur was needed to translate Devol's thoughts into hardware. He set about filling that role by convincing his company to take a preliminary license under Devol's patents. Devol did not become an employee. Instead, his contract stipulated that he would continue to apply for patents, which Manning, Maxwell, and Moore would buy out on a long-term basis. Ironically, Devol had approached Manning, Maxwell, and Moore three years earlier but had been turned down.

Engelberger was now in charge of two divisions that often worked in tandem. The aerospace division, now called

Consolidated Controls Corporation, produced jumbo jet components and nuclear control systems and grew quickly. In seven months it was in the black and today it has a 74 percent return on investment. A $120 million business, it is now the largest supplier of control systems to the nuclear navy, a major supplier to cruise missiles, and contributes thirty to forty components in every jumbo jet. Says Engelberger, "If you're in one of those jumbo jets, and you lose altitude in the cabin and a little mask drops down but you don't get your oxygen, the last thing you say before passing out is 'That son of a bitch, Engelberger.'"

In contrast, progress for the robot division was slow and choppy. Looking back, Engelberger analyzes events according to results of a 1967 air force study, "Project Hindsight." Examining the reasons why some innovations had succeeded and others had failed, the study concluded that a successful innovation had to have perceived need, appropriate technology and confident technologists, and adequate financing. If any one of these three was missing, the innovation would die.

Perceived need for industrial robotics came much earlier than adequate technology, Engelberger says. In 1936 Charlie Chaplin "blew the whistle on the Industrial Revolution," with his film *Modern Times*. "He really saw the poignant thing that was wrong—that the human was now being paced by the machine, working for the machine. His lifestyle was oppressed." But the technology to lift that oppression was not available and labor was intimidated and cheap. Asimov's Three Laws also added to the perceived need and remain a guiding influence today. "The more intimately our robots get involved in the world today, the more critical his laws are," says Engelberger.

In search of a design standard for a machine that could make more than one specific product, Engelberger and Devol conducted a market survey. They visited factories and watched people and machines perform various production processes, always weighing new machine designs against observed constraints. Some constraints resulted from norms accepted during the fifties that would not have applied today. For example, at the time women worked for far less money than men, and their jobs often involved light work using two hands asynchronously. In contrast, men were better paid and used two hands simultaneously to lift heavy parts. So while economic justification required going after male labor, the cost of a two-armed machine would still

Charlie Chaplin in his 1936 film Modern Times. *Says Engelberger of the comedian, "He really saw the poignant thing that was wrong—that the human was now being paced by the machine, working for the machine. His lifestyle was oppressed."*

have been prohibitive. They decided to go for a single-armed machine.

Engelberger was appalled by working conditions in many of the factories. In one plant that produced furniture casters, he saw women tied to machines by straps around their wrists. When a woman put two halves of a caster in an open press, the straps would yank her hands away before the press closed. "It was really very unwholesome," he recalls, "and there were two hundred machines clattering away in that tremendously noisy place. It was so dramatic. The foreman pointed out two older women and he said, 'See those two? If I don't shake them at the shoulder at the end of the shift, they'll go right on to the next shift.' They'd had hypnotic labotomies, effectively. So you *know* their children aren't going to take those jobs. That's for sure."

After visiting six Chrysler plants, seven Ford plants, five General Motors plants, and twenty other factories, the group drew up specifications for a prototype industrial robot. It was the first servomachine. The construction of today's Unimate 2000 is very much like the 1956 prototype.

Looking for customers, Engelberger made several proposals to Ford Motor Company's vice president for manufacturing, Del Harder. Harder was a legendary figure who, with John Diebold, is generally credited with coining the word *automation*. When he saw the robot specifications, Harder told Engelberger, "You know, we could use two thousand of them tomorrow."

This was wonderful news, but Manning, Maxwell, and Moore checked the team's excitement by resurrecting their earlier doubts about the promise of industrial robots. In 1957, the company decided to abandon its aerospace and nuclear control businesses, preferring not to continue as a government contractor. During a Friday-afternoon conference, the day before Engelberger was to go on vacation, he was told to liquidate his business the following Monday.

The accompanying offers of a big promotion and a considerable salary increase were tempting, Engelberger recalls. Now, suddenly, Engelberger and Devol's innovation lacked adequate financing. And yet they perceived the need for the innovation, were in the process of developing the appropriate technology, and they had confident technologists.

"I balked," Engelberger remembers. "I said, 'Wait a minute, I don't think you know what you're doing, liquidating this business.'" To make certain, he traveled down to

New York City, bought five books on finance at Barnes and Noble, and ploughed through them in one weekend. Then he consulted an accountant and concluded that Manning, Maxwell, and Moore's presentation was unsound—by liquidating they would lose far more money than they had estimated.

Engelberger knew he had to act swiftly, so his next move was to call his company's outside directors and ask them to wait four months before liquidating. In the meantime he would chase Wall Streeters to raise money to buy both the aerospace and robot businesses.

While canvassing for dollars, Engelberger was pleased to find several people interested in the robot concept, but they were uninterested in aerospace. They reasoned that Manning, Maxwell, and Moore was abandoning the business because they knew something that Engelberger didn't. "That's a very hard thing for a young guy getting started sometimes, if he's leaving a big company," Engelberger says. "The assumption is that he's a young idiot and the big guys know much more than he does, and therefore, let's not touch that mess." There were offers to buy just the robot business, but Engelberger, then thirty-two years old, refused. " 'I said I won't do that because I've got 140 employees and I'm trying to save their jobs. You don't get the robot idea unless you get the whole package.' "

After a series of introductions through Devol's contacts, financing for the whole package finally came from Norman Schafler, founder of Consolidated Diesel Electric Corporation, a military-vehicle manufacturer now called Condec. Engelberger's divisions became a subsidiary, Consolidated Controls Corporation. Since Engelberger took all his robotics playfellows with him, Manning, Maxwell, and Moore could no longer make use of Devol's patents. Engelberger made a deal with them so that his new company could take out a license and start the robots project again. Today, Engelberger delights in teasing his daughter, who recently received her MBA, saying that he got *his* degree in a matter of days.

Meanwhile, the robot prototype project was at a standstill, and yet Ford had been so interested. According to Engelberger, "They said, 'Well nothing is going to happen to this. This whole wonderful idea is going to go to hell.' They took our whole document, our entire proposal, put the Ford Company name on top of it, and sent it around to other companies that they thought would be logical to do it."

The other companies included American Machinery

One of the first Unimates, a contraction of "universal automation," now on exhibit in the Henry Ford Museum in Michigan.

and Foundry (AMF), Borg-Warner, General Mills, Hughes Aircraft, Bendix, IBM, Sunstrand, Western Electric, and many others. With the specifications in circulation unbeknownst to Engelberger, and Engelberger himself making rounds, a potential robot producer would hear supply and demand. "I'd be going to AMF through the back door because I'm the little guy trying to find out. In the front door comes Ford. They hear from me 'A good idea would be to develop robots.' They'd hear from Ford, 'We'd like to buy robots.' So there was reinforcement going on."

That was the positive way Engelberger looked at the situation. But it also worked against him, he says, because when he finally obtained adequate financing, he also faced potential competition. "I didn't *need* any competitors. We'd just as soon have had people leave the idea alone. But they were reinforced by what they thought were two independent views."

Engelberger's document was proprietary, he says, but it did not have big stamps all over it. "There was no secrecy agreement, so they just usurped it," he says. He was busy doing development and "when you're raising money, you've got to spill your guts. You can't hold anything back—you've got to tell everyone what you're doing." And while the material could have been copyrighted, Engelberger explains, "You're out there trying to convince people, and at the same time the world is coming unglued. So you don't think about that."

Had Devol and Engelberger not taken a technological gamble, the potential competitors might have become real. While the fundamentals of servo theory—the means of providing power to machinery—remained unchanged after World War II, there was progress in the ways to both compute and record information. Even though Remington Rand had needed a faster recording system than Devol's playback patent offered, that system was capable of recording either digital or analog signals. In the 1950s, analog computers that ran on vacuum or radio tubes were state of the art, but engineers were beginning to use the transistor, the precursor of today's solid-state digital chip. It was still an analog world, however, and Engelberger says it was difficult to arrive at an economically sound analog control system even though radio tubes cost 30 cents and transistors cost $1.70.

In keeping with Devol's early patent, the Engelberger/Devol specifications that Ford circulated called for digital signals, but the robots that the other companies built were designed to run on analog systems. In contrast, Engelberger's team heeded a Bell Telephone Laboratories study predicting that the price of transistors would have to come down. It was a difficult decision, says Engelberger, who did not imagine that today they would cost a fraction of a penny. "We never would have thought that at the time. We just thought 'Well, it will come down.'" So in 1958, Consolidated Controls went digital.

During the next few years, the design was perfected with the help of several outside consultants, including Professor John R. Ragazzini, who had taught Engelberger at Columbia University. When it looked like their robot was "technically on," Consolidated Controls was ready for the big battle—that is, winning over the conservative manufacturing community.

Engelberger began "a very hard sell," facing the first of three major institutional barriers—innovation by invasion. Generally, innovations made *by* an industry *for* the industry tend to catch on quickly. But Engelberger was an outsider with an innovation, and so was looked upon as a smart aleck trying to tell people how to run their business. "We were invaders," he says. "We said robotics is good for industry. And we were trying to stuff it down their throats." Even when a younger, less conservative fellow liked the idea, his superior was not likely to listen. "His boss would look at him and say, 'Haven't I given you enough work to do? You've gotta give me this science-fiction crap?'"

In 1959, General Motors was the first to install a test model Unimate in its Turnstead die-casting plant. But orders for more Unimates did not come until 1961. That year, Engelberger again faced the need for financial backing. Condec decided that it needed more research and development money for the robot business and set about looking for a partner. Engelberger tried companies that he thought would be the logical sources for venture capital, like AMF, IBM, United Shoe Machine. He also tried Champ Carry, chairman of Pullman Corporation and an acquaintance of Devol's. Engelberger had learned that he had to go straight to the top. "Forget everyone else," he says now. "They're going to NIH you to death." Furthermore, you have to arrive when the top man has just cleaned his desk. "He's got to be taking a deep breath. He can't be up to his ass in alligators, you know," says Engelberger. "He's got to say, 'Now, what am I going to do *now?*'"

While the Condec board was meeting to evaluate three

These 1960 Hughes Aircraft robots, called "Mobots," were designed "for environments that are beyond man's capacity and for tasks beyond man's capabilities." They could be used as remote manipulators—an operator would watch images sent by two television cameras and control two three-jointed arms with lever-type toggle switches. But Hughes also said "designs for computer control of repetitive operations can be made available."

offers, a messenger arrived with a $100,000 check from Champ Carry to bargain in good faith. They did. The result was a joint venture, with Pullman having bought a 51 percent interest for $3 million. The new company was Unimation, Inc.

Looking back on the many years that it took to secure financing for robotics, Engelberger likens his experience to that of other entrepreneurs. In 1947, for instance, Joseph C. Wilson bet his firm, The Haloid Company, on the Xerox process, but was unable to offer a product until 1959. E. H. Land's Polaroid camera, invented in 1947, produced messy prints at first and took years to perfect. These and other innovations took up to fifteen years to get off the ground. Although they were technologically feasible, they were considered economic liabilities, Engelberger says. There was a man who might have made the story of robotics entirely different had he lived, Engelberger says with regret in his voice. Morehead Patterson, chairman of AMF, was a "long-term thinking guy." But Patterson died in 1962 and the AMF executive Engelberger approached "didn't have the staying power." So when Engelberger became discouraged, he would remember what Wilson had once said, that in the final analysis, choosing an innovation is an act of faith.

Despite having two major corporations behind him, throughout the early 1960s Engelberger found himself up against two more institutional barriers. One was the zone of indifference arising from the average middle managers' fears that robot installations would be too troublesome and economically unjustifiable. The second phenomenon was an overall inertia that also had the peculiar effect of being cyclical. Firms would not recognize the need to automate unless their competition did.

In 1963, Engelberger and Devol held a press conference at the Biltmore Hotel in New York City, hoping that publicity would help their fledgling company. By 1964, Unimation had sold only thirty robots and its biggest customer, General Motors, had been downplaying installations because it feared labor opposition. Progress was also hampered by the failures of all the other early product lines, save AMF's Versatran model. That made potential customers wary of purchasing robots. They did not have the assurance of continuous future servicing nor the experience to maintain the robots. "We would have been much better off at that time if we'd had successful competitors," claims Engelberger.

To determine how industrial robotics could catch on faster, Engelberger commissioned the consulting firm Arthur D. Little, Inc., to build a model of the market. The model took into account such factors as furthering potential buyers' awareness and understanding of the product. It also factored in the decision-making process leading to an appropriation for a large capital investment and the time it might take for a board of directors to pass it. It was hoped that the model would help in planning short-term strategy, but just getting it to accurately reflect the current scenario was no easy task.

When first run on the computer, the model showed that Unimation would not be able to sell any robots for another three years. But Unimation *had* been selling robots, so an unnecessary limitation had to be governing the model, making it inaccurate. The model makers must have inadvertently excluded profiles of whomever *was* buying. It turned

A different Hughes aircraft Mobot.

out that the model was too rational—it didn't allow for an irrational buyer, "the guy that could come up with the money without risking his job, who'd say 'Hell, get one,'" remembers Engelberger. So they cranked him into the model.

The next step was to measure the market's price sensitivity. Varying the price of a robot from $18,000 to $25,000 did not seem to change the market much, but at $15,000, "the model suddenly jumped, the market suddenly became six times as large," says Engelberger. Again the model seemed flawed. Going back to analyze and review several estimates revealed that the number of workers per factory shift was critical. The computer had crunched out price-sensitive figures according to government data assuming that most of the work force labored on the first shift, 17 percent on the second shift, and 6 percent on the third shift. At $15,000 per robot, the economics paid off in the first shift alone. The sixfold market increase was indeed correct. Says Engelberger, "There was nothing wrong with the model. It was just that our Bureau of Labor Statistics figures said, 'Hey, your economic justification just crashed the barrier.'"

With this armamentarium, Engelberger kept his backers convinced that one day the robot business would be as good as his aerospace business. Moreover, with the right robot price and such high economic justification, middle and upper management zones of indifference were expected to shrink. Without good justification, says Engelberger, "nobody needs a robot . . . there isn't anything that a robot can do that a willing human being can't do better." As long as it made economic sense to hire more people or simple machine tools to increase capacity, employers would do so. But with the right economics, the picture gradually began to change. "Ultimately, forget about the nobility crap," says Engelberger. "Nobody puts a robot to work because they want to make life easier for their employees. They put it to work for economic savings."

By 1966, Unimates were being put to work in the diecasting industry and General Motors had been testing robots in spot welding for two years. Shortly before he was to appear on the Johnny Carson show, Engelberger got what would be his biggest order for the next eight years—sixty-six spot-welding robots for GM's Lordstown, Ohio, plant. So on national television Engelberger was happy to announce that his company was making twenty robots a month. That was true, but only for the moment. "Of course, once we shipped those sixty-six, we were back to three or four a month again," Engelberger says. But the competition of Engelberger's few customers began to perk up.

In the meantime, the Japanese were taking an interest in industrial robots. "While we were agonizing in '66, the Japanese... were looking at what was happening and they came over, company after company," Engelberger recalls. Wasting no time, the Japanese government invited Engelberger to tour the country and to lecture in Tokyo the following year.

When he arrived in Tokyo to lecture, his hosts were concerned that after his address, the audience might not be inquisitive enough. So to be polite, they made up three or four questions before the audience arrived. Accustomed to speaking before eight or ten people in the States, Engelberger found himself in front of seven hundred engineers and executives. He began talking at 1:30 in the afternoon and was "dragged off the dais" at 6:30 at night.

One reason for their enthusiasm was in fact due to nomenclature—they picked up on Engelberger's machines because they were called robots. A second reason was that the year before, an exhibit in Japan resulted in the purchase of seventeen AMF Versatrans. Says Engelberger, "People just bought the machines and copied them," and AMF ended up with seventeen eager Japanese competitors.

So in 1968, when firms like Hitachi, Mitsubishi, and Kawasaki expressed interest in Unimates, Engelberger was prepared. "One thing you learn in Japan is that there is a certain honor among thieves," he says, and with that perception, AMF's experience, and Arthur D. Little's knowledge of Japanese-American relations, negotiations began. Engelberger also drew on his own past conclusion—that it was best to deal with the man at the top. Having the attention of Kawasaki's chairman of the board, and also knowing that very large Japanese companies protect their licensors' property, Engelberger granted Kawasaki the right to build Unimates in exchange for royalties.

Engelberger says that the institutional barriers he was up against in the States did not exist in Japan. "They are implementers," Engelberger says. "They went ahead and used the technology." Japanese managers have an advantage over their American counterparts because they "are on a longer timestring," Engelberger explains. "They can make a five-year plan. But in the States if you plan that wonderful thing to contribute to your business, and it's going

In 1977, Joe Engelberger presented the first Robot Institute of America Engelberger Award to Professor Yukio Hasegawa. The annual award became "awards" in 1981—three are now given for applications, technology development, and education.

to be good five years from now, I guarantee you your successor will get the benefit—because we go by *quarters* in this country. What can you do for me *now?*" Engelberger agrees with the Club of Rome, the think tank famous for *Limits to Growth,* that "almost anything you do that is good in the future has a valley up front, before it catches on to make a benefit."

Another advantage is that the Japanese engineering community respects its applications engineers, whereas engineers in the United States look down on their applications engineering brethren. "In general, we have had a tendency to feel that the designer is the elite," says Engelberger. "The user, the manufacturing engineer, the industrial engineer, is not." Engelberger recalls how strong this attitude was when he was enrolled at Columbia University. "I *knew* that the industrial engineering department was where you put your football players to somehow get them through."

Furthermore, the immense practical experience of a machine loader who works his way up to foreman and then industrial engineer is not often recognized. But in Japan and Germany the opposite is true. Says Engelberger, "In Germany, a guy who's the head of manufacturing can be Herr Doktor Professor, and be teaching as part of a job that is very prestigious."

Back in the States, interest in robotics gradually began to increase. The first international symposium on industrial robotics was held at the Illinois Institute of Technology in 1970, and thereafter such meetings and exhibitions became more and more frequent. As such forums further increased awareness, the irrational buyer seemed to slowly evolve into the more regular customer who was willing to order several robots, rather than a token one to experiment with. Though not yet profitable, Unimation's cumulative sales volume increased from $2 million as of 1967 to $14 million as of 1972, representing revenues from an installed base of 105 robots worldwide to 698 robots worldwide.

Researchers at universities also began to focus their attention on mechanical arm designs. One Stanford University graduate student, Victor Scheinman, turned up at a 1975 trade show, The Fifth International Symposium of Industrial Robotics, in Chicago, Illinois, carrying a small electric arm. Engelberger remembers seeing Scheinman "standing outside with his nose pressed against the window" because he couldn't afford a booth. Already familiar and impressed with Scheinman's work, Engelberger invited him to share a

corner of his table, saying, "Well, Vic, come on in. What the hell—you're not going to hurt us."

But not everyone agreed. As Scheinman's arm wriggled around and attracted a lot of attention, AMF's people in the booth next door "got mad as hell," according to Engelberger. As he tells it, they said, "That guy is stealing all our thunder with that rascal arm." So Engelberger had to make Scheinman leave because "they were being poor sports."

Having a keen eye for inventions, Engelberger watched Scheinman as he struggled to keep his new company, Vicarm, Inc., afloat. General Electric and Cincinnati Milacron, a machine-tool manufacturer, were also interested. But at another robotics conference in Warsaw, Poland, in 1976, the two men met again just before Scheinman was to confer with the other companies. After a stroll around

At a luxurious press conference in 1978, General Motors unveiled the programmable universal machine for assembly (PUMA) system that included conveyors, parts feeders, and robots small enough to work alongside humans. But it was the small robots in that system, supplied by Unimation, that became known as PUMAs.

a lake, Engelberger and Scheinman clinched a deal with a handshake—Unimation would buy out Vicarm and Scheinman would become general manager of Unimation's new West Coast development division. Vicarm's thunder was now Unimation's.

While Scheinman had been building his arm in the laboratory, General Motors had been conducting an in-house survey of its car subassembly operations. GM's analysis showed that 35 percent of its workers were involved in subassemblies like window cranks and dashboards. They also found that 90 percent of the parts in their automobiles weighed less than five pounds. While window cranks and dashboard styles were likely to change, a three-thousand-pound car would probably remain the sum of many small parts. So GM concluded that small programmable machines that could accommodate changing subassembly styles and work alongside humans would be a worthwhile investment.

GM wrote specifications for a programmable universal machine for assembly (PUMA), with the same space intrusion and reach as humans. They sent specifications to everyone they thought would be interested in building it. There were twelve bidders, including Unimation. "The beauty of it was that we had it," says Engelberger; the Vicarm was what GM wanted. Unimation won a development contract to modify the Vicarm into the PUMA and in 1978 the first one arrived at GM's Technology Center in Warren, Michigan.

At that time, the American automotive industry was under fire for allowing the Japanese to capture much of the U.S. market and for failing to innovate. GM had also been hurt by bad press coverage of its Lordstown plant and labor relations. After years of maintaining a low profile where robots were concerned, says Engelberger, GM suddenly turned around. At a lavish press conference, GM unveiled an assembly system that included the robot arm, conveyors, and parts orienters. The system itself was billed as the PUMA, but to the press, "all the other crap was just conveyors." To them, "that thing, that arm, *that* was the PUMA," Engelberger says, "and there was no changing it." After that great send-off, says Engelberger, "our market just burst."

Engelberger claims that it was fortunate GM was not considering going into the robot business, but even so he found himself with another fight on his hands. Because of the press conference results, Engelberger wanted to call his new robot a PUMA. He told GM, "We can't help it and you can't help it, but the word you coined is the word that applies to our product." GM contended that it owned the trademark even though, by law, a trademark cannot be registered unless the registrant is offering the product for sale. Engelberger spent a year trying to convince GM to let him secure the rights to the name. He succeeded, but maintains that he could not have won the case had GM been planning to enter the robot business, at that time. GM eventually formed GMF Robotics Corporation in 1982. This was a joint venture with Fanuc Limited of Japan.

Although GM entered the market relatively late, other large corporations began to move in during the mid-

In this laboratory demonstration, a PUMA installs light bulbs in the backs of instrument panel cluster cases.

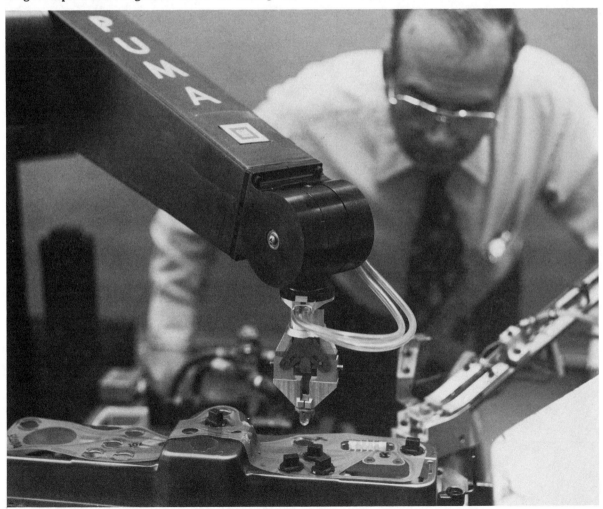

seventies. In the mid-sixties, Cincinnati Milacron Corporation in Lebanon, Ohio, introduced a system for directly controlling several machines with a central computer. Then, in 1974, it unveiled a mini-computer–controlled robot, the "T³," which stood for the "tomorrow tool today."

Prab Conveyors, Inc., in Kalamazoo, Michigan, installed its first robot in 1969 and as it gained acceptance the company created a robotics division in 1978. Losing clients to Unimation and AMF, Prab bought AMF's Versatran line for an undisclosed amount the following year. It reorganized itself in 1981 as Prab Robots, with Prab Conveyors as a wholly owned subsidiary. Such a flip-flop in nomenclature underscored the company's commitment to robotics.

By 1980, six companies commanded 94.3 percent of the then $90 million market. The following year the market almost doubled to reach $155 million and was still dominated by the same leaders. Although the 1982 market did not expand as much as the previous year's, those six companies found themselves sharing that $190 million market with a host of newcomers, who captured 25 percent of the year's sales.

Engelberger says his critics acknowledge that he did "a hell of a promotional job" for industrial robots, but point out that the wrong people got the message. Instead of customers heeding Engelberger's call, the leaders of the machine-tool, high-technology, and automotive industries caught on. Electric and electronics firms like GE and IBM saw advantages in building robots for their own labor-intensive light assembly operations, such as printed circuit board assembly. With car manufacturers like GM, Renault, and Volkswagen in the game, the robot industry was confronted by its biggest customers turned competitors.

Furthermore, Engelberger asks with a laugh, "Can you imagine an executive going to the country club and teeing off and somebody asking, 'Are you making robots?' and he's going to say, 'Gee. Sorry, no.'" Robotics became a corporate status symbol. And while by now there have already been 100 or so abortive efforts around the world, there are still about 230 robot manufacturers.

When the 1982 recession hit, machine-tool cancellations, including robots, exceeded orders for six months, according to Engelberger, and Reagan's incentives were not meaningful, because tax credits and rapid depreciation were only useful if a company was making a profit. The robot industry suffered because "you can't convince somebody to buy a piece of equipment to get a tax credit when he's losing money," Engelberger explains.

Besides Unimation's troubles, Condec's smoke-stack industries, like bronze and steel valves for housing and machinery for making car tires, were not doing well. The construction industry was at a standstill and cars were not in demand. This, coupled with "the big people joining in the robot game," meant that Condec could not adequately support Unimation. In 1981, Condec had issued approximately 5 million shares of Unimation stock, 20 percent of which was sold to the public, raising about $17 million at the offering. When in 1982 financial advisers suggested selling a property, Condec did not want to part with Unimation. Engelberger's companies were once again considered for sale. Either Unimation or Consolidated Controls had to go.

Condec negotiated the sale of Unimation with companies that included GE, IBM, Litton, Westinghouse, and several European concerns, including France's Matra, as active bidders. Engelberger had the power to veto an inappropriate would-be purchaser so that he could safeguard Unimation and protect the people who had worked for him. None of the companies were objectionable, and in December 1982 Westinghouse made the highest bid—$107 million, including stock that was bought back from the public at $21 per share. Engelberger signed a contract containing a five-year noncompetition clause, which required him not to go into a business that would rival the new, wholly owned Westinghouse subsidiary. Engelberger was content with the deal. "I made out quite well," he says, "with a golden handshake and a big new boat." And though he didn't have to work for Westinghouse, he chose to do so.

In January 1984 Engelberger resigned as president of Unimation. He preferred to act as a Westinghouse consultant for its Energy and Advanced Technology Group. Besides negotiating the Kawasaki deal for Unimation and Westinghouse's Mitsubishi and Kamatsu agreements, Engelberger reviews and evaluates research activities at Westinghouse. He also lectures to divisions on the process of innovation and how to encourage it. In addition, Engelberger is devoting time to his new venture capital firm, Technology Transitions, Inc., in Hartford, Connecticut.

Back in the Unimation boardroom just off his office, Engelberger had been able to sit at the conference table and gaze across at a kitchen unit against the wall. When Uni-

An example of the Versatran robot line that was developed in the late 1950s by American Machinery and Foundry and bought out in 1979 by Prab Conveyors, which is now Prab Robots.

mation was on the market, Engelberger preferred to let Westinghouse officials think he was just "a jerk who didn't put the kitchen in a room." Engelberger figured that it was best not to emphasize his ambition to watch his robot butler, to be named "Isaac," make coffee, serve Danishes, and clean up. When the kitchenette was installed in 1980, Engelberger imagined that Isaac would emerge from a closet on the opposite wall and surprise board members by preparing a meal under voice communication. That plan will be resurrected, he says. "You've got to ease them into this," he says, "so we'll get back to it a little bit later than I thought."

There is no question in Engelberger's mind that one day industrial and personal robotics will converge. "You can come from the top with the expensive, rugged, strong industrial robot earning its keep and you can come from the bottom with the personal robot.... All these ideas will come together ... and we'll find this meeting ground in the service arenas in the household role."

In the not-too-distant future, Engelberger says homes will have a "great big massive computer in the robot pantry." That computer will communicate with larger computers so that if a robot is doing maintenance on a dishwasher, for example, and the robot gets stuck, it can call the larger computer for instructions. "It's going to take a modem to call up the factory and say, 'You know, I'm stuck,' and a smarter robot there can say. 'There's a little bit of that going around, right?' And then he'll tell him what to do."

You will be able to tell the same home robot what meal you want to cook and it will prepare the necessary cooking utensils and ingredients. Says Engelberger, you will tell the robot that your main course is number 133 and dessert is number 67, and it will look them up on the computer and check for ingredients in the larder. The robot will also know the age of all your condiments and it will know what is or is not ripe. Anything that is out of date will be thrown away, and it will order what is needed from the grocery store. "Now you're the artist who's coming home—you go in there and make your beautiful gourmet meal. You sit down and enjoy it with your family or friends, and when you're through, you get up and go in the sitting room for a brandy and a coffee. The robot comes in and cleans up. It washes the dishes and does the dirty work."

Household robots are not yet capable of preparing gourmet meals and, since soft materials are difficult to handle, they could not make beds as easily as they could wash dishes. But most robots are capable of handling labor-intensive activities, like fast-food delivery, if certain operations are modified. When Engelberger and a McDonald's executive vice president reviewed that company's operations, they determined that industrial robots could make french fries and cherry pies. But since a robot lacks the sensory perception to separate paper sticking to hamburger patties, McDonald's would have had to alter its procedures. "Eventually it ended up that the robots could do it, not only like Pizza Time, where you have entertaining robots. The robot could actually cook and prepare the food and deliver it," Engelberger says.

Besides changing procedures one can alter the solution, that is, the robot. But Engelberger says, "It's still a very serendipitous thing that you have a solution looking for a problem." Engelberger respects fortuitous discussions and recognizes that they can lead to new applications. He lectures to many trade groups, no matter how obscure. Sooner or later, Engelberger says, someone wondering if robots could help him will come along and ask, "Do you suppose you could?" That is what happened with investment casting. "We never thought of investment casting—the way the Greeks made statues. It's one of the loveliest things for a robot to do," says Engelberger, "...because the human can't do it as well as a robot can." Engelberger believes that through lecturing he will continue to find people willing to try something new. Then, "You change the solution a little bit and give it a little vision or change it physically and make it fast."

Engelberger has been skeptical, however. In 1973, an Australian research scientist telephoned him to inquire about the possibility of robots shearing sheep. Engelberger said, "You're nuts," but the scientist arrived at Unimation and presented a preliminary plan for a robot, about the size of the PUMA, to shear immobilized sheep.

The Australian wool industry perceived shortages of human shearers and was already facing competition from the synthetic textile industry. So to protect Australia's largest export commodity, accounting for $1.7 billion in exports from 135 million sheep, several universities are tackling the problem with funding from the Australian Wool Company. Despite having significant technical hurdles to overcome, particularly in sensors, the company says "the robotic solution has the most promise in the medium term." Says

Engleberger feels that robots will one day do "the dirty work" at home. This RB5X personal robot is already able to vacuum floors and rugs with the help of a special attachment.

Engelberger gleefully, "You tighten up the skin, don't catch the wool, and watch out for the fact that some are male and some are female."

Engelberger also has in mind a robotic gas station. Bemoaning the current twenty-four-hour and self-service offerings, he says, "Gas could really be pumped fast, but they have that slow thing to give the guy a chance to polish the windows and shoot the bull with you.... When I go to a gas station, I want *gas*. I don't want a lot of crap and I don't want to hear the same conversation I've had all my life with the gasoline station attendant." Self-service stations "are a lousy deal—your hands smell of gasoline, you've gotta get out and pay the clerk, and when you go to one of those places at night, the dregs of the earth work there so you're afraid of getting rolled."

One gasoline company that Engelberger spoke with said the solution is for the customer to remain in the car. If the customer had a credit card that identified him as well as the car, Engelberger imagines, he could stay behind the wheel. The card would tell the gas station " 'I am a 1981 Chevrolet,' and it would immediately know where the gas tank is." Then a robot would find it and pump the gas. Again, the robot would need some sensory perception to weigh the car, for example, or to adjust to motion if there are three kids in back jumping up and down. And Engelberger adds, "You certainly don't want it to start pumping gas in the window." The idea is very logical, he says, because almost every town wants a twenty-four-hour island. And while there are still some technical problems, "that robot station should be a hell of a business."

Fruit picking is another possible application for robots that is of particular interest to the Italians and Israelis. In the United States, one way of harvesting is to shake the base of a tree and allow ripe fruit to fall. Bruised oranges could then be used for orange juice. But Italy and Israel want fruit handled like gems, says Engelberger, since the market is more aesthetically oriented. Computer simulations, a special robot hand, and visual aids are being developed by Unimation, under contract to an Italian firm. Engelberger says that these will help determine characteristics, like fruit color or the shape of surrounding leaves, so that robots can do the picking.

Noting the U.S. loss of textile and garment industry jobs to Singapore and Taiwan, Engelberger sees robotics as a means of providing unique services rather than recapturing low-technology industries. "Everyone is all excited—'we've got to save the garment industry, it's going offshore.' Now I can make a good point to say that I'm my brother's keeper, we cannot ignore the Third World anymore. It's not ignoring us, so we just can't put our blinders on. But it may very well be that all low-technology/high-labor industries *should* go to the Third World." Then if we want to retain something that is good for us in a highly industrialized world, he says "let us do something different. Let us have an automated salon [where] they take a hologram of your body and you choose a Pierre Cardin that's not on the shelf. You sit and drink coffee, and while you're waiting, you pick your cloth, just as you would with a tailor or seamstress, and you get something *built for you*. Now, you can't do that in Taiwan."

While any technology is transferable, Engelberger says that it is very difficult to compete with a service, like the salon, that is on site. "That's a direction you could go in to say that we *do* want to provide some unique services to people, and we're going to get it with our flexible automation because we're going to deliver it on the spot. Think of the inventory savings. Think of all the damned designer things that they steal from couturiers in France that are no damn good. They're stuck and become dust rags."

What does the flexible manufacturing factory of the future look like to Engelberger? How soon will it arrive and what are the social implications? The methodology for unmanned manufacturing is definitely here, he says. "You'll end up with people from the factory who will do the judgmental things," he says, and products will be designed so that they can be made by robots. The factory of the future will be a turnkey system: If a customer wants to make widgets, the supplier will be able to say, "Stand back. Let me give you all the machinery, build the factory for you, and then I'm going to give you the key."

But while people are now thinking of robots as just part of such a system, Engelberger says robot capabilities will improve in ways that people don't yet see on the frontier. "The minute you give the robots sensory perception—vision, touch, voice communication, you're going to get closer and closer to what Asimov was all about when he talked about robots," he says. "A robot becomes more and more robotic the more and more it emulates the human being."

On the other hand, even though the Japanese "look you straight in the eye without cracking a smile and say that by

"The minute you give robots sensory perception—vision, touch, voice communication—you're going to get closer and closer to what Asimov was all about when he talked about robots. A robot becomes more and more robotic the more and more it emulates the human being."

the turn of the century we'll have only knowledge workers,'' that is a noble goal that will not succeed, Engelberger says. Removing everyone from rote activities will take a while— for instance, as agriculture became mechanized, it took one hundred years for farmers and farmworkers to decline from 47 percent to 4 percent of the total work force. According to *Scientific American,* it went from 64 percent in 1850 to 3.1 percent in 1982. Perhaps it will take fifty years for 29 percent of the nation's labor force in manufacturing to reduce to 5 percent. "Ultimately, I don't know what the time base is," he says. "I hope it will be gentle."

There are several constraints that will reduce the speed, he explains. There is, of course, concern over unemployment, but while displacement will occur, it need not be massive, as it was when the automotive industry faltered. Robotics can happen gradually, taking and creating jobs in an array of different industries. There are also capital-formation constraints. "You've got to form capital and it takes an awful lot of capital to accomplish automation." Furthermore, he observes, echoing Alvin Toffler in *Future Shock,* people resist change. "There is a limit to how much change people can adapt to. We need a more efficient means of creating our material wealth," says Engelberger, "that is not only more efficient in labor, but more efficient in the use of capital and raw materials. Those are the three elements of productivity." The difficulty, he says, is distributing the benefits, which have never been evenly distributed in the past. A union might try to convince Engelberger to build a plant in Detroit, where there is unemployment. And he can, as he did, choose instead to build in Waterbury, Connecticut, where plenty of skilled but unemployed workers also live. That has been a personal effort at distributing benefits, but Engelberger thinks statesmen are needed for this purpose.

Above all, however, this man wants to see increased productivity rates. "I'm completely convinced that we end up with more benefit than cost in the transition [to automation]," he says. "I take the fundamental stand that the gain of productivity is always good."

THE NEW INDUSTRIAL REVOLUTION: THE APPLICATIONS AND USES OF INDUSTRIAL ROBOTS

3

Anything that is manufactured is manipulated. Every part is manipulated while it is made. Every part is manipulated while it is assembled. A part is manipulated when it is delivered from a plant. Everything is manipulation.

George C. Devol, Jr. (interview, 3/11/83)

hrough the ages, man has prepared objects for manufacture with his hands, the most dexterous manipulators in the animal kingdom. In fact, the words *manufacture* and *manipulation* have their roots in the Latin word for hand, *manus.* Now, however, those words have come to mean the handling of materials by hands or mechanical means. Since the Industrial Revolution, one result of the introduction of machinery has been the rise of mass production and the decline of artisanry. Now, as sophisticated robot manipulators and other automated equipment are introduced in factories, we are moving toward unmanned manufacturing. Besides sounding paradoxical given the origins of these words, a factory with few human workers would seem to entirely eliminate customized goods. In fact, this is not necessarily so.

Another result of the industrial age has been the assembly line's effect on workers. Spending one's working life guiding machines in their repetitive and uninspiring activi-

More than 50 percent of Texas Instruments' calculators are manufactured in a highly automated assembly facility in Abilene, Texas. The system assembles calculator keyboards, metal-oxide semiconductor integrated circuits, displays, circuit films and cases. At this point in the system, visually aided inspection robots test each calculator as it comes down the assembly line.

John Deere & Company, in Davenport, Iowa, uses three Nordson robots to paint logging and earth-moving equipment. Increased productivity, material savings, and reduced energy consumption were bonuses for Deere.

ties stultifies the human brain. Those in charge of machines, feeling no interest in their work and filled with dull resentment at the unrewarding nature of their jobs, cannot be expected to labor for quality. Shoddiness often seeps in. The advent of robotics can alleviate this.

The advantages of the Industrial Revolution can now be fully realized. The use of robots will prevent humans from being forced to function like robots. Incapable of weariness and resentment, robots can labor indefinitely, not only producing more objects, but ensuring that there will be little or no variation in product quality and safety. Uniformity will persist, but flexible manufacturing will enable more product customization than previous industrial manufacturing methods. Special features can be added to a product by temporarily altering a robot's computer program and the changes will not affect quality. Thus, a new means of production, allowing large runs of personalized products, has arrived.

In factories today, industrial robots perform such tasks as welding, machine loading and unloading, material handling, spray finishing, assembly, and machining applications. In nuclear power plants and other facilities where radiation is hazardous to humans, robotic arms that are partly human-controlled and partly computer-controlled are used for maintenance, repair, and waste removal. Similar robotic arms on diving vehicles facilitate undersea salvage and exploration by the world's navies and the offshore oil industry. As the technologies of such remote manipulators and robotics converge, hazardous waste and salvage operations will also become more automated.

Recently, with the advent of two-dimensional vision systems, certain factory material-handling operations have been improved and parts inspection has been introduced. But the majority of industrial robots currently installed in plants are not "smart" or "intelligent" manipulators, largely because their ability to sense objects in their environment is still primitive. Since they do have computer memories, these robots can "learn" to do certain tasks, but they can only act effectively with what they have learned if the objects to be manipulated are placed at specific, consistent locations.

Mechanical, electrical, and applications engineers, who are responsible for installing robots, have tended to match robots with items designed for production by other means. This approach, along with robotic deficiencies in vision and touch, has limited the implementation of robots.

Products are now beginning to be designed so that robots can produce them more easily. The application most likely to expand as a result of this new approach to design is light assembly.

In all that immediately follows, think of robots as machines that do the heavy work, the dangerous work, the tedious work, as machines have done from the first use of the lever and wheel. But think of them also as special kinds of machines, imbued with the capacity to seem as though they make decisions and show judgment of a limited kind. Since they can do work of a complexity and delicacy no machines could do before, a whole spectre of labor is thus lifted from the back of humanity.

APPLICATIONS
WELDING

Industrial robots (IRs) can perform two types of welding operations—spot and arc welding. Spot welding's ancestry dates back to techniques used by blacksmiths who welded wrought iron by heating two pieces almost to their melting point and hammering them on an anvil until they became one. Today, two metal sheets are welded by laying one sheet on top of the other and fusing them with an electric gun at several points—hence the name "spot welding." This

Ford uses German-made KUKA robots for assembling Escorts in its European plants. In this Saarlouis, West Germany, plant, Escort fender aprons are spot-welded to cross and side members at Station 1, creating a transportable basic unit. At Station 2, bulkhead and radiator panel assemblies are attached to the previous assembly with a conventional welding press. Five robots weld engine compartments at Station 3, and more conventional welding occurs at Station 4. At Station 5, two robots sharing a turntable weld the rear chassis. The front end, center floor, and rear floor are then joined at the other remaining stations.

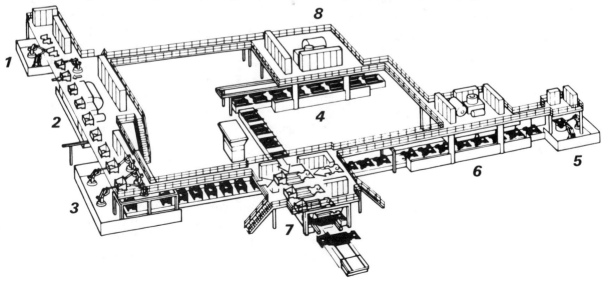

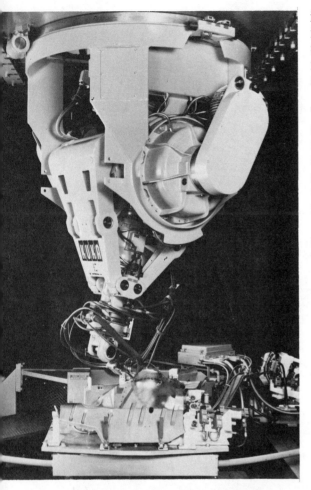

This ceiling-mounted robot can spot-weld highly curved workpieces that floor-mounted robots might not easily reach. The robot, a KUKA 200, is the first of its kind on the world market. It can also be used for material-handling operations.

is a difficult and unpleasant task for humans because welding guns are heavy. Also, assembly lines only allow a short time period to manipulate the gun and welds can easily be missed or placed inconsistently. This affects product quality and possibly safety.

There are two ways to make use of a welding robot. The robot can move while the parts to be welded are stationary, or the parts can move on a conveyor and a stationary robot can weld them as they pass. The second method, line tracking, is gaining wide acceptance because it requires less sophisticated conveyor equipment. The IR's computer control system measures the speed of the parts and adjusts the robot arm to variations in line speed.

To complete a weld, a robot must follow a sequence of steps. First, the two sheets must be pressed together by the welding gun electrodes with a force of 800 to 1,000 pounds per square inch. Next, an electric current of large amperage but low voltage is passed through the sheets, generating heat and creating the weld. The electrodes maintain the pressure until the weld cools. The sequence then begins again at a new "spot."

The robot's computer memory must store variables for the sequence, such as the time it takes to position the gun perpendicular to the spot to be welded. In some instances the robot must perform a group of welds close together. In such a case, another role of the computer might be to control the arm so that distances between welds are evenly spaced. Each movement contributes to a precise total cycle time.

In addition, several sequences for welding different models of a product must be remembered and programs for these sequences must be called up when a different model appears on the line. When several robots work along a production line, one centralized computer can coordinate their activities. For example, the computer will call up programs for individual robots working on different styles along the line. It can also record production statistics such as the number of welds completed in a given time period by one or all of the robots. This monitoring capability also extends to overall production figures such as the number of models completed per hour, day, or month.

Spot welding is not useful for long-path joints between two side-by-side metal sheets. Instead, arc welding is used. In this process, metal sheets are butted together and a thin tungsten wire at the tip of an electrode is brought close to the surface. Current is passed through, creating a spark, or electric "arc." Inert gases are required to sustain the electric arc and prevent oxidation, so arc welding is sometimes called the "tungsten inert gas" process (TIG), the "metal inert gas" (MIG) technique, or "gas metal arc welding" (GMAW). The gas insulates the weld area from air, which otherwise would cause oxidation. Oxidation would threaten weld integrity.

The resultant heat, sometimes as much as 6,500 degrees Fahrenheit, melts the edges of the metal sheets. The electrode wire also melts, adding to the molten pool, and the pieces are fused. Because the wire melts, it must be continuously fed.

Since 1979, Hayes-Dana, Inc., a division of the Dana Corporation in Barrie, Ontario, Canada, has been using arc-

An Advanced Robotics robot of the type used at the Hayes-Dana plant.

welding robots to manufacture axle housings for its trucks and buses. In the company's Barrie, Ontario, plant, eighteen Cyro robots supplied by Advanced Robotics Corporation arc-weld thirty-three different axle housings. The robots perform five different weldments at six stations.

Arc-welding robots can also be used to manufacture robots. Unimation uses its Apprentice robot to arc-weld Unimate trunk columns to their bases. The Apprentice is an aid to skilled human welders, hence its name. The welder must guide the robot to weld the seam each time. While this Apprentice is welding, the human welder can move to another Apprentice. Alternating between the two allows him to prepare one robot for a weld while the other robot completes a weld.

MATERIAL HANDLING

Material handling is the second largest IR application. A common material-handling task in manufacturing processes is palletizing parts as they come off a conveyor and depalletizing parts in order to put them on a conveyor. Pallets are platforms on which arrays of items can be transported and stored. Usually they are designed to be moved by a forklift or crane.

This application, which cuts across many industries, involves complex robot programming. In palletizing, four situations can occur when a pallet arrives at a robot station. An empty pallet can be partially or completely filled by the robot. A partially filled pallet can arrive and then be partially or completely filled.

There must be a way of indicating to the robot which of the four situations is at hand and what program to use. This can be done by labeling the pallet with a bar code like the labels used on supermarket products. An operator holds a wand that reads the label so that he knows which button on the computer controller to push for the appropriate program. Some robots having two-dimensional vision can recognize the pattern of filled or unfilled spaces and determine on their own what program to use .

Once the appropriate program has been selected, it can tell the robot where to place parts at different positions

The machining applications of industrial robots include: cutting, grinding, polishing, drilling, sanding, buffing, deflashing, and deburring.

A Thermwood robot, equipped with a special suction cup gripper, loads a plastics-forming machine and stacks flat plastic sheets.

A2

A Prab Model 4200 robot loads and unloads 40-pound cylinder heads from two multispindle machine tools. The workcell is one of seven machining stations at a manufacturing plant where diesel cylinder heads are made for military tank engines.

Fourteen Cincinnati Milacron T³-586 robots spot-weld J-car bodies at a General Motors Assembly Division plant in South Gate, California. The robots spot an average of 400 welds on each body and complete seventy-two bodies per hour. Four different J-car models can be welded on the same line.

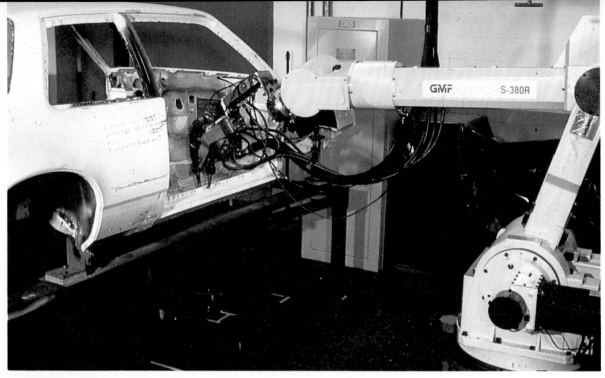

A robot spot-welds a car body. Note the claw-shaped tool mounted on the robot's wrist—these are the electrodes through which electricity passes, heating the metal sheets and joining them at one point.

Palletizing parts as they come off a conveyor is a common material-handling task performed by industrial robots.

This large Prab Model FC robot is capable of handling loads of up to 2,000 pounds and was designed to dip wax cores into a series of slurry and sand baths for investment-casting processes.

This three-handed Model FC has just dipped molds into a tank of fluidized sand, which sticks to the previously applied slurry.

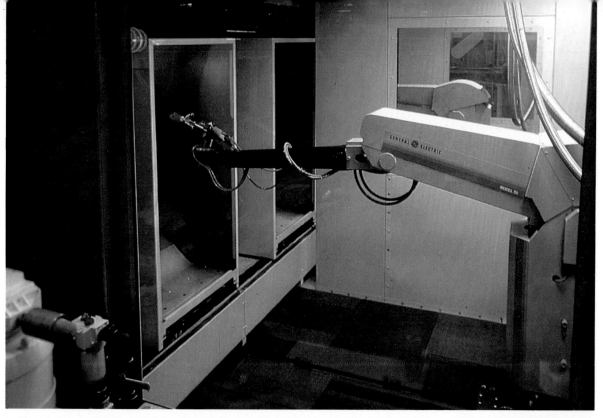

Isolated in its own booth, this hydraulically powered General Electric S6 robot, built by Hitachi, applies a releasing agent to refrigerator cases. Besides using the reach of its arm, the robot can approach and retreat from a workpiece by moving on a track.

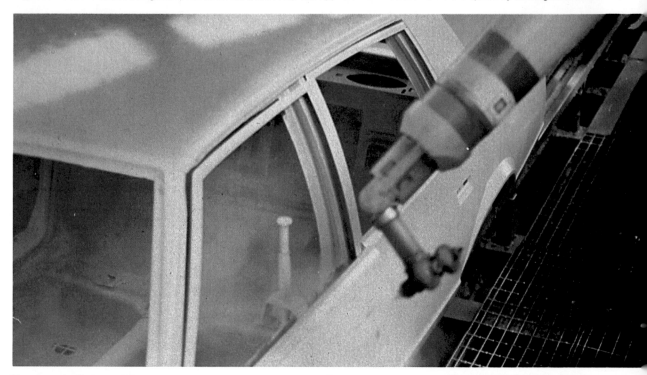

Two numerically controlled painters, robots originally developed by General Motors and now offered by GMF Robotics, spray paint pickup trucks on both sides of this General Motors line. The robots are oblivious to the paint particles, which would be very hazardous to humans.

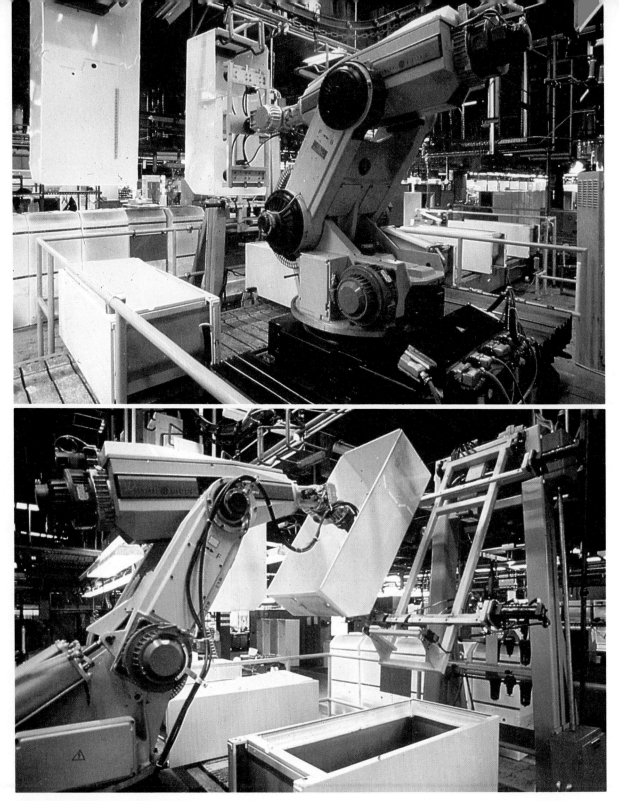

Here, with the help of a rectangular-shaped end effector, a GP132 (GP stands for general purpose) robot lifts a refrigerator liner from an overhead conveyor for insertion into the outside case. The electric robot, built by Volkswagen, can handle up to 132 pounds and can also spot-weld, palletize, and perform material-handling operations.

At General Electric's appliance manufacturing plant in Louisville, Kentucky, Cincinnati Milacron's T³-566 robot transfers refrigerator compressors from one moving conveyor to another. The compressors hang on yokes, which the T³ locates with its two optical sensors. The robot lifts a yoke from one conveyor and hangs it on hooks on the second conveyor. Then the robot's tracking ability allows it to follow the conveyors so that it "knows" the moving yoke's position. When a yoke has completed the conveyor loop, the robot returns it to the first line.

At General Motors, ASEA robots equipped with laser scanners verify dimensions of openings in car bodies.

This mock-up shows two of the Los Alamos Meson Physics Facility's bilateral force-sensing master/slave manipulators attached to a longer arm (coming out of the page). With these manipulators, workers can perform maintenance tasks, like soldering, electrical wiring, some welding, and handling of delicate radioactive materials, without risking the effects of radiation.

Robots depalletize 8-foot projectiles being built for the United States Army.

on the pallet. Similarly, in depalletizing, the program tells the robot where to reach for an object to unload it from the pallet. Some robots can grab a part gently, with the help of sensors that indicate how much force a gripper should apply to the object in order to lift it. The program also tells the robot how to orient the part in order to fit it on the pallet when palletizing, and how to approach a positioned part on a pallet when depalletizing.

MACHINE LOADING AND UNLOADING

Machine loading and unloading robots pick and transfer parts to and from machines. These robots are mainly used in foundries.

The die-casting industry uses robots to remove parts from die-casting machines. The die-casting process forms parts by forcing molten nonferrous metals, like lead, aluminum, zinc, magnesium, copper, and brass alloys, into molds. These molds are made of metal and are called "dies." One die consists of two halves that are pressed together by the die-casting machine. Molten metal is pumped into the closed die halves so that every cranny fills. When the metal solidifies, the die is opened and the casting ejected. The casting is then quenched in water and placed in a trim press. Flash, the extra metal that has overflowed from the die cavities, is then trimmed off. This is done by blowing off extra material with air jets.

The working environment in this operation is unpleasant for humans because of the heat generated. But for a die-casting operation to run smoothly, the dies must be lubricated and cleaned. This requires a worker to place his hands inside the dies, which introduces risk since the dies might close due to some malfunction. Also, despite cleaning and lubrication, a casting can still stick to the dies, requiring that it be removed manually. Again, this can be dangerous to the worker.

Casting, removal, quenching, and trimming are suited for a pick-and-place robot because the path traveled between points is not important. Of the four steps in this sequence, removal contributes most to the cycle time. Die-casting cycle times with human operators are generally under fifteen seconds, but 50 to 75 percent of this results from humans' efforts to remove castings. Robots that reach in and grab castings have increased the productive capabilities of die-casting machines by 200 to 300 percent. Because robots can work more consistently than humans, the rate of operation results in more uniform die temperatures. In turn, this results in less flash to be trimmed. Since standarized grippers can be used, the orientation of the parts is inherently consistent, and since users do not need to change existing equipment when a robot is installed, this application is widespread.

A second machine-loading and unloading application involves the investment-casting process. This technique for making intricate parts is sometimes called "precision casting" or the "lost wax process." It dates back to ancient times and was used by the Egyptians after 2500 B.C. to make jewelry and art objects. In manufacturing, this technique results in very accurate parts production.

Investment casting involves six steps. First, a wax facsimile of the part must be made, usually by injecting wax into a machined metal mold. The wax model is dipped into a slurry of chemical binders and then into a bed of fluidized sand over and over again. (Fluidized sand is just sand in a tub that has air pumped into the bottom. The air causes the sand to behave like a liquid so it will coat the wax evenly.) Alternating between chemical binders and sand builds a multilayered sand mold around the wax. This mold is cured in an oven at over 1,000 degrees Centigrade, the molten wax is poured out, and the resulting female mold is ready for molten metal to be poured in. After the metal cools, the sand mold is broken away.

Unlike die-cast parts, investment-cast parts require little flash removal. There are no join marks resulting from two mold halves being pressed together, so machining the part after it has cooled is minimal. And since the original metal die tolerates wax better than molten metal, it can be

The Prab Model FA robot flips an automobile floor panel in a mock-up at Prab's plant.

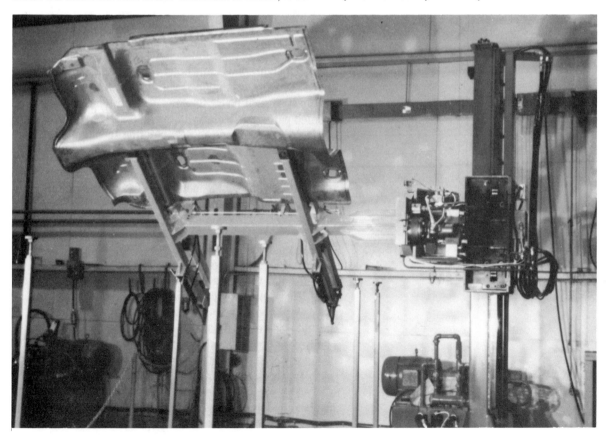

spray gun could be connected to five hoses, which would in turn be connected to five tanks of paint. The program could say "stop white," "pass air and paint solvent through the gun" (to clean it), and then "spray red." If the robot were operating in a highly automated plant with a master controller, the robot's controller could instruct the larger computer to tell an automatic paint changer to make the switch.

Besides spraying consistently and automatically switching paint, spray-painting IRs can save paint by supplying an electrostatic charge. The charged paint particles are attracted to electrically grounded parts, thus material savings costs alone can be between 10 and 30 percent.

Although finishes can be applied with greater consistency, some complicating factors enter the picture. Sometimes the IR cannot allow for changing conditions, and the characteristics of the finishing material, such as its viscosity, solids content (the amount of solid paint versus the amount of thinner), air pressure, substance pressure, and temperature must be maintained at exactly the same level day after day.

These complicating factors are specific to spray-finishing IRs and make their installation more complex than is true for other applications. They share requirements of consistent part placement and gun orientation. And as in spot welding, parts can move and the IR can be stationary, or the parts can be stationary and the IR can reach to spray them. So spray-finishing installations are generally more complex and expensive than other installations.

 MACHINING

achining includes cutting, grinding, polishing, drilling, sanding, buffing, deflashing, and deburring. Machine tools like lathes can cut, grind, and polish more accurately than robots. Some of the other machining tasks that have been done manually can be done by robots, but in general, most IRs are not yet accurate enough. Those engaged in drilling, for example, require templates to guide them to points that must be drilled—as is true for human drillers. A template is used in the same way that a tailor uses a pattern to cut a shape out of cloth or to locate buttonholes.

For drilling, the template can be a sheet, with holes punched out, that overlays the sheet metal to be worked on and indicates the points to be drilled.

While most machining applications are too precise for IRs, some IR manufacturers (notably ASEA) consider deburring the second most important applications growth area next to welding. Deburring is the removal of excess bits of metal after a part has been through some earlier machining. At the present time, most IRs are set up to remove burrs whether there are burrs or not. They cannot "see" whether a burr exists, so they "assume" that it was left on a part after milling, and follow a program to remove it. Some deburring IRs can touch-sense a large burr or determine that no burr exists on a portion of a part. In the latter case, they can skip the section of the program for deburring that particular portion of the part.

There are two approaches to installing a deburring IR, according to Lars Gustafsson, applications engineer at ASEA. The IR can handle the part and manipulate it against

An ASEA robot deburrs a stationary differential housing.

a tool that does the deburring, or the IR can hold the deburring tool and manipulate it around the stationary part. One advantage to the first approach is that several tools, such as carbide cutters and rotating files, can be used without replacing one for the other on the robot's arm. The tools, mounted on hard machine equipment, remain in permanent locations within the robot's reach. These tools can also have unlimited horsepower, which is not the case when they are powered by a robot.

One limitation, however, is that if the part to be handled is large, the robot will also have to be large in order to manage the payload. This means that IR movements will be neither as accurate nor as speedy as they are when handling small parts. Since deburring requires great accuracy and speed, IRs that handle the part are most suitable for light parts where multiple high-powered tools for deburring are required.

The second approach, having the tool robot-mounted, is advantageous because there is then no limitation of part weight, because the IR isn't doing the lifting. In this case the IR can be smaller (and therefore cheaper) since the tools it holds are not heavy. The difficulty occurs when a robot-mounted tool must be changed, and while some automatic tool-changing procedures have been developed, an IR that handles a tool is still preferable for deburring heavy parts that don't call for tool changes.

In either approach, tools wear, and this must be compensated for either by the robot or the interfacing machining equipment. Automatic compensation for tool wear is easier when the IR handles the part. If the part is to be ground, for example, the IR can adjust for changes in the grinding wheel's diameter as the wheel wears. The IR will maintain the same relative contact position between parts and the wheel throughout a batch, compensating for changes in the wheel's size. This leads to greater uniformity of ground parts.

ASSEMBLY

ssembly by means other than welding includes fitting together parts, and holding them together with nuts, bolts, screws, bonding, or other means. This is a relatively new application for IRs and many assembly robots still exist in the research and development (R & D) or early application stage. Nevertheless, robotic assembly could lead to enormous changes in manufacturing techniques and labor force distribution. Eighty-five percent of all manual labor expended in U.S. industry can be classified as assembly. According to Joseph Engelberger, in 1981 40 percent of the blue-color work force was engaged in assembly.

Unlike welding IRs, assembly IRs are small and so have small payloads. They are designed for light-duty, very precise assembly and perform at very high speeds. Some have 2-D vision that allows them to determine part orientation, some have tactile sensing that allows them to control the force of their grippers, and some have both.

A worker operates the computer controls of an assembly line at Chrysler's St. Louis assembly plant.

The first IRs developed especially for assembly include Unimation's PUMA (programmable universal machine for assembly); the SCARA (selective compliance assembly robot arm), developed in Japan; The Pragma, by Digital Electronic Automation (DEA), Turin, Italy, and Olivetti's Sigma.

Today, three PUMAs of different sizes make up part of the Unimate line. They all have five and some have six degrees of freedom—that is, five or six fundamentally different directions in which the robot can move. The smallest, the 260 Series, has a payload of 2 pounds (.9 kilograms). The largest, the 760 Series, has a payload of 22 pounds (10 kilograms). These robots have been enhanced over the years, with the middle and oldest PUMA, the 560 Series, being upgraded to a second generation PUMA and rechristened the Unimate PUMA Mark II.

Although the PUMA was initially designed as an assembly robot, PUMAs now perform many of the applications described so far. Examples of PUMAs in assembly include small-appliance assembly, electrical component insertion, and wire harness wrapping.

The SCARA robot was developed by Professor Hiroshi Makino of Yamanashi University, with the support of thirteen Japanese companies, including Nitto Seiko, Pentel, and Sankyo Seiki, which now produce SCARA types. Because the SCARA robot was designed with the sizes of electric appliances in mind, electric appliance manufacturers showed more of an interest in the SCARA than did automobile manufacturers. Many Japanese electric appliance manufacturers, who have declared that they intend to robotize 50 to 75 percent of their assembly operations by 1985, have set about building modified versions of the SCARA. Sankyo Seiki, for example, has developed a system called "SKILAM" that has two sets of SCARA-type arms. One company employs it on a micromotor assembly line for television sets. The system is also employed for fitting various kinds of components onto electronic substrates, assembly of automotive parts like carburetors, and assembly of optical equipment parts.

Nippon Electric has developed several assembly robots, one of which is very similar to SCARA. Two models are used for assembly and inspection of telephone receiver components, assembly and bonding of integrated circuits, and assembly of keyboard switches for personal computers.

DEA's Pragma robot, also known as the Allegro (named for its speed), which GE builds under a DEA license, can be fitted with up to four arms, each with three to five degrees of freedom. GE had several experimental installations in November 1981 that had tactile sensors attached to the robot's grippers. This means that if a part is faulty or in a wrong position, the robot can sense that, try to complete the task by pushing hard, and, if that fails, reject the part or sound a warning. Tactile sensing also permits detection of missing components and rejection of substandard parts. Pragmas now in European factories assemble sealing valves for refrigerators, motor cylinder heads, and track rods.

Westinghouse has an exclusive license to manufacture, sell, and service Olivetti's Sigma robots. They are sold as Westinghouse's Series 5000 robot and can have one, two, or three arms that are attached to a pair of precision overhead rails on a steel frame. The arms can act independently or in collaboration, along the horizontal length of the frame. The frame provides the rigidity needed for accurate and precise assembly.

The system has vision through solid-state cameras, mounted on its arms, that determine the displacement and orientation of randomly placed workpieces on the conveyor. Examples of products assembled by the Series 5000 are cassettes, thermostats, and printed circuit boards. Olivetti's Sigma robot tasks are: assembly of printed circuit boards, color ribbon cassettes for typewriters, shock absorber components, electric plugs, feelers for electric typewriters, insertion of feelers into keyboards of typewriters, assembly of pistons and connecting rods.

This bench-top robot, built by Control Automation and called "MiniSembler," is designed for electronic assembly operations. The arm moves from side to side, back and forth and up and down. The tip of the arm is the lower metal cylinder, which rotates 320 degrees and can position electronic components to within ± 0.001 inches. The camera, mounted parallel to the arm tip, is part of the vision system, which gauges and inspects components.

INSPECTION

Some assembly robots also function as inspection robots. Hitachi's assembly IR, which has a twenty-five-step memory capacity and a 7-ounce (200-gram) payload capacity can fit together different components one by one in a specified order. The robot moves fast, and takes only one to two seconds to fit together workpieces. Its gripper can grasp parts gently and a special searching function automatically detects the holes of workpieces. The special search enables the gripper to properly fit parts even when position-

ing is not accurate. An automatic rejecting function prevents assembly of defective workpieces.

Automatix has developed a vision system, Autovision 4, that is capable of statistical process and quality control. The system inspects products by taking three-dimensional readings and does a statistical analysis to determine if the dimensions are drifting out of tolerance. If, for example, a car subassembly like car-door-to-car-body gap is on the verge of becoming too tight or too loose, the vision system communicates this to earlier stations on the assembly line. Since it can predict the time it will take for the subassemblies to become unacceptable, the system can prevent their occurrence altogether. This ongoing statistical quality control diminishes rejections when final assemblies are inspected, and so can lead to large savings.

REMOTE MANIPULATORS
IN HAZARDOUS ENVIRONMENTS

Master/slave manipulators, arms that humans can control with joy sticks as well as with some aid from computers, are used in hazardous land, sea, and space environments. The nuclear industry handles radioactive fuel and wastes with these devices. The mining industry is beginning to employ them for waste disposal. Sea salvage operations that would otherwise have been impossible have been successfully carried out. And the Space Shuttle's robotic arm recently helped astronauts launch a satellite. As these devices become more robotic, they will expand man's experience, allowing him to explore heretofore inaccessible environments.

Three robotic manipulator arms are used to maintain the linear accelerator, or "atom smasher," at the Los Alamos Meson Physics Facility in Los Alamos, New Mexico. When protons are accelerated to 800 million electron volts and interact with target material, strong radioactivity is induced. Even if the accelerator is turned off, radiation is still high and hazardous to humans. To shield Los Alamos workers from radiation, the target area is buried and covered with twenty feet of steel sheets from old battleships.

To maintain the target area, workers use remote manipulators built by TeleOperator Systems of Bohemia, New

York. The arms, which have seven degrees of freedom, hang from a large hydraulic truck over the target area. Cables from the arms are routed through a twenty-foot shaft to a trailer, which houses the controls. The human operator sees what is going on below by watching a television monitor, and is further aided by being able to feel what the manipulator feels. This is accomplished with bilateral force reflection. TeleOperator's president, Carl R. Flatau, explains: "We have a controller, which is called a 'master,' and a manipulator, or robot arm, which is called the 'slave.' You can push the master and the slave will follow, and you will feel in the master what happens in the slave. You could also have the slave push the master around, doing the whole thing in reverse. So there is symmetrical power flow and in that sense it is bilateral."

Bilateral force sensing also allows the manipulator to have small collisions with objects it is working on and yet still continue working. It absorbs the shock the same way that a human hand does when catching a ball. To catch a ball, you automatically move your arm back—if you did not, the ball would bounce off your hand.

With the manipulators, workers can do almost all the things people would do but without risking the effects of radiation. Soldering, electrical wiring, some welding, and handling delicate materials are some of the maintenance tasks achieved.

Flatau says his bilateral force sensing master/slave manipulator, built in 1977 and the first of its kind, remains state of the art. Some minor functions are controlled by small analog microprocessors, and now TeleOperator Systems is developing a completely microprocessor-controlled version. It will be possible to record movements for operations, making the device more robotic than before. Says Flatau, "Furthermore, the capability of processing signals before they are fed into the feedback network is at hand, and this will give us a variety of more flexible ways of doing things." Flatau and his colleagues at other remote manipulator companies, including Barbara Plonski of GA Technologies in San Diego, California, and Will Boehlke of GCA Par Systems in St. Paul, Minnesota, agree that remote manipulators and robotics are converging.

There are approximately twenty to thirty bilateral force sensing master/slave manipulators operating around the world, according to Flatau. Five work under water and Flatau supplied half of the total. There are far more of

GCA PaR, a subsidiary of industrial robot manufacturer GCA, makes remote manipulator arms for land and undersea vehicles. Two arms such as the one on this mobile land unit have been used on Lockheed's submersible, Sea Quest, *since 1968. Another GCA PaR arm is used on the Navy's* Curved III *unmanned submersible since 1974.*

This sixties-vintage submarine was built by General Dynamics for research activities. Now defunct, the tenton Star III had a bow manipulator with interchangeable "hands" and two television cameras, and operated at depths of 2,000 feet.

another class of remote manipulators that operate closer to hazards. Numbering about four thousand to five thousand, these manipulators are used in hot cells where nuclear fuels are developed and tested. Operators manipulate the arms from behind a wall that shields the workers from radioactive materials. Central Research Laboratories, a division of Sargent Industries in Red Wing, Minnesota, is a leading supplier.

In deep-sea activities, where the hazard is not the object to be retrieved, but depth itself, remote manipulators are also being used. Seventy-five percent of all offshore oil rigs are maintained by divers, who generally can work well at depths of 300 feet. Humans can withstand depths up to 800 or 900 feet, but this can be hazardous, and the offshore industry is waiting for technology that will enable it to maintain wells at 6,000 feet.

One device called "Wasp," a cross between a diving suit and a submarine with two insectlike arms, has assisted in several discoveries. Bruce H. Robinson, an oceanographer at the University of California at Santa Barbara, began developing Wasp for the offshore oil industry nine years ago. Wasp can work at depths of 2,000 feet. A human pilot inside the suit can walk on the sea floor and look around through the Wasp's plexiglas dome. The device is powered by a 3,000-foot-long umbilical cord to a ship on the surface.

In October 1982, when Wasp was used for the first time in a pilot program ten miles off the coast of Santa Barbara, it enabled humans to discover a dense layer of tiny crustaceans spread across the Santa Barbara Basin, which is 1,500 feet deep.

Wasp also assisted in the exploration of a nineteenth-century shipwreck 340 feet beneath the Arctic Ocean. Divers used the Wasp to determine that a three-masted British ship, *The Breadalbane*, was remarkably well preserved and then they recovered the ship's wheel. The wreck is the northernmost one yet found. According to a *New York Times* article, Phil Nuytten, president of Can-Dive Services, was the first man to reach the wreck. Two of the masts were still standing, the wheelhouse was intact, and its two compasses were still mounted. "It looked like you could sail it away," he said. "If you could somehow make the water vanish, you could probably repair it in a couple of weeks and sail it back to England. It looked great."

Several companies are currently making remotely operated vehicles (ROVs) that dive to the ocean's depths without a human inside. These tethered vehicles and their arms are operated by humans aboard ships. Ametek-Straza in El Cajon, California, markets two ROVs called "Scorpio" and "Scorpi," which look like snow sleds but can operate at 3,000 feet below sea level. Both have master/slave arms, built by Kraft Ocean Systems in Kansas City, Missouri, which can also be programmed. Scorpio's two arms lift up to 250 pounds water weight, and Scorpi's can lift 110 pounds with its single arm.

In 1981, Scorpio explored waters 150 miles off the Russian coast to photograph the wreck of the British cruiser, HMS *Edinburgh*. The ship was carrying $72 million in gold bullion when it was torpedoed in 1942 and sank 800 feet, cargo and all. With Scorpio's help, the bullion, which by then represented forty-year-old lend-lease payments, was retrieved from murky, ice-cold waters.

An RCV-150, another ROV made by Hydro Products (a division of Honeywell) in San Diego, California, came to the rescue of AT&T. The company's $1.7 million SEA PLOW IV, which it used to bury undersea cables, had been lost off the Irish coast. It was thought that the PLOW was resting in 800-foot waters near the wreck of a Greek freighter that had been torpedoed in 1940. Fishing nets had caught onto the ship's hull and would have snagged human divers' towlines. Instead of risking accidents to humans, the RCV-150 was used to detect and photograph the PLOW. It took several false starts to retrieve the craft, which was dropped a few times, but eventually it was saved, as was a great deal of money.

There are several multimillion-dollar research and development projects under way to improve ROVs so that they can dive to depths of 6,000 feet. Besides the need to salvage costly equipment, the offshore oil industry hopes to use ROVs to maintain rigs. Some companies know of oil fields at these depths but have postponed constructing rigs since they await advances in ROV maintenance equipment.

INDUSTRIES USING INDUSTRIAL ROBOTS

The automotive industries in Japan and the United States have bought the most robots. Within this industry

The Scorpio, a remotely operated vehicle that dives to depths of 3,000 feet, recently helped retrieve gold bullion from the Edinburgh, *which sank off the coast of the USSR. The manipulator arm below in front can be remotely controlled by a human or it can be computer controlled.*

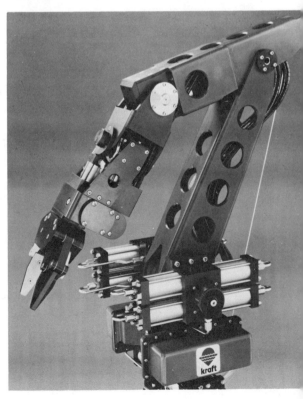

welding and machine loading and unloading continue to be the favored tasks for robots. In 1982, the U.S. auto industry accounted for 40 percent of the U.S. IRs, and of these, 70 to 80 percent were used for welding. The remainder were used for machine loading and spray finishing. The heavy equipment industry, which includes construction and agricultural equipment companies, uses IRs for similar applications.

Applications in the automotive industry are likely to dominate the market for the next decade, with GM committed to invest over $1 billion in 15,000 new IRs during this period. Chrysler plans to increase its number of IRs by 31 percent per year through 1988, bringing its total to 987. Ford plans to have 5,000 to 7,000 IRs operating by 1990. In addition to welding, IRs are being used increasingly for assembly, part transfer, and machine loading.[7]

The foundry industry followed the automotive industry with 20 percent of the U.S. inventory engaged in material handling and machine loading and unloading.[8] The foundry industry overlaps with the automotive industry to a large extent since many foundries are operated by auto equipment companies. IRs were first used in foundries for machine loading and unloading and die casting.

Light manufacturing, which includes plastics, food, pharmaceutical, and cosmetics production, is the next largest industrial user of IRs. In the plastics industry IRs are used mainly for machine loading and unloading. Food, pharmaceutical, and cosmetics manufacturers use IRs for material handling like stacking and packaging.

Electrical and electronics industries use IRs for such work as laying wire for wiring harnesses for appliances and computers, painting these products, assembling printed circuit boards, and inspection of loaded boards.

Aerospace firms accounted for only 2 percent of IRs in use, with applications mainly in painting, some machining such as hole drilling, and some assembly.[9]

NASA and the DOD are IR users to the extent that they have bought IRs to develop manufacturing processes that have been transferred to the private sector. With Milacron robots the air force has developed IR systems for drilling and routing operations on aircraft panels as part of its Integrated Computer-Aided Manufacturing program (ICAM). As a result, such a system has been installed in a General Dynamics plant.

MATCHING INDUSTRIAL ROBOTS TO TASKS

Until recently, there have been two main justifications for using IRs. It is preferable for a robot, as opposed to a human, to work in a hot, hazardous, boring environment. And production volumes can dictate whether a machine tool or robot is more cost efficient.

In manufacturing, production volumes are described as "mass," "batch," and "piece." For parts that are small

Robots at Chrysler's completely retooled Jefferson assembly plant in Detroit apply nearly 3,000 welds to each K-car body cycled through the system.

and relatively simple to make, mass production involves lot sizes of over ten thousand and machine tools are usually used. Batch production lot sizes range from three hundred to fifteen thousand, and piece lot sizes range from one to three hundred. First-generation IRs were thought to be most economical for batch production, but now it seems that reducing unit cost can be achieved for smaller production volumes.

Nevertheless, those industries still associated with batch and some mass production continue to be the biggest IR users. The automotive industry is a large batch and mass producer. In contrast, the aerospace and aircraft industries are piece producers, which explains why they have not yet used many IRs.

Besides differences in volumes of lots to be produced, different applications demand different kinds of IRs with varying ranges of capabilities. It might not be necessary, for instance, for a material-handling robot to follow as smooth a path when moving between points as for a welding robot to do so. A welding robot might not have to be as precise a manipulator as an assembly robot, and will probably have to carry a heavier load. A robot arm used for material handling might not need as many joints as that for a spray-finishing robot. An IR will be chosen on the basis of different degrees of sophistication depending on the nature of the application.

The path that a robot follows between points depends upon two types of controls, nonservo and servo. Nonservo IRs use mechanical stops to indicate points that the arm should reach. The mechanical stops are the program, in a sense, but the program is not stored in a computer memory. The arm is physically prevented from moving beyond end points, but it cannot stop between these points. This positioning limitation confines nonservos to simple, pick-and-place applications. The mechanical stops provide high speed and repeatability, which is a robot's ability to achieve the same position from cycle to cycle. Nonservo IRs are mainly used in material-handling operations that are simple and repetitive, like moving parts from one conveyor to another.

Servorobots can be of two types, point to point or continuous path. They do not rely on mechanical stops, but have computer-stored programs that direct the robot arm where to stop. Feedback devices allow the robot to compare its arm position with the desired position stored in the memory and to correct that difference by moving to the desired point. This can be done by moving to that point in a series of steps, as in the point-to-point servorobot. The steps to get to that point are not stored in the memory because only the end points are relevant to the task to be performed.

If the steps in between are important to the task, and a smooth path is necessary, the entire sequence can be programmed and every point in the memory will be compared with the actual arm position. For that reason, we speak of a "continuous path."

Point-to-point IRs are used in a wide variety of applications, including material handling, machine loading and unloading, and assembly. Continuous path IRs are used mainly in spray finishing, certain kinds of welding, and some machining applications.

Servo and nonservo IRs can have three types of power supplies: hydraulic, pneumatic, and electric. These provide "muscle" to the robot arm and also determine robot size and accuracy, and the application the IR is most suited for. Hydraulic drives use high-pressure fluid as a power source. They allow high levels of force and power and are best for carrying heavy weights, but they are noisy. In the early 1980s, hydraulic-driven IRs were the most popular. Now, they account for 29 percent of IRs built. Pneumatic systems use compressed air as a power source. Previously found in almost a third of IRs, they are now in only 15 percent of IRs built. They are installed mainly in machine shops where compressed air is already used and familiar to personnel. Pneumatic IRs are not as precise as hydraulic IRs and are therefore used in light-duty operations requiring speed but not a high degree of accuracy. Electrically powered IRs— the most accurate and the most quiet—have become more and more popular. They are used in about 20 to 30 percent of installed IRs and account for 56 percent of IRs built.

Although they cannot lift loads as heavy as the other two power supplies discussed, the trend is toward more electric IRs, largely because they are best for growing light applications, such as electronic assembly.[10]

Besides the kind of path a robot arm can travel and the type of power supply, every IR has a list of more detailed specifications that further determine whether it is suited for a particular job. These specifications, or "performance characteristics," describe how precisely an IR can act. Among specifications manufacturers list are their robots' positioning accuracy, repeatability, payload capacity, and work envelope.

Positioning accuracy is a measurement of an IR's ability to position a tool or gripper at a point in space

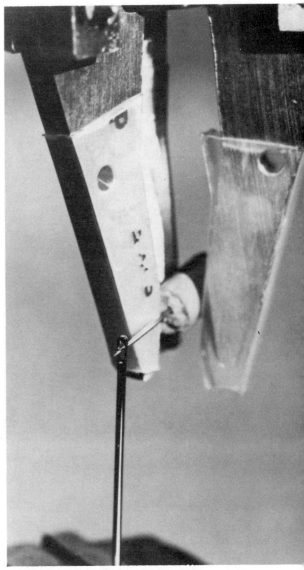

To demonstrate accuracy and dexterity, American Robot engineers thought of the ancient craft of sewing. Here, a gripper on the end of the robot arm demonstrates some industrial magic by threading the 0.009-inch eye of one needle with the 0.007-inch-wide tip of another.

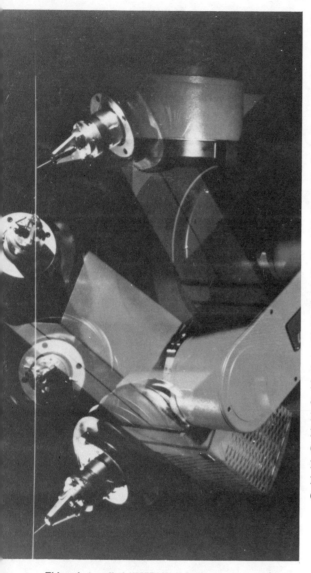

This robot, called ''MERLIN,'' has an accuracy of ± 0.008 inches and its repeatability is ± 0.001 inches.

specified by its computer. This measurement reflects the difference between the mechanical ability to reach a point and the theoretical position of that point. The idea is similar to what we consider successful hand-eye coordination in humans. When the hand reaches an object according to the brain's estimate, we consider the operation accurately carried out. But for a robot, the operation's accuracy is measured by comparing the aim of its arm and hand with a computer-calculated destination. For those applications where the difference is tolerable, the robot will perform successfully. Accuracy is specified as a range: For example, it can be accurate to ± (read plus or minus) 0.001 inches or ± 0.025 millimeters, so that the robot may "expect" to be no further from the desired point than those distances.

Payload capacity is the maximum weight a robot can carry and includes the weight of the gripper or tool at the end of the arm. Payloads range from 1 or 2 pounds to well over 2,000 pounds. The heavier the gripper and/or the object to be manipulated, the larger the robot needed to do the job. Users must consider both the load capacity needed and the space they have to install the IR.

Another consideration also related to space is the IR's *work envelope*. This is the greatest region accessible to a robot when its arm extends to its fullest reach at various angles and degrees of rotation. This is a function of how many axes an arm can move through. The greater the number of axes, the more agile the arm and the more extensive the envelope. This is important for selecting a robot's position in relation to the workpiece, other equipment in a workcell or line, and the area within which workers can safely move while the robot operates.

INSIDE THE ROBOT: HOW IT WORKS

hat gives an industrial robot degrees of freedom? Where does it get the muscle to lift a certain payload? How does it perform a task with high accuracy and repeatability? Moreover, how does it use feedback and "learn" to perform a task? These capabilities result from integrating various arm designs, power sources, and computer controls.

To understand what is inside a robot making it tick, we will take you inside a Unimation plant in Danbury, Connecticut, where robots are built. Although several kinds of robots are assembled in this particular plant, here we will focus on one electric robot, the PUMA 560. (See Fig. 4.1.)

Before describing the construction of this robot's arm, its anatomy should be understood relative to other, less sophisticated designs. Besides the SCARA-type mentioned in chapter 3, simpler robot arms can be "rectangular," "cylindrical," and "spherical." The PUMA is a "jointed-arm" robot and comes closest to the human arm's anatomy. All of these designs, or configurations, determine the axes around which an arm is free to rotate or extend, hence the phrase "degrees of freedom."

Rectangular configurations are sometimes called "Cartesian" because the arm's axes can be described by using the X, Y, and Z coordinate system first developed by

Fig. 4.1.
PUMA System: Information Flow

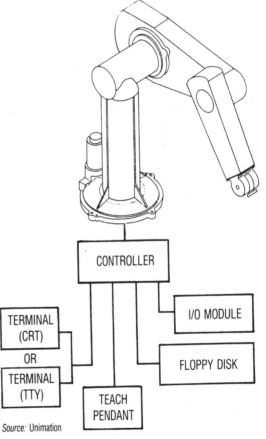

Source: Unimation

Fig. 4.2.
Cartesian Coordinate System

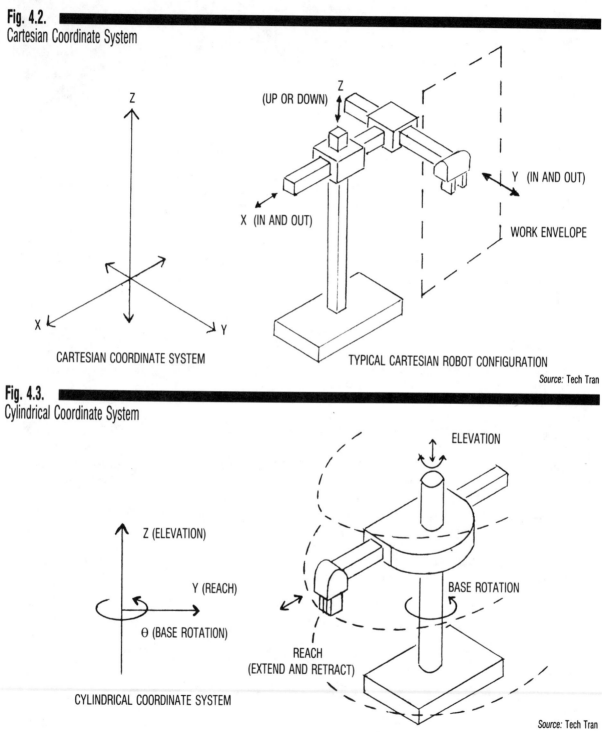

CARTESIAN COORDINATE SYSTEM

TYPICAL CARTESIAN ROBOT CONFIGURATION

Source: Tech Tran

Fig. 4.3.
Cylindrical Coordinate System

CYLINDRICAL COORDINATE SYSTEM

Source: Tech Tran

Fig. 4.4.
Spherical Coordinate System

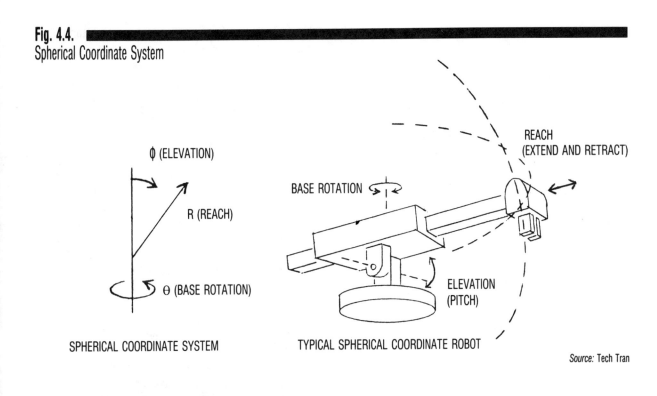

φ (ELEVATION)

R (REACH)

θ (BASE ROTATION)

BASE ROTATION

REACH
(EXTEND AND RETRACT)

ELEVATION
(PITCH)

SPHERICAL COORDINATE SYSTEM

TYPICAL SPHERICAL COORDINATE ROBOT

Source: Tech Tran

Fig. 4.5.
Robot Arm: Member Identification

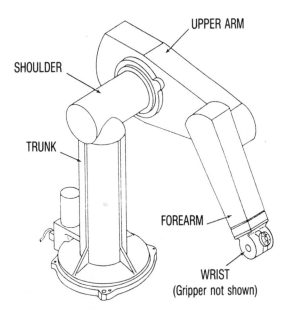

UPPER ARM

SHOULDER

TRUNK

FOREARM

WRIST
(Gripper not shown)

Source: Unimation

Descartes. Just as you can describe a point's location on a graph with reference to X and Y axes, arm movements can be described as in and out along an imaginary Y axis, and from side to side along an imaginary X axis. Up and down movement along an imaginary Z axis (which, on a graph, would run through the graph paper and describe depth) adds the third dimension.

You can think of these axes as somewhat akin to a sailboat's mast and boom, with the mast as the Z axis and the boom the Y axis. Movement occurs by sliding the Y axis up or down the Z axis, as if the boom were sliding up or down the mast. Another movement occurs by sliding the Y axis back and forth to extend or retract, as if the boom were cutting across the mast, which of course a real sailboat's boom does not do. To make up for the Y axis' inability to swivel (the way a mast swings from starboard to port), the X axis acts as a second boom that also cuts across the Z axis. (See Fig. 4.2.)

If a pen were attached to the tip of the robot arm it would draw a rectangle as the arm moved. That shape—the area that the arm can reach—is called the "work envelope." Because it moves along three axes, such an arm is said to have three degrees of freedom. According to a report by Tech Tran Corporation, 22 percent of industrial robots in use in 1983 were of the rectangular configuration type.[11]

A cylindrically configured arm also has three degrees of freedom, but it moves linearly only along the Y and Z axes. Its third degree of freedom is due to rotation at its base around the Z axis, hence its work envelope is the shape of a cylinder. Here the sailboat analogy works better. The Y axis does swivel like a sailboat's boom, and an X axis is not necessary. But the Y axis can slide up and down the Z axis and extend and retract, which a boom does not. Because it swivels, extends or retracts, and slides up and down, a pen at the end of this type of robot arm would draw cylinders of various length radii and heights. (See Fig. 4.3). In 1983, 19 percent of IRs had this cylindrical configuration, according to Tech Tran.

A spherical configuration replaces up and down movement along the Z axis of a cylindrical configuration, with a rocking motion of the arm. There is no longer a mast, but only a boom that rocks, swivels, and extends and retracts. A pen at the arm's tip would draw partial spheres of various length radii. According to Tech Tran, 13 percent of IRs in use in 1983 had spherical configurations. (See Fig. 4.4.)

The jointed-arm configuration is the most popular, according to Tech Tran, at 46 percent of IR models in use in 1983. The members of the arm are the trunk, shoulder, upper arm, forearm, and wrist (see Fig. 4.5). Whereas a spherical configuration arm has just two rotational motions, all joints of the jointed-arm configuration rotate. Joint 1 swivels around an imaginary axis running vertically through the trunk. Joint 2 rotates around an imaginary axis running horizontally through the shoulder member and perpendicular to the trunk. Joint 3 rotates around an imaginary axis that runs parallel to joint 2's axis. (See Fig. 4.6.)

So far, these movements give the arm three degrees of freedom. The remaining three result from types of wrist motion. The best way to understand these movements is to imitate them with your own wrist while extending your index finger. If you were to draw an imaginary line up and down using wrist motion only, your wrist would rotate around an imaginary axis parallel to the axes that joints 2 and 3 rotate around. This motion is called "pitch." Because this motion occurs by bending your wrist, it is sometimes referred to as "bend."

If you rotate your hand from left to right and back again, as if you were drawing the path of a swerving car, your wrist will have rotated around an imaginary axis running perpendicular to the axis of the wrist bending motion. This movement is called "yaw."

Fig. 4.6.
Robot Arm: Degrees of Freedom

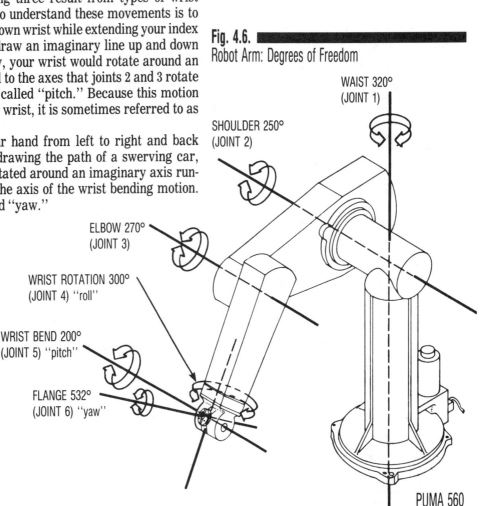

WAIST 320°
(JOINT 1)

SHOULDER 250°
(JOINT 2)

ELBOW 270°
(JOINT 3)

WRIST ROTATION 300°
(JOINT 4) "roll"

WRIST BEND 200°
(JOINT 5) "pitch"

FLANGE 532°
(JOINT 6) "yaw"

PUMA 560

Source: Unimation

Fig. 4.7.
Robot Arm: Operation Envelope

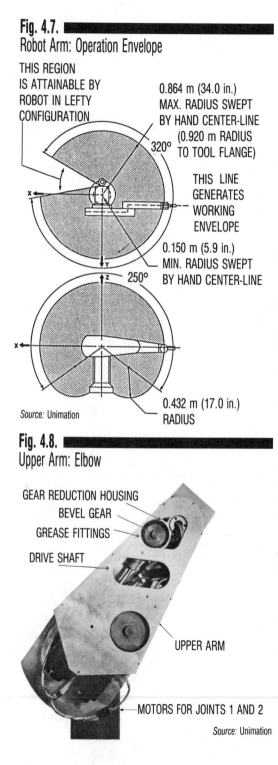

THIS REGION IS ATTAINABLE BY ROBOT IN LEFTY CONFIGURATION

0.864 m (34.0 in.) MAX. RADIUS SWEPT BY HAND CENTER-LINE (0.920 m RADIUS TO TOOL FLANGE)

320°

THIS LINE GENERATES WORKING ENVELOPE

0.150 m (5.9 in.) MIN. RADIUS SWEPT BY HAND CENTER-LINE

250°

0.432 m (17.0 in.) RADIUS

Source: Unimation

Fig. 4.8.
Upper Arm: Elbow

GEAR REDUCTION HOUSING

BEVEL GEAR

GREASE FITTINGS

DRIVE SHAFT

UPPER ARM

MOTORS FOR JOINTS 1 AND 2

Source: Unimation

Now imagine rotating your entire forearm as if you were drilling a hole with your finger. To do so, your forearm would have to rotate around an axis running through the center of your wrist bone to your elbow. This motion is called "roll."

These motions, pitch (or bend), yaw, and roll, are also used to describe the orientation of an airplane. They give the PUMA 560 a total of six degrees of freedom. Work envelopes for PUMAs are also partial spheres. (See Fig. 4.7.)

At Unimation's plants, robots are built from the base up. First, the arm's mechanical structure is built, and later assembly operations marry the mechanical aspects of the arm to a computer and other electronic devices. Then the fully assembled robot is sent to the test bay area. If a customer requires special features, such as vision or customized grippers, and wants his computer program test run before the robot is delivered, the robot is sent to another plant where applications engineers customize it.

The PUMA 560 is built member by member or joint by joint. Each joint has its own direct-current (DC) servomotor, gears, gear trains, and drive shaft, to name the most basic components. The motor that powers joint 1 is located outside the trunk on the base casting. Motors for joints 2 and 3 sit side by side at the shoulder of the upper arm. (See Figs. 4.8 and 4.9.)

The elbow of the forearm has three motors, three drive shafts, and so on for joints 4, 5, and 6. (See Fig. 4.10.) Placing these motors near the elbow instead of at the wrist minimizes the weight that joint 3 must lift and so lessens its size and power requirements. (See Fig. 4.10.)

All the joints are connected by a wire harness running from the arm base to the arm tip. (See Fig. 4.11.) The wire harness connects to a cable that runs from the base to the computer controller. Together, these connections create a two-way communication link. Signals travel between the arm and controller. Signals from the arm to the controller are generated by incremental optical encoders that sit on top of each motor. (See Fig. 4.12.) They feed the controller information about the position of each joint. So encoders are an important link in the continuous flow of information that is known as a closed feedback loop.

An incremental optical encoder measures how much a joint has rotated by determining the number of times the encoder's light source is interrupted as the motor rotates. It also measures the *rate* that the light source is broken and

Fig. 4.9.
Joint 1 Assembly Detail

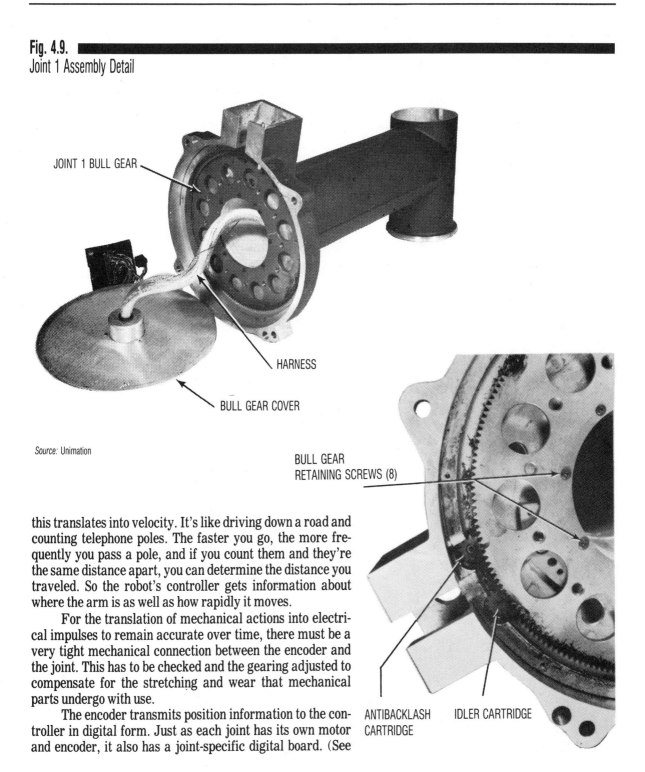

JOINT 1 BULL GEAR

HARNESS

BULL GEAR COVER

Source: Unimation

BULL GEAR
RETAINING SCREWS (8)

ANTIBACKLASH
CARTRIDGE

IDLER CARTRIDGE

this translates into velocity. It's like driving down a road and counting telephone poles. The faster you go, the more frequently you pass a pole, and if you count them and they're the same distance apart, you can determine the distance you traveled. So the robot's controller gets information about where the arm is as well as how rapidly it moves.

For the translation of mechanical actions into electrical impulses to remain accurate over time, there must be a very tight mechanical connection between the encoder and the joint. This has to be checked and the gearing adjusted to compensate for the stretching and wear that mechanical parts undergo with use.

The encoder transmits position information to the controller in digital form. Just as each joint has its own motor and encoder, it also has a joint-specific digital board. (See

Fig. 4.10.
Wrist Articulations: Joints 4, 5, and 6

Fig. 4.11.
Upper Arm

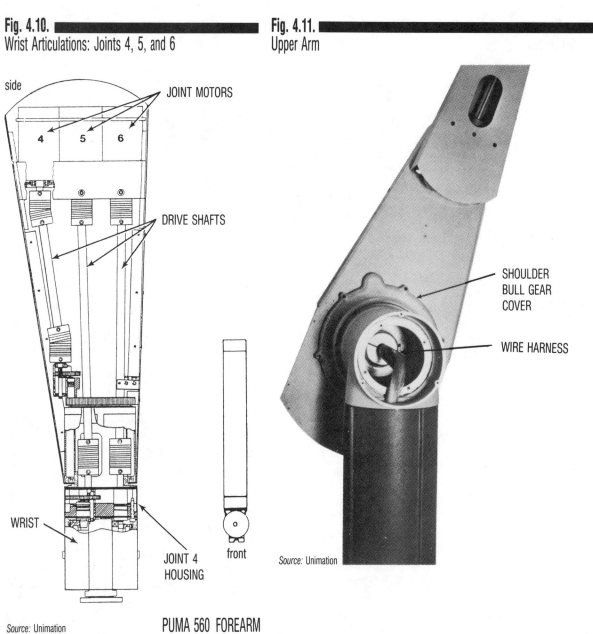

side

JOINT MOTORS

4   5   6

DRIVE SHAFTS

WRIST

JOINT 4
HOUSING

front

Source: Unimation

PUMA 560 FOREARM

SHOULDER
BULL GEAR
COVER

WIRE HARNESS

Source: Unimation

Fig. 4.12.
Optical Encoders

A low-resolution encoder with only one rotor

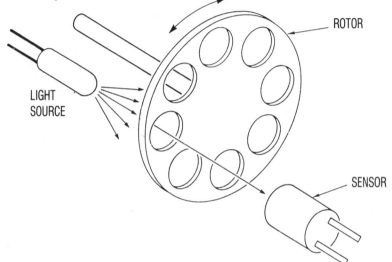

A high-resolution encoder with a rotor and stator which eliminates edges or fingers

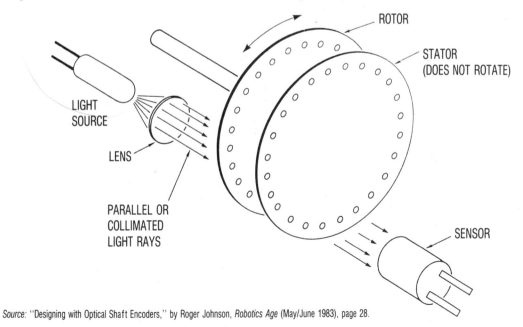

Source: "Designing with Optical Shaft Encoders," by Roger Johnson, *Robotics Age* (May/June 1983), page 28.

Fig. 4.13.
PUMA Control System, Block Diagram

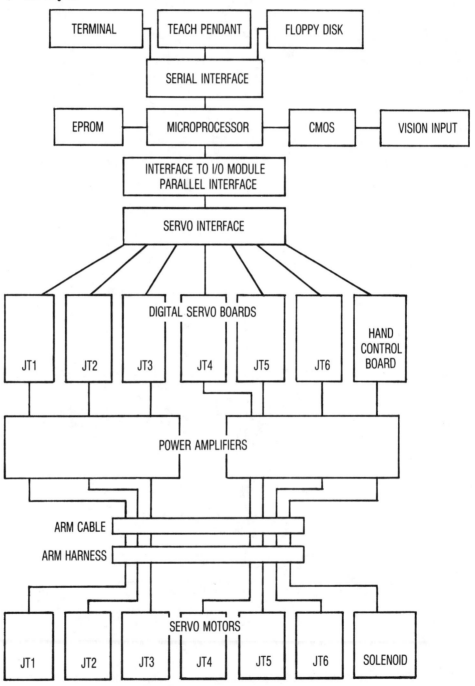

Source: Unimation

Figs. 4.13, 4.14, 4.15.) To use encoder information to *move* the arm, the arm's actual position must be *compared* with a commanded position stored in the controller's memory. Then the difference between the positions will be calculated and power can be sent from the controller to the arm to make appropriate changes in joint position.

For a moment, let's leave the information flow from the arm to the controller and look at the equipment that sends information from the opposite direction—from the human operator to the controller. First we will see how one joint can be commanded and moved using feedback. Then we will see how several joints can change positions simultaneously, just as you can rotate your elbow while bending your wrist.

Fig. 4.14.
PUMA Control System, Summary

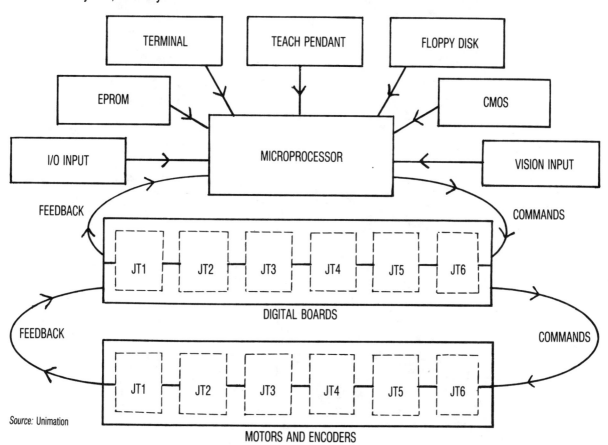

Source: Unimation

Fig. 4.15.
Controller: Board Location (Top)

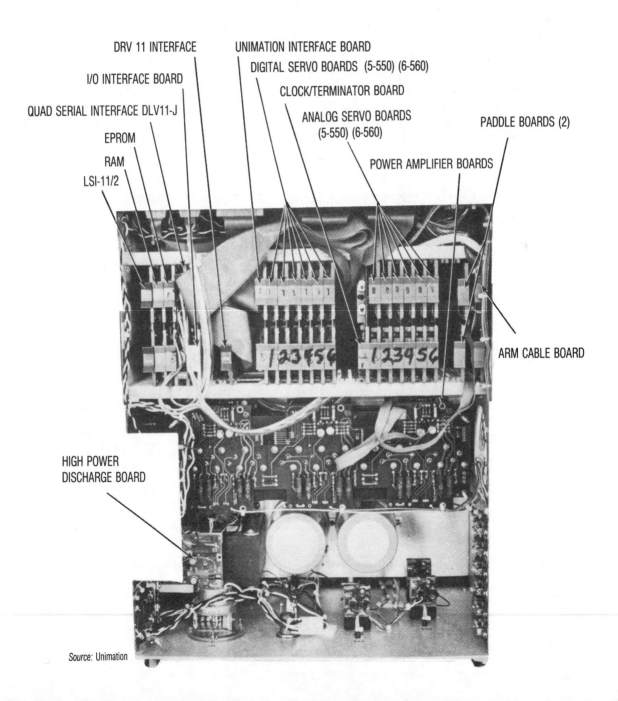

DRV 11 INTERFACE

I/O INTERFACE BOARD

QUAD SERIAL INTERFACE DLV11-J

EPROM

RAM

LSI-11/2

UNIMATION INTERFACE BOARD

DIGITAL SERVO BOARDS (5-550) (6-560)

CLOCK/TERMINATOR BOARD

ANALOG SERVO BOARDS
(5-550) (6-560)

POWER AMPLIFIER BOARDS

PADDLE BOARDS (2)

ARM CABLE BOARD

HIGH POWER
DISCHARGE BOARD

Source: Unimation

In the electrical assembly area of the plant, the arm is hooked up to the controller and the controller is connected to peripheral components. These are a teach pendant and a terminal, which are required, and a floppy disk drive and an I/O (input/output) module, which are optional. (See Fig. 4.1, p. 75.)

The teach pendant and terminal serve a similar function—they are two different ways of inputting program instructions for arm movement into the controller. Programming a robot with a teach pendant is sometimes called "leadthrough" because the arm is led through each motion. Using a terminal, having either a screen display or printer, is called "keyboard" programming since instructions are typed in. The floppy disk drive stores programs on the same kind of disks used with most personal computers.

The I/O module is a communication link that synchronizes activities between the PUMA and other machine tools. In a cell where a PUMA needs to pick up a part after a machine tool stamps it, the I/O module would send a signal to the PUMA "telling" it that the machine tool has finished stamping and that the part is ready for pickup. The PUMA controller can receive information from four I/O modules.

Whether you use the terminal or the teach pendant to program the PUMA, the destination of the arm's tip must be described as a point in space. But points in space are meaningless unless they are described either in relation to a fixed point or relative to one another. Point positions therefore need reference systems, and the PUMA gripper's position can be indicated using one or a combination of reference systems.

On the teach pendant (see Fig. 4.16), there are three buttons corresponding to three reference systems, or *modes*. These are "joint," "world," and "tool." There are also six buttons "X/1," "Y/2," and so forth on the thinner part of the pendant that correspond to the arm's six joints and which rotate the joints when pressed.

To indicate these modes when using the terminal for programming, you must type in the commands of Unimation's programming language, which is called "VAL."

When a mode is chosen, the controller's microprocessor (see Fig. 4.13) calculates position data using that mode's reference system. It calculates according to instructions of the master VAL program, which resides in a permanent memory unit, called erasable and programmable read-only memory or EPROM (shown to the left of the microprocessor in Fig. 4.13).

Fig. 4.16.
Teach Pendant Controls and Indicators

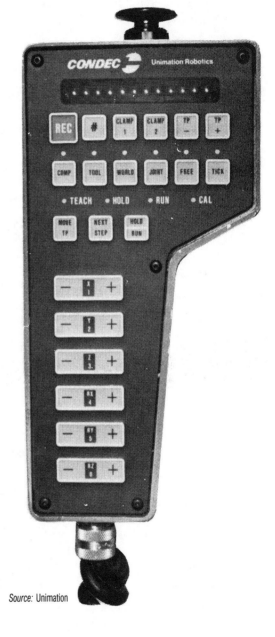

Source: Unimation

Fig. 4.17.
Degrees of Rotation

The lines through the joints represent 0 points from which degrees of rotation are measured.

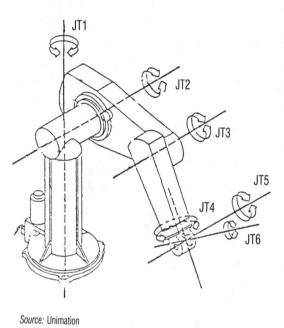

Source: Unimation

The "joint" mode uses only the amount of rotation around each joint to define the destination of the tip of the arm. Pressing one of the six buttons causes its corresponding joint to rotate for the duration the button is pressed. If the right side of the button (+) is pressed, the joint rotates clockwise, and if the left side of the button (–) is pressed, the joint rotates counterclockwise.

The reference system is just based upon an arbitrary zero point—the encoder measures degrees of rotation from that point to the destination point. For example, joint 1 could be said to be at 0 degrees when the upper arm is aligned with the trunk, and at 90 degrees when it is perpendicular to the trunk. (See Fig. 4.17.)

Using the teach pendant, you can position one joint at a time based on your own visual approximations. Pressing the REC (record) button would send precise degrees of rotation data to the controller.

If you wanted to see the numbers, you could call them up using the terminal. Or if you were programming just with the terminal and knew in advance what the numbers should be, you could key them in. The description of joint angles for the arm tip to reach its destination, which we'll call "point A," would constitute one line in the program memory. Typing in the VAL command "HERE #A" could show a description of joint angles on the terminal screen or printout like this:

JT1	JT2	JT3
90.406	10.448	147.711

JT4	JT5	JT6
0.159	-54.695	57.99

The number symbol is the VAL command for joint mode. Each column indicates the direction and degrees of rotation (to the third decimal place) of each joint (JT1, JT2, etc.). So the first column indicates that joint 1 is to be rotated clockwise 90.406 degrees and the fifth column indicates that joint 5 is to be rotated counterclockwise 54.695 degrees.

The "world" and "tool" modes use degrees of both rotation *and distance* to indicate the tip's point in space. Like degrees of rotation, distance must be measured from a point of reference.

In world mode, distance is measured from a Cartesian coordinate reference system that is fixed in the arm base.

(See Fig. 4.18.) Looking at Fig. 4.19, we want to know the lengths in millimeters of lines X, Y, and Z. These describe the distance from the tip, where a tool would be *mounted* (called the "tool mounting flange"), to the origin of the coordinate system where X, Y, and Z intersect. For the moment, we are not going to concern ourselves with joints 4, 5, and 6, which control the tool's position.

These distances are calculated by the microprocessor, using the actual lengths of the arm's members and the joints' degrees of rotation as indicated by the encoders. So the degrees of rotation for joints 1, 2, and 3 in the previous example can be transformed into linear measurement. Or linear measurement could have been used in the first place. On the computer terminal, the program line in world mode using the VAL command "HERE A" would be:

X	Y	Z
153.63	658.19	-485.88

Since there is no number symbol (#) preceding the A, this is a world mode VAL command. X, Y, and Z in the column headings correspond to the lines in Fig. 4.19. The numbers express length in millimeters and the minus sign indicates that the tip (or tool mounting flange) sits below the shoulder rather than above. Since we are not concerned with the orientation of the tool, the columns for JT4, JT5, and JT6 are not shown.

In tool mode, the reference system's coordinates are fixed in the tool. (See Fig. 4.20.) The origin is at the center of the tool mounting flange. Instead of measuring distance from the tool mounting flange to a fixed point in the shoulder for each new position, as in world mode, tool mode measures the distance from the *previous* flange location, "point A," to its *new* location, which we'll call "point B." The position of the tool coordinate system at point B is measured relative to the tool coordinate system at point A. (See Fig. 4.21.)

In this case, the gripper has moved 50 millimeters along the X axis to get from point A to point B. There have been no changes along the other axes, so on the terminal, using the command "HERE A:B," instructions would look like this:

X	Y	Z
50.00	0.00	0.00

Fig. 4.18.
World Coordinate System

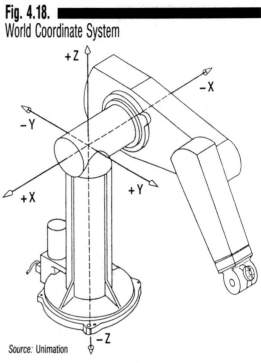

Source: Unimation

Fig. 4.19.
Additional Degrees of Rotation

Distances are measured from the origin of the system to the tip of the arm (tool mounting flange).

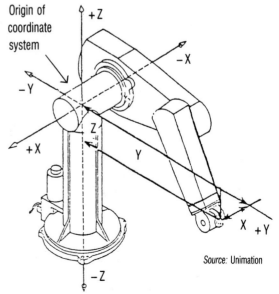

Source: Unimation

Fig. 4.20.
Tool Coordinate System

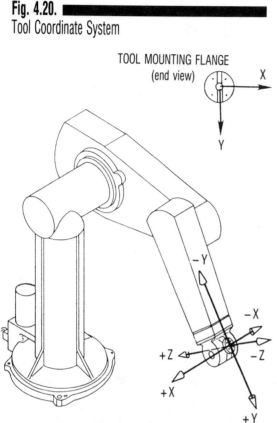

TOOL MOUNTING FLANGE
(end view)

X

Y

−Y

−X

+Z

−Z

+X

+Y

Source: Unimation

Because the location has been defined using two location names separated by a colon, the controller "knows" that now the X, Y, and Z stand for tool coordinate axes and not world coordinate axes.

Three additional references can be used to describe how the tool coordinate system sits relative to the fixed world coordinate system. These references tell the system whether the tool points up or down, which way the tool rotates, and which compass direction the tool faces.

The teach pendant has one other mode that the terminal does not share—"free" mode. This allows the arm to be programmed by actually taking it by the hand and showing it the needed motions. This method, used mainly for programming a robot to spray paint, is sometimes called "walkthrough."

A program created in any of these modes is stored in a memory unit called "CMOS" (to the right of the microprocessor in Fig. 4.13, p. 84). CMOS, which stands for complimentary metallic oxide semiconductor, stores information so that the program is easy to troubleshoot and modify. The final program is sent to the microprocessor, where calculations are performed according to instructions sent from the EPROM. The resulting desired, calculated position is sent from the microprocessor to a digital servoboard, where it "meets" the actual, measured position data sent by the encoder.

So coming from the opposite direction, we have now arrived at the point in the feedback loop where we left off. Now the comparison of actual and theoretical joint positions can take place, the difference determined, and power allocated to generate movement.

Commands and comparisons are made very quickly. Every 28 milliseconds the microprocessor commands each joint to move to a new position at a specified velocity. The digital board breaks these commanded positions and velocity changes into thirty-two smaller changes during the same time period. As the arm moves, the encoder returns signals indicating the actual position and velocity achieved. Any deviation between actual position and speed and a microprocessor-commanded position and speed is taken into account by the digital board when it issues the next set of incremental commands. The digital board oversees the performance of VAL commands and makes continual updates to ensure that real world arm actions match the theoretical concepts of the microprocessor.

The correction signals that result from this comparison are sent from the digital servoboards to power amplifiers so that voltage and current levels are high enough to drive the direct current motors. The cable feeds these signals to the motors.

But what if you wanted several joints to move simultaneously so that the arm could perform its task faster? Suppose you wanted one joint to move 32 degrees in one second and another joint to move 10 degrees in that same second. To synchronize these movements, the microprocessor would command the first joint to move 1 degree and tell the second joint to move 1/32 of 1 degree. This way, the joint that has more degrees to move is "told" to move at a faster rate than the joint with fewer degrees. The result is that both reach their destinations at the same time.

So far we have concerned ourselves with the control and power system for the arm's joints. There is also a smaller, separate power system that provides "muscle" to the tool or gripper mounted on the tool mounting flange. This system uses pneumatic rather than electrical power—it opens and closes grippers, using compressed air. Unlike the electrical control system, it does not have a feedback loop. Although the microprocessor controls the system, the controller does not "know" the force with which a gripper grasps an object and so it cannot modify that force. The only way to lessen or increase force is for the human operator to lessen or increase the air pressure.

Instead of sending command signals to a digital servoboard as it would to control a motor, the microprocessor sends signals to a hand control board. The hand control board then sends signals, via the wire harness, to a solenoid. (See Fig. 4.22.) The solenoid opens or closes a pneumatic valve according to the VAL commands "OPEN," "CLOSE," "OPENI," "CLOSEI." The first two commands set up open and close signals pending an arm motion. You could write the program so that the gripper opens or closes *when* the arm tip begins to move toward point A. In contrast, the "I" at the end of commands "OPENI" and "CLOSEI" tells the gripper to open and close *immediately*.

Now the arm and its tool or gripper "know" how to move so the entire computer-controlled assembly moves "intelligently." But the assembled robot must prove its performance in the test bay area before being shipped to a customer or before customization at another plant. Testing can last as long as one hundred fifty hours during which the

Fig. 4.21.
Tool Mode

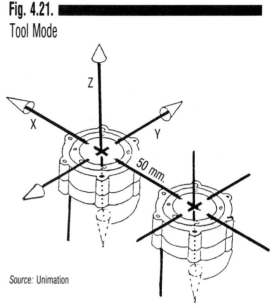

Source: Unimation

Fig. 4.22.
Solenoids

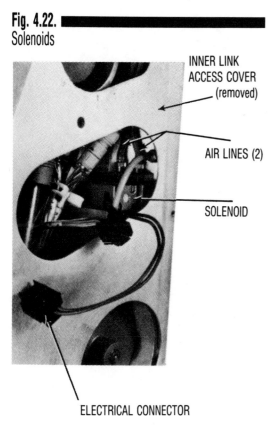

INNER LINK
ACCESS COVER
(removed)

AIR LINES (2)

SOLENOID

ELECTRICAL CONNECTOR

Source: Unimation

arm twists and swivels at various speeds according to the kinds of VAL commands described above. It does so while carrying various loads at different room temperatures. Having passed these tests, the robot can go on its merry, manipulative way.

At customization plants, software engineers test CMOS programs supplied by users and, if necessary, modify the master VAL program that resides in the EPROM. For example, a customer might need a PUMA to take bottles from a conveyor and palletize them into a case that can hold twenty-four bottles. Suppose the case has six rows and four columns (a total of twenty-four pockets, with one pocket for each bottle). For this pick-and-place operation, the PUMA can be programmed to make the same "pick" motion for the remaining twenty-three different places. And that effect can be multiplied for any number of cases.

Unimation supplies standard grippers for certain operations. But what if the objects to be moved have an unusual shape or size? And what if the objects to be moved must be distinguished from other nearby objects? If a customer's operation requires special grippers, Unimation will help design, build, and test them. Should vision be needed, Unimation can connect the PUMA to its Univision I or II vision systems.

Built by Machine Intelligence Corporation of Sunnyvale, California, one of the first vision system suppliers, the Univision I system allows the robot to "see" in two-dimensional, black-and-white silhouette images. It consists of a vidicon camera, a vision image processor, and a graphics display monitor. The vision image processor is connected to the robot's CMOS and so, in turn, connects to the microprocessor. (See Fig. 4.23.)

Suppose that instead of picking up bottles from a conveyor, a PUMA was supposed to pick out wrenches lying among other objects on a conveyor. The camera would be placed above the conveyor and would show all the objects in black and white on the display monitor. The vision processor would translate the images into digital information, but there would be no way for it to distinguish the wrench from the other objects. For the system to recognize the wrench and "tell" the robot arm where the wrench is, the vision system must be "taught" the object image.

To "teach" the wrench image, the camera takes a picture of a wrench at a particular orientation in space. The processor records differences between the light the wrench

Fig. 4.23.
Univision I System Concept

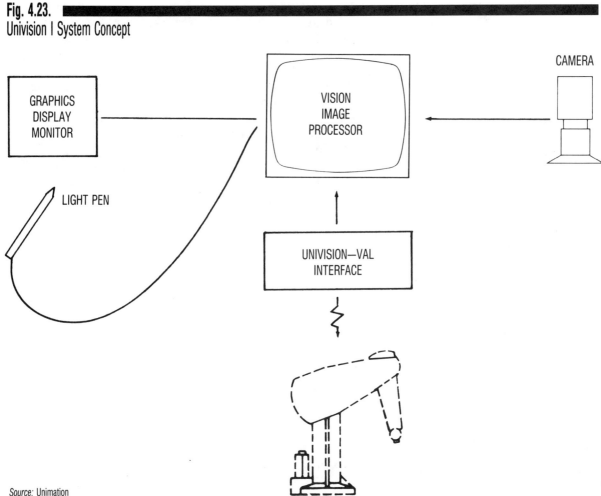

Source: Unimation

reflects and light reflected by the other objects. The camera also records light reflection differences between regions of the wrench itself. Then the processor does a statistical study drawing out certain characteristics of the wrench, such as its outline and breaks in continuity. This creates a description of the objects, which is stored in the vision system's own memory.

After the system has "learned" an image, it must determine whether the wrench it "sees" matches the wrench stored in its memory. There are two comparisons to be made—the differences of their shapes as well as their orientations in space must be determined. If the system determines that it has indeed "seen" a wrench, it must then calculate the difference between the remembered wrench's coordinates and the actual wrench's coordinates. If, for example, the actual wrench is offset by 2 inches in one direction and 3 inches in another, this information is translated into X and Y coordinates of the world system.

The vision processor sends this information to the CMOS and the microprocessor so that it can incorporate the object's orientation coordinates into the program. Now the PUMA not only "knows" that the wrench has been found, but also "knows" where to reach for it.

THE NEW BREED: PERSONAL, PROMOTIONAL, AND HOBBY ROBOTS

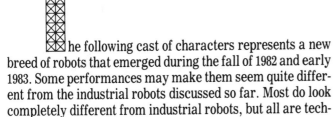he following cast of characters represents a new breed of robots that emerged during the fall of 1982 and early 1983. Some performances may make them seem quite different from the industrial robots discussed so far. Most do look completely different from industrial robots, but all are technologically related to robots in working factories.

Woody and Chip race through a maze while students at a California junior high school cheer them on. The contestants are fairly matched—both share the surname RB5X. So as the twenty-three-inch-high cylindrical relatives wheel around corners, the onlookers' chants could be "May the best-programmed win." That would also apply if Topo, B.O.B.™ or F.R.E.D.™, members of the Androbot family, were racing.

MEET HERO

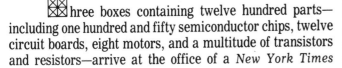hree boxes containing twelve hundred parts—including one hundred and fifty semiconductor chips, twelve circuit boards, eight motors, and a multitude of transistors and resistors—arrive at the office of a *New York Times*

Unveiled in September 1982, this rotund robot, RB5X, was the first mass-produced personal robot. Although RB5X cannot yet read a newspaper, it can deliver one.

reporter. Two weeks later, after eighty-seven hours of soldering and assembling according to the instructions in a manual, the science writer tests the fruit of his effort. After he flicks a power switch, the metallic-sounding voice of his creation says, "Ready." A display panel flashes letters spelling "Hero"—not to praise the laborer, but to announce that another Heathkit Hero 1 has been born.

MEET MINIMOVER

iniMover sits on a desk, tethered to a personal computer. Also on the desk are two trays of different-size ball bearings. The computer screen shows a list of instructions in the language BASIC. Sitting in front of the screen is the program's author, who types in "@RUN." As the program runs, it tells MiniMover's shoulder, elbow, wrist, and gripper to reach for ball bearings in one tray and put them in another, sorted by size. When all the ball bearings are sorted, MiniMover is ready for a new program, poised for another task.

Devices like RB5X, the Androbots, and Hero 1 have been called personal and educational robots; they will bring robotics technology to the home. They are also educational, because in order to play with your electronic companion or make it work, you have to learn about it. You might even want to build it, as in Hero 1's case. So these devices have been marketed as both educational tools and the latest in consumer electronics and home entertainment. For simplicity, we will just call them "personal robots."

Miniature industrial robots, such as MiniMover, can sit on office desks, dining-room tables, or wherever the family personal computer sits. But because they are designed and produced *purely* as training devices for future robotics experts, we do not include them among personal robots, calling them instead "instructional robots."

Whatever the machines are called, manufacturers of both personal and instructional microrobots say that once laypeople become familiar with the technology, they can then use all robots to extend—if not enhance—human capabilities.

Many other devices draw on robotics but do not strictly qualify as robots because they are only partially computer controlled or are not reprogrammable. These range from armless automatic carts that deliver office mail to simple remote manipulator arms used by bomb squads to handle explosives. The most sophisticated of these devices, such as the Space Shuttle's robotic arm, are described as having a man-in-the-loop and as master-slave manipulators. The shuttle arm relied on instructions from an astronaut as well as computer calculations to launch a satellite in the spring of 1983. We include this range of devices here because before long these devices and robotics will be more fully combined.

Finally, we include entertainment, promotional, and hobby (meaning strictly home-grown) robots. In some instances, science-fiction robots that appeared in stories and films inspired and influenced actual personal robot design. Perhaps we can't quite say that life imitated art, but technology approached what was previously seen in the mind's eye.

Heath Company unveiled the Heath Educational Robot, Hero 1, for short, in December 1983. The robot comes assembled or in kit form, and is controlled by its own on-board computer. Its electronic sensors enable it to detect light, sound, motion, and obstructions in its path.

PERSONAL ROBOTS

Some industry experts say that the arrival of personal robotics is analogous to that of personal computers. By 1982, ten years after their introduction, personal computers had become a multibillion-dollar business. *Time* magazine chose one for its January 1983 cover, substituting a "Machine of the Year" for the customary "Man of the Year." By mid-1983, the demand for personal computers in America had mushroomed into a $7.5 billion market, or about 4.2 million units. Estimates for the number of personal computers in use by the end of the century run as high as 80 million, *Time* reported.

Most personal robot manufacturers see their products as extensions of personal computers, so many designed the first generation to be programmed via Radio Shack's TRS-80 and Apple Computer's Apple II and Apple IIe. They expect to tap part of the present personal computer installed base and the growing market by offering the robot as a computer extension, or peripheral. But some manufacturers also offer robots that incorporate enough computing power to be programmed without a personal computer, using on-board microprocessors instead.

But whether microprocessors are internal or external to robots, manufacturers say that the first users of personal robots are in the same position as early personal computer owners. Initially, there were very few programming packages for personal computers, so personal computers seemed to have little use except for balancing checkbooks. New uses such as word processing and electronic game playing became possible when programs to harness the hardware were developed. Now there is a paucity of programming for personal robots, so people say, "What can you do with a personal robot? It's more than a personal computer, but it's not yet a domestic servant."

According to personal robot manufacturers, the answer lies in software development. As the first personal robot owners experiment with their devices, they will develop programs for new uses. Some personal robot manufacturers expect a cottage industry devoted to developing personal robot program packages to spring up, just as it did for personal computers. Right now, buying a personal robot means programming it yourself. The hardware for a robot sentry is here, and that for a robot maid on its way; meanwhile, they await instructions—just as the computer accountant, computer wordsmith, and video game did.

As of this writing, most personal robot manufacturers are just completing negotiations with distributors—mainly vendors of personal computers. Some vendors say they can't fill robot orders fast enough. Others say that these robots will have to be more than toys or educational tools in order to catch on. We don't know when a robot will appear as "Machine of the Year," but here we introduce and highlight the capabilities of gadgets that made some people call 1983 "the year of the personal robot."

Introduced in September 1982, the RB5X became the first mass-produced personal robot. Created by a handful of entrepreneurs at RB Robot Corporation in Golden, Colorado, the robot is the brainchild of the company's president and chairman, Joseph H. Bosworth. Bosworth recognized that robotics did not have anything similar to personal computers that people could take home, learn from, and be comfortable with—a kind of "window on technology." "If you wanted to do that in robotics, you had to buy a $40,000 to $80,000 industrial robot," he says. RB5X costs about $1,495.

The need for an inexpensive way to learn, coupled with inspiration from George Lucas's *Star Wars* fantasy robots R2D2 and C3PO, led Bosworth to conclude that this was the time for "the revolution of robots in the home as well as in the factory."

In designing RB5X, Bosworth and his vice president of research and development, Dan L. Prendergast, were careful not to make their robot resemble a human being. To anthropomorphize would be misleading, they felt, because robots have the potential to do more than just mimic humans.

RB5X does not yet have vision, but it can sense its environment with touch sensors and make decisions based on what it senses. While the external design resembles R2D2, and Prendergast freely admits that influence, he also says that RB5X's shape was dictated by its projected capabilities. The cylindrical shape turned out to be the best way to distribute the bumpers that tell the robot when it has touched an object. The cylinder was also best for turning—the robot spins on its axis.

Like R2D2, RB5X has a dome on top, but RB5X's is transparent so that people can see the microprocessor in-

Dingbot, Omnibot, and Verbot, three personal robots manufactured by Tomy Corporation. Dingbot is a bump-and-go toy robot. Omnibot is a pre-programmable electronic robot with an on-board microcomputer and tape deck. Verbot is a voice activated electronic robot that responds to eight separate verbal commands.

side. The microprocessor stores information in programs that are written on a personal computer. These programs have to be a written in the language Tiny BASIC and are sent to the robot's memory via an RS-232 interface. (An RS-232 interface is a standardized communications link that sends signals from one device to another. Frequently it is used to connect terminals of different brands to a large central computer. In this case the link connects the robot to the intelligence of the personal computer.)

The programs so far developed are based on software principles that allow RB5X to make decisions about the environment based on experience. These principles, formulated by hobby roboticist and author David L. Heiserman, who is a consultant for RB Robot, allow the robot to generalize from specific incidents. He calls the robot learning that results "evolutionary adaptive machine intelligence" (EAMI).

Here is an example of EAMI. Suppose RB5X travels down a hallway until bumper 2 touches an object blocking RB's path. The robot knows from its program that it can try to continue moving by turning left or right, backing up, or stopping briefly. It chooses randomly to back up, and finds that it can keep moving. If RB stores this information and ranks that response superior to the other choices, it will have reason to back up the next time bumper 2 touches an object. Later solutions to bumper 2's signal are no longer based on trial and error, because RB has learned from the earlier experience.

The word *evolutionary* in EAMI is used because the robot at first sought a solution based on primitive, random selection, but later could seek a solution based on ordered, ranked selection. This is adaptive behavior.

Describing himself as one who likes to live his dreams, Bosworth sees RB5X as the first robot in a long series to come. His version is reflected in the robot's name. While "RB" was inspired by the then in-vogue practice of naming major characters with initials (like Spielberg's "E.T." and "J.R." of television's "Dallas"), "5" and "X" have special meaning. "We anticipated that the premier robot would be 'RB6'" says Bosworth. "That is, over a period of anywhere from three to five years, the ultimate personal robot that could interact in a very simple, voice-response manner would evolve." Development of robots that could hear orders would proceed through RB5, RB4, and so on. Since the first model was not engineered for the average consumer, but "for the enthusiast and software developers out on the frontier," the robot was also dubbed "X," for experimental. Bosworth hopes to drop the X when he can offer a model that is practical enough for consumers who want to become robot literate.

HERO 1

In December 1983, the Heath Company in Benton Harbor, Michigan, unveiled Hero 1 and a companion Robotics Educational Course manual. A unit of Zenith Radio Corporation, Heath is the world's largest manufacturer of do-it-yourself electronics kits. According to Heath's president, William E. Johnson, Heath saw the need for a product that could help society prepare for a growing demand for engineers, designers, technicians, and workers who understand the application and maintenance of robots. Says Heath's director of educational marketing and development, Douglas M. Bonham, "Hero is intended as an educational device, first, last, and always. We didn't really produce the first personal robot. We introduced an educational robot, and the world proclaimed it a personal robot." "Hero" stands for Heath Educational Robot, and company officials found out by accident afterward that Hero of Alexandria wrote about automata circa A.D. 1.

Hero 1 costs about $1,500 in kit form and $2,495 if bought fully assembled. In its final form, Hero 1 has an on-board microprocessor, a keyboard, an arm, the ability to speak, a limited sound sensor, and light and motion detectors.

Hero 1's arm has seven axes of motion. Its shoulder is attached to a rotating turret at the top of the robot's body. The turret provides one axis of motion, since it rotates 360 degrees, allowing the arm to reach anywhere around the robot (axis 1). The shoulder itself pivots much as the human arm does, and can be raised about 180 degrees (axis 2). Although the arm does not have an elbow, it can extend and retract five inches, adding another axis (axis 3). The wrist can rotate clockwise or counterclockwise, and it can wave back and forth (axes 4 and 5). When the arm is rotated 90 degrees, the back-and-forth waving motion changes orientation (axis 6). Finally, the wrist holds a gripper that opens

Hero 1 made his way through the halls of Congress to testify before the Senate Commerce, Science, and Transportation Committee in June 1983. Said Hero:

"I have many of the same capabilities as my larger industrial brothers. We can work well with humans. But we all have limits. We need better sensors, mechanical systems, and user-friendly software. We can serve you better with better technology. We need your help to become more useful. Mr. Chairman, I join the IEEE in supporting S. 1286, the Manufacturing Sciences and Technology R&D Act of 1983. Thank you very much."

After all, there is nothing quite like lobbying in person.

and closes (axis 7). The arm can lift up to a pound when it is retracted and up to eight ounces when fully extended.

To speak English, Hero 1's speech synthesizer generates sixty-four tiny, basic elements of sound, called "phonemes." Strung together, they create words in English. Hero can also speak foreign languages, but for any tongue, you have to do the stringing together yourself, according to codes that Heath provides in a dictionary in the instruction manual, and by sounding out other words and coding them. Then the codes have to be punched into Hero 1's keyboard. So that Hero 1's speech does not sound too robotlike, it has four levels of inflection. Without them, Hero 1's voice would be monotonous and it could not sing.

Hero 1's sonar, sound and light detectors, give it an awareness of its environment. From up to eight feet away, it can measure its distance from any size object and be accurate to a quarter of an inch. Beyond eight feet, Hero 1's ability to sense the object depends on the object's size.

Hero 1's sound detector does not provide it with the ability to hear your voice, but it can detect 256 levels of sound. For example you can program it to count how many times you clap your hands or tap it on the head. Bonham says, "He can hear the difference between *Coke* and *Pepsi* because one is a one-syllable word and the other has two syllables. But he can't hear the difference between stop and go."

These features allow Hero 1 to fetch objects, tell jokes, act as a security guard, or roll around like a super-duper mobile alarm clock. And it seems that it may even compete with R2D2 and C3PO, having been offered roles in two movies. One stars the comedian Steve Martin. The other film will be a "science-fiction space opera," according to Bonham.

Hero 1 played a very real part in the legislative process in June 1983, when it delivered a speech on behalf of the Institute of Electrical and Electronics Engineers to members of the Senate who were holding hearings on a bill to promote research and development of manufacturing technologies.

To encourage users to develop software, Heath is holding a contest and offering a gift certificate for the best Hero program. As a result of customer requests, Heath will provide an RS-232 interface so that Hero can be hooked up to a personal computer for programming. Also planned is an expanded on-board memory and an "explore" mode to let Hero wander around autonomously.

ANDROBOT

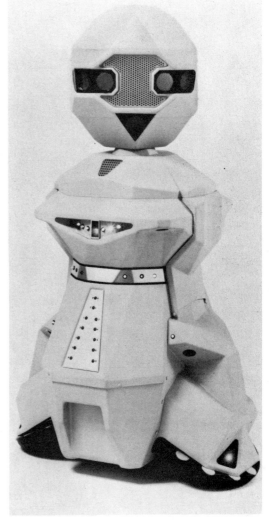

January 1983 marked the beginning of the year 1 A.B.—"After B.O.B."—according to Androbot in San Jose, California, which unveiled personal robots B.O.B. and Topo. The more sophisticated of the two is B.O.B. ("brains on board"). Like Hero 1, B.O.B. has built-in microprocessors so that it can be programmed without a personal computer. The bulk of Topo's intelligence, like that of RB5X, resides in a personal computer. But neither B.O.B. nor Topo comes with arms.

Six months later, Androbot announced F.R.E.D. and AndroMan. F.R.E.D. stands for friendly robotic educational device. AndroMan is a scaled-down version of B.O.B. and Topo.

Like other companies' personal robots, these products are designed to perform useful tasks in the home, educate, and entertain. But the orientation of Androbot's founders and the users they have targeted for each robot emphasize some purposes more than others.

Androbot (a combination of *android* and *robot*) was founded in 1981 by Nolan K. Bushnell. Bushnell is no stranger to high technology. Known as the inventor of video games, he thought up Pong and founded Atari back in 1972. After selling Atari to Warner Communications for $28 million in 1976 and agreeing not to compete with the company for seven years, Bushnell turned to nurturing start-up technology companies.

Androbot is just one of about twenty such companies. With the seven-year video-game hiatus drawing to a close, some Androbots have been designed to participate in what the company calls three-dimensional video games. With 17 million Atari 2600s in American homes and their owners looking for new ways to use them, robots and video games seem a "natural marriage," says Androbot's marketing manager, Rick Gibson.

Both Topo and AndroMan can take the action in a video game off the screen and into the three-dimensional realm. One game will involve navigating the robots through a crater-filled moonscape. Just as the direction of a hungry yellow Pac Man creature on a video display terminal is controlled by a joy stick, both Topo and AndroMan receive joy-stick instructions. These are transmitted from a per-

Dubbed "B.O.B.™," for brains on board, this personal robot offers the same computing power as IBM's personal computer. Besides cerebral talents, B.O.B.™ senses body heat with infrared sensors. That way, the robot avoids humans.

sonal computer to the robots via infrared signals.

Whereas AndroMan is built for adventures on 3-D gamescapes, Topo has other capabilities. This robot receives keyboard commands as well as joy-stick commands through an infrared link. A language called "TopoForth" allows users to write original programs on the keyboard, which can be saved on a diskette so Topo will remember them. Thus whether you have written step-by-step instructions in TopoForth telling Topo to go to the patio, for example, or if you have taught Topo to travel to the patio by moving the joy stick in the appropriate directions, the personal computer will save the information. The next time you want Topo to go to the patio, you call up the file containing the program and send it by infrared signals to the robot, and it will perform.

B.O.B. is a smarter version of Topo because programs can be processed by an on-board computer. The circuit boards are housed in its chest and there are slots to plug in cartridges that contain programs. These cartridges serve the same purpose as diskettes, in that they contain instructions. They are just another, more compact way of storing information. If, for example, you would like B.O.B. to act as a sentry, you could buy and plug in a cartridge, soon to be offered by Androbot, called AndroSentry. You could also create your own sentry program by learning Androbot Control Language, which is similar to TopoForth, keying the program into a personal computer, and sending it to B.O.B.

These robots sense their environment with ultrasonic and infrared sensors. The ultrasonic sensors determine the position and range of objects to within half-inch accuracy. Infrared sensors detect body heat so that the robots can avoid warm-blooded creatures.

Neither B.O.B. nor Topo has arms. Instead, they have two appendages attached by hinges to their sides. These can be pushed down manually and objects can be placed on them. Even though Androbot acknowledges that the state of the art for arms is here, the company says that the coordination and judgment required to use them are lacking. The optics for getting a robot to find and pick up a black sock on a black carpet are not yet sufficiently developed, says Gibson, and programming a robot to judge what is or is not clean requires a great deal of computer memory.

Androbot is researching these matters, but for the next three to four years it will concentrate on financial rewards in entertainment, education, and companionship. Attachments are being offered to provide some manual capability to the robots. For example, an Androwagon adds on to B.O.B. and Topo, allowing them to carry objects. And an Androfrig that attaches to the refrigerator dispenses drinks in cans so that the robots can carry them on their arm appendages.

F.R.E.D. is intended for six- to fourteen-year-olds. F.R.E.D. and another robot, the Tasman Turtle, are meant to teach children geometry. The Tasman robot, made by Flexible Systems of Hobart, Australia, made its U.S. debut in January 1983; it has been available in Australia since 1980. Both F.R.E.D. and the Tasman Turtle are programmed with the language Logo.

Logo is the result of artificial intelligence research headed by Seymour Papert at the Massachusetts Institute of Technology. In the 1960s, Papert, who studied with the renowned child psychologist Jean Piaget, began developing a computer language especially designed for use by grade-

Children can learn to program a robot by practicing with a Tasman Turtle, which responds to instructions in the computer language Logo.

school children. The purpose of that language, now called Logo, was to teach children geometry as well as familiarize them with computers. A child can direct a triangular character, called a turtle, in any direction across a computer screen and have it create a shape. If the child types in "RIGHT 90," the turtle turns 90 degrees to the right. The command "FORWARD 50" sends the turtle about 50 millimeters forward. Papert told *Time* magazine that Logo "convinces the child that he can master the machine. It lets him say, 'I'm the boss.'"

Children learn programming by getting F.R.E.D. and Tasman Turtle to draw geometric shapes in the real world instead of just on a computer screen. Unlike the screen turtle, these robots can sense and respond to the environment. Witness what happens if Tasman Turtle bumps into an object, as Ross J. Harris's turtle did when he was experimenting with it. "It's bumper closes a microswitch, one of the four switches on the turtle's front, sides, and back.... The commands FTOUCH, BTOUCH, LTOUCH, RTOUCH allow you to check the state of the switches. By using a conditional statement in Logo procedure [program] you can command the Tasman to react to meeting an obstacle." Harris gives an example of such a conditional statement:

```
TO AVOID
□ TFD 20                    (meaning take 20 steps forward)
□ IF FTOUCH THEN            (meaning if the front sensor was
  TBK 20                    touched, go back 20 steps)
□ TRT 30                    (meaning turn right 30 degrees)
□ AVOID
END
```

Harris's program gives the turtle the ability to respond to its surroundings. "This ability to make something new happen as a result of contact with the real world allows you to program the robot turtle to interact with its environment, simulating a kind of 'intelligence,'" he writes.

Some personal robot manufacturers say that people will adapt the way they do things in the home to suit the capabilities of their personal robots. For example, if you have stacked dishes haphazardly in the dish rack, you might begin stacking them in a specific order each time. Then, a robot with minimal senses could be programmed once to always recognize the stacked-dish pattern. It could remove the dishes from the rack and put them away with the same preprogrammed arm movements. The idea is similar to redesigning products so that they can be assembled by industrial robots. Right now, "Our homes are designed around what our capabilities and needs are," says RB Robot's Prendergast. "Things will begin to adapt for both our and our robots' capabilities and needs. I don't think that's too far-out a thing to require." Perhaps it is not too much to ask that home design be robot-friendly.

In this multiple exposure of the desk-top instructional robot, Alpha, made by Microbot, Ben DuBois programs its arm motions using a hand-held teach pendant.

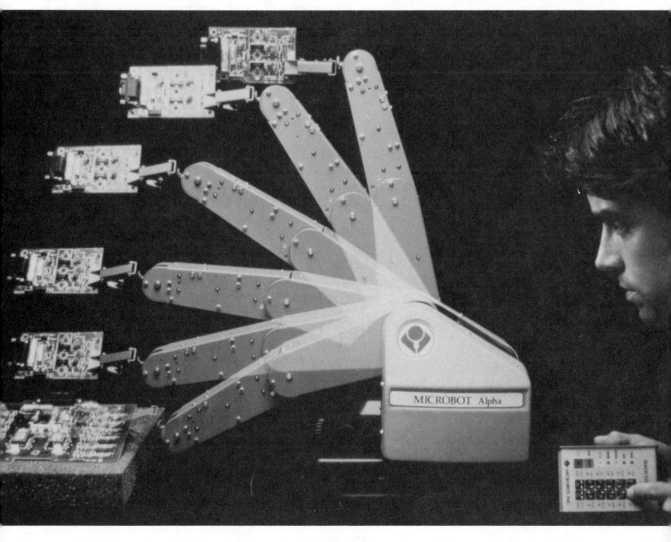

In the 1960s, Americans watched events in a televisionland house inhabited by the zany Addams family. The Addams's eccentricity was in part expressed by their peculiar pets, one of which was a hand called "Thing." Thing lived in a box that sat on a table. When he wanted to communicate, he lifted the lid of the box and expressed himself by using sign language or grabbing relevant objects on the table. Occasionally, Thing answered the telephone.

Instructional robots might seem like mechanical Things, but they are not quite as mysterious or macabre. They are miniature industrial robot arms that have five or six degrees of freedom. They are an inexpensive way for hobbyists, schools, universities, and research laboratories to experiment with robot programming languages and to simulate some manufacturing applications.

Although Microbot of Mountain View, California, was the first to demonstrate the market for miniature industrial robots, other companies, such as Rhino Robots of Champaign, Illinois; Mitsubishi Electric of Tokyo, and M. T. Hikawa of Toyoake, Aichi, now make instructional robots.

John W. Hill, a founder and now vice president of Microbot, says that his desire to create a computer attachment to draw and build things started out as a hobby. While working in SRI International's bioengineering, biomechanics, and robotics laboratories, Hill and three associates built three small robot arms that could be programmed on Radio Shack's TRS-80 personal computer. They rented a booth at the 1980 West Coast Computer Fair in San Francisco and were surprised to find themselves swamped. "We were six people deep and everyone wanted to program the robots. People were climbing on top of each other."

With that enthusiastic reception, they made eight distribution deals and incorporated Microbot. Now over twenty distributors sell three products, MiniMover 5 ($1,700), TeachMover ($2,500), and Alpha (under $8,500).

MiniMover and TeachMover are purely for instructional purposes, whereas Alpha is capable of handling light materials in factories. The arms of all the robots reach to no more than eighteen inches when extended and can lift up to one and a half pounds.

When completed, Roberta delivered a graduation address at Dekalb. Here the robot's arms, two MiniMover instructional robots mounted sideways, are visible.

The robots can be programmed with the same kinds of instructions as their bigger industrial brethren. But to create inexpensive miniatures, Hill relied on a different mechanical design, called "tendon technology." Electrically driven industrial robots have a motor in each joint to power that joint. This means that the motor at the shoulder must be powerful enough to lift the motor at the elbow. This drives up the cost of the entire arm. To keep his mini-robots inexpensive, Hill put all the motors for the joints in the robot's base. The motors drive cables, or tendons, that act like pulleys on the joints and manipulate the arm to $\pm$ 0.02 inch. Putting the motors in the base also makes the arm more stable, so the robot does not have to be bolted down to keep from toppling over.

The MiniMover can also be programmed with an Apple II by Apple Computer or a PMC-80 by Personal Micro Computer, using a language that Microbot developed called "ARMBASIC."

TeachMover, like many industrial robots, can be pro-

British painter Harold Cohen also builds programmable drawing devices, thus creating a kind of robot art. While a visiting professor at the University of California, San Diego, in 1968, Cohen learned computer programming from a friend and hasn't put his own hand to paper since. Instead, his turtle, AARON, does the drawing, and its works went on tour—here it is shown at Documenta Kassel, West Germany, in 1977—and were exhibited at the Brooklyn Museum in 1983.

grammed with an attachment called a "teach pendant." Teach pendants look something like hand-held calculators. They have buttons that rotate joints clockwise or counterclockwise for as long as they are pressed. The computer memorizes the sequence of buttons pressed just as it would memorize lines of instructions that had been written on a keyboard.

Microbot mini-robots have been bought by corporations that have gone into industrial robotics or are actively involved in robotics research. Microbot numbers IBM, Hewlett-Packard, Western Electric, Bell Laboratories, Syn-

tex Laboratories, Ciba-Geigy, Du Pont, and Westinghouse among its clients. It also supplies to an increasing number of high schools and universities that offer courses in robotics. Seventh-graders in Wood River Junior High in Idaho learned to manipulate a TeachMover in one class period. At the University of Southern California, Los Angeles, students in a course called "Basic Robotics Laboratory," offered by the Department of Engineering, spend up to ten hours a week programming mini-robots. They are assigned exercises like stacking, palletizing, and synchronization of multiple arms, which they carry out with two MiniMovers and two Apple II computers.

A miniature assembly system using the MiniMover was created at the University of Alabama in Huntsville, where a simulated manufacturing workcell was built to assemble two-and-a-half-inch-square paperweights bearing the university logo. The assembly process starts when a video camera locates a blank paperweight in a bin. An image analyzer sends information about the paperweight's location to an Apple II computer, which instructs a Mini-Mover to pick up the part and transfer it to a small positioning table, a mobile platform called an X-Y table because it can slide backward, forward, and from side to side on rods. It positions the paperweight under a drill, which bores four holes in the paperweight. Then the robot moves the paperweight to a final assembly platform. The robot picks up a magnet, which it uses to attract and hold the university's steel logo plate. The robot brushes the logo against a glue sponge and places the logo on top of the paperweight.

Rhino Robots introduced its first instructional robot, the XR-1 ($2,400), at the end of 1981 and has since sold six hundred units, for a total of $2 million. President Harprit Sandhu says that U.S. installations represent 1 percent of the industrial robot (IR) market. The demand for instructional robots is so great, says Sandhu, that his company now does $46,000 a week in sales. He proudly announces that no industrial robot manufacturer did that kind of business in units or dollars in the last year and a half.

Two robots, the XR-2 ($2,850) and the Charger ($20,000), have since been added to the product line. A third new product, the Scorpion, will compete with F.R.E.D. and Tasman Turtle.

The XR-1 and XR-2 are similar models designed purely for instructional and research purposes, whereas Charger is a small industrial robot. The XR series stand

Rhino writes, demonstrating its dexterity.

This is Rhino Robots' latest addition, Scorpion, which also runs on Logo.

thirty-two inches high and can lift five pounds. They are slightly bigger and stronger than the Microbot arms. The XR-2 has a unique feature (or nonfeature), since it is a naked robot. Sandhu decided to expose its gear mechanisms to allow students to "see that there is no magic about robots and that [they] can build one too." The motors and gear drives are the same as those for industrial robots, and the mechanisms can be taken apart and reassembled.

The XR series can be programmed on any personal computer that takes the RS-232 interface and with any computer language. Like the Microbot TeachMover, it can also receive instructions through a teach pendant. But Rhino has another feature that makes its robots faster than other instructional robots—its Mark II controller. This is known as a slave controller, because it assists the computer by sending specific instructions to arm joints. This frees up the computer, which can work on the next calculation in the meantime. "It's not unlike the factory manager who tells someone to bend a wire, and while the worker is bending it, the manager is thinking about the next thing to be done," Sandhu explains."

The XR series is used in schools, universities, and company laboratories. One firm decided to use its XR-1 as a psychological personnel-management device. To introduce employees of the Brown Shoe Company in St. Louis to automation and robotics, Charlie Wolfersberger, of the research engineering department, takes his Rhino on tour. He has given demonstrations to five hundred groups of about twenty employees each who asked him to make the robot do such tasks as drop a lump of sugar into a coffee mug. The demonstrations help relieve employees' fears and usually open discussions on issues related to automation.

The Charger is a rugged Industrial Robot that can lift fifty pounds and is accurate to within one millimeter. Sandhu introduced it to fill the need for a "medium-technology, medium-accuracy robot that doesn't cost an arm and a leg," a need that was expressed at a 1983 robot trade show. "Everybody wants to sell you a $250,000 robot that shakes your hand, talks to you, goes to dinner, and can thread a camel through a needle's eye. That's not what everybody needs," says Sandhu.

The Charger is programmed with an Apple computer. Consequently, all the thousands of kids who know how to program Apples can now program robots, says Sandhu. And the Apples' three thousand accessories are now accessories for the robot.

ROBOT CARTS

ust as some flexible manufacturing systems in factories have self-propelled carts to bring materials to machining stations, robot carts are being used to carry hazardous materials. In safe environments they've also been used to speed up interoffice or interdepartmental deliveries.

The New York City Police Department recently acquired a mobile remote manipulator that members of its bomb squad use to remove bombs and suspicious packages. When detectives on the squad got the device in March 1983, they fondly named it "E.T.," but the manufacturer, Pedsco Canada of Ontario, Canada, calls it the Mark-3 Remote Mobile Investigation Unit, or RMI-3.

RMI-3 consists of an arm with a television camera mounted on a six-wheeled cart that is connected by two hundred feet of cable to an operator's dolly. The dolly has a television monitor that lets the operator see what the camera sees. With that perception, the operator can manipulate the arm and direct the cart using a joy stick on a control box. Unlike the bilateral force reflecting manipulator, like those used for handling nuclear waste, the operator cannot feel what the arm feels. But detectives on the squad have used it with considerable success. During its first three and a half months on the force, detectives used it to remove twenty-six out of sixty-five suspicious packages, says bomb-squad commander Lieutenant Charles Luisi. It could not be used on twenty-eight assignments due to physical limitations, and on the remaining eleven occasions, packages were identified as not hazardous.

In 1984, Carl R. Flatau of TeleOperator Systems introduced a vehicle that carries two bilateral force reflecting arms for use in nuclear power plants and to assist police bomb squads. The vehicle is able to reach areas too hazardous for humans to investigate without closing down an entire power plant. It will save humans from exposure while preventing very expensive shutdowns—the costs of which are passed on to consumers. Besides its sensitive arms, its wheels allow it to jump a three-foot-wide trench and climb stairs. It is able to open a door and maneuver through a thirty-inch doorway.

After four bombs exploded on New Year's Eve 1982–83, the New York City Police Department bought two robot carts so that officers could use them to handle hazardous packages while maintaining a safe distance. Here, bomb squad detectives test one of the devices, which they call "E.T."

The Automated Systems Division of Bell and Howell in Zeeland, Michigan, has been supplying insurance companies, banks, pharmaceutical houses, and other businesses with its Mailmobile delivery vehicle since 1976. The idea originated with Sears, Roebuck in Chicago, which had difficulty keeping people employed in the tedious job of picking up and delivering mail and office-supply requests. Lear Seigler, an aerospace firm, developed the Mailmobile, and then the firm was taken over by Bell and Howell.

The Mailmobile is often referred to as a robot, but is really an armless vehicle that carries sorter trays along a chemical path on an office carpet. It travels at a speed of about one mile per hour, makes a soft humming sound and has flashing blue lights to announce its presence. It is programmed to stop at departments for twenty seconds so that workers can remove or load mail. If necessary, workers can stop it for a longer time interval before it continues on its way.

The Mailmobile can have on-board intelligence so that it can make decisions at path intersections, and two Mailmobiles with machine-to-machine communication via radio transmitters can avoid colliding. Bumpers that wrap around the cart stop it when an object is touched, and the cart waits ten seconds before continuing its run.

At Citibank headquarters in New York City, where every floor has a Mailmobile (the company calls them "Citipages"), savings of $25,000 a year per unit have been reported. Citibank paid $10,000 or $20,000 for each cart, and programs them to make rounds every twenty minutes. "Even when we had ten [human] pages per floor, deliveries were usually made every hour or two," says John G. Anderson, Citibank's vice president for premises and office management. Productivity has increased, because people try to complete work on time for the next run, he told *Corporate Systems* magazine.

Another robot cart is hard at work at the Yale–New Haven Medical Center, delivering a different kind of mail. Designed by Dr. David Seligson, chairman of laboratory medicine and clinical laboratories, the robot's purpose is to quickly transport specimens to the laboratories where they are to be analyzed.

Under the old transport system, hospital staffers would collect patient samples and send them through a pneumatic tube to a collection station. There, a messenger would pick them up and take them to the appropriate laboratory. The test turnaround often took as long as two hours, inspiring Dr. Seligson to speed up the system. In large hospitals like Yale–New Haven, the long distances between laboratories and clinical areas can be detrimental. "When a patient is in the emergency room in a diabetic coma, the physician needs to know several important values in the patient's blood," Seligson told *Clinical Chemistry News.* Waiting for laboratory results of course delays diagnosis and treatment. This can be fatal. Yale–New Haven's emergency room is a quarter of a mile from its labs, but building a special emergency room lab would have been too expensive.

Clancy, a compact eighteen-by-twenty-four-inch robot carrier with a keyboard and sixteen photocells to sense a guide tape on the floor, provides an inexpensive solution. Built at a cost of $1,000, Clancy makes rounds from one station to another in three minutes and has reduced turnaround to ten minutes. After loading Clancy with samples, hospital staffers punch in destination codes on the keyboard. Upon arriving, Clancy beeps to alert a lab technician. Soon Clancy's beep will be replaced by a voice.

Clancy doesn't dawdle in the hallway to chat with passersby. It does the work of five deliverymen, and it is polite. If it senses people along the path, it stops six inches away and waits until its path is clear.

Yale–New Haven finds Clancy so successful that two clones are planned. These robots will carry samples by elevator to labs on different floors.

PROMOTIONAL ROBOTS

ust as Vaucanson entertained nineteenth-century crowds with his mechanical duck, ShowAmerica and International Robotics today create automatic crowd pleasers. There are animated figures in Disneyland and Epcot Center. Robots promote products at trade shows. Hollywood has created robot film characters, and an Andy Warhol robot will soon make its Broadway debut. There is a kind of "information ricochet" (to use Tom Wolfe's phrase) among developers of these robotlike amusements, who become inspired by one another's creations.

One day while walking through New York's Pennsyl-

The H. J. Heinz Company considers this promotional robot its ambassador and fondly calls it "H.J." An attraction at trade shows, fairs, and baseball games, the robot has distributed Heinz Pickle pins, continuing the tradition of the company's founder who handed out a million pins, now collector's items, at the 1893 World's Fair.

Instead of diamonds, up to 20,000 electronic components are this girl's best friends. Low-pneumatic valves controlled by a microcomputer give "New Monroe" facial expression and body movement. Although gemless, New Monroe was first exhibited at the 1982 Osaka Jewel Fair.

vania Station, Broadway producer Lewis Allen happened upon a promotional robot for Columbia Picture's film *The Greatest.* The robot was a Muhammad Ali look-alike that so fascinated Allen that he imagined it could come to life. Allen had also been reading two books by pop artist Andy Warhol, *Andy Warhol's Exposures* and *The Philosophy of Andy Warhol,* and was searching for a way to adapt them for theatrical production.

Allen perceived Warhol as trying to reduce himself to a camera and a tape recorder. Since Warhol has often said that his ambition in life is to become a machine, Allen decided to build a robot in Warhol's image. He approached Walt Disney Productions, but they were gearing up for Epcot Center and were themselves looking for technicians. Allen also approached George Lucas, but the *Star Wars* producer was interested in robots for film only. Finally, Allen hired computer consultant Gerald Feil and Alvaro Villa, a one-time Disney engineer, to build the robot. Both had experience in special effects and animation design for films and live tours of animated figures. Work on the robot's hardware began in Villa's company, AVG Productions in Valencia, California, in 1981, while Robert Shapiro, president of Meta Information Applications in New York City, began working on the software. The screenplay was being written by playwright-producer Peter Sellers, who had worked on Allen's most recent Broadway hit, *My One and Only.*

The Warhol mechanical clone will star in a show called *Andy Warhol's Overexposed: A No Man Show* that will open on Broadway in September 1985. The robot will have fifty-four movements, ranging from facial expressions to folding its arms. These will be synchronized with recordings of Warhol's voice. All of this will be controlled by a specially built computer, "because nobody builds one for animated figures," says Villa.

The robot will be seated on its bed in Warhol's room, surrounded by its dog, a telephone, and two television sets. It will interact with these as well as with the audience. When a member of the audience asks a question, the robot will have five preprogrammed answers to choose from.

Besides being entertaining, Allen says, the show may indicate that art and technology are not necessarily pitted against each other. Other questions Sellers says it may raise are: What is the difference between a robot and a human being? What happens when a human being becomes a robot?

What happens when a robot tries to become a human being?

Other robots in the image of famous personalities, including Thomas Edison, have been created by Shunichi Mizuno, president of the Japanese company Cybot Corporation in Osaka.

In 1982, New Monroe, a facsimile of Marilyn Monroe, was introduced at the Jewel Fair in Osaka. Though not as sophisticated as the Warhol robot, New Monroe has forty movements, enabling it to laugh, sing, talk, and strum a guitar. Cybot also created a fairy and a mermaid, which were both used in department store displays.

Another Japanese company that makes robots to amuse people is Namco Limited in Tokyo. Visitors at amusement parks can challenge mechanical kendo players to a duel for a small fee. The company also makes toy robots that look like R2D2. Some have wheels, others have three legs.

ShowAmerica in Chicago is the world's oldest and largest manufacturer of promotional robots, the kind that caught Lewis Allen's eye at Penn Station. These are not robots in the true sense, because their speech and movements are radio controlled by an actor behind the scenes.

For thirteen years the company has been making robotlike replicas of products that move among crowds. A turning point for ShowAmerica came in 1976, after Lucas's *Star Wars* was released, says President J. W. Anderson. It stimulated such interest in robots that 1977 was the biggest year, and business has doubled in the last three years. Eighty percent of the robots appear at trade shows, and the remaining 20 percent take part at grand openings, groundbreakings, hospitality suites, etcetera.

The most popular robot is the Quadricon, a humanoid type with head and arm movement and flashing lights. A company can lease the robot for $850 a day, plus shipping expenses and a charge for a customized outer shell that makes the robot resemble the company's product. ShowAmerica's robots have been used by Exxon, General Electric, Rockwell International, H. J. Heinz, and Pfizer, to mention a few. They have appeared all over the world, and so, Anderson says, "they are marvelously enjoyable entertainment communication devices that transcend all nationalities and all age groups."

ShowAmerica also rents out electronic talking parrots and electronic talking mannequins like the ones made by Walt Disney Productions. A line of electronic talking cartoon characters is being developed now. These will have eye,

Here Jamie Farr, of the television series "MASH," clowns with a ShowAmerica robot that plays goalie for the Los Angeles Kings hockey team and is sponsored by the greater Los Angeles Toyota dealers.

After Everett's robot, Robart I, came to the attention of Vice Admiral Earl B. Fowler, the position of special assistant for robotics was created for Everett at the Naval Surface Weapons Center in White Oak, Maryland. There work progresses on a vision system and other improvements for Robart II.

mouth, and head movement. Their bodies will slouch and straighten up. They will pivot at the waist and also have shoulder and elbow movement.

Although Lucas's film robots stimulated the public's fascination with robots, Anderson says they raised unrealistic expectations about real robots. There were several versions of R2D2 used in the filming of *Star Wars*. When a scene called for a certain capability, the appropriate model was used. While there is not one robot in existence that can do what R2D2 does on film, says Anderson, "when it was all put together with the camera and in the projection room, it looked like the world's greatest thing since the wheel." Perhaps it was, if so many people were inspired by it.

HOBBY ROBOTS

obby roboticists, people who have realized their personal vision of a robot using home-grown methods, have also participated in information ricochet. John W. Gutmann, head of the Atlanta Computer Society's Robotics Special Interest group, and his friends Bill Dodd of Hobby Robots in Hazelhurst, Georgia, and Robert Wagoner teamed up to build a promotional robot for a California store owner. Gutmann, an AT&T computer maintenance employee, provided the electronic skills needed for the robot's "nervous system." Dodd, whose training is in industrial automation, handled the mechanics. Wagoner designed the software. Their $12,000 to $15,000 creation, named "Oscar," after the Computer Shack store owner who requested the robot, attracts customers by announcing sales and specials.

Gutmann has also offered his skills as a hobby roboticist to a community college, Dekalb Technical College, by guiding students in the construction of a robot called "Roberta." Roberta has radio controls and an on-board computer. Its arms are two MiniMovers that are mounted on its sides and can reach in front, and up and down. Roberta also has speech, and a year ago was programmed to deliver a graduation address at the college.

Another robot, Robot Redford, built by hobby roboticist William Bakaleinikoff, president of Superior Robotics of America, Petaluma, California, delivered a speech at the

Hero 1 has a small arm that can lift one pound when it is retracted and up to eight ounces when fully extended. The robot can also be programmed to speak by stringing together tiny sound elements called "phonemes."

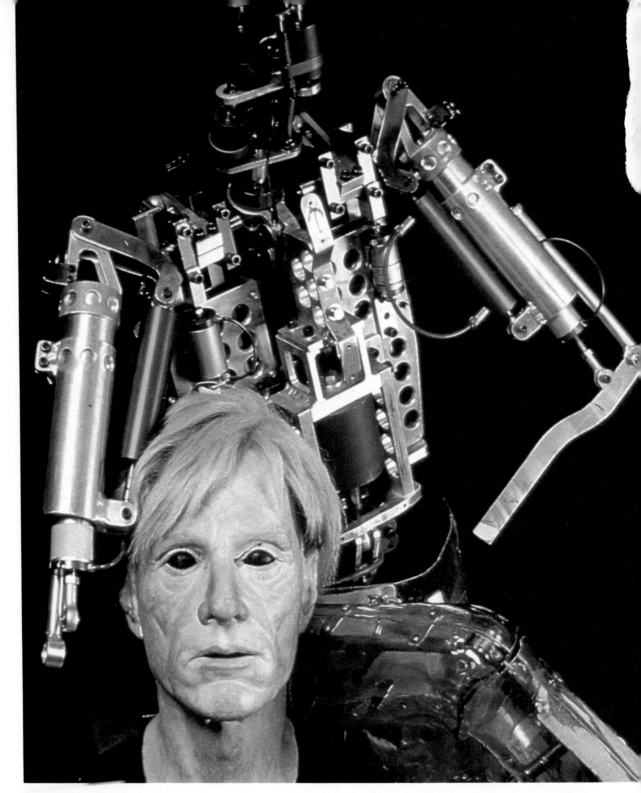

Pop artist Andy Warhol has often expressed his lifelong ambition to be a machine. Heeding his call, Broadway mogul Lewis Allen hired special effects and animation experts to construct a Warhol mechanical clone. It will debut in September 1985 on Broadway in Andy Warhol's Overexposed: A No Man Show. *Lewis Allen's other shows include* Annie *and* My One and Only.

B2

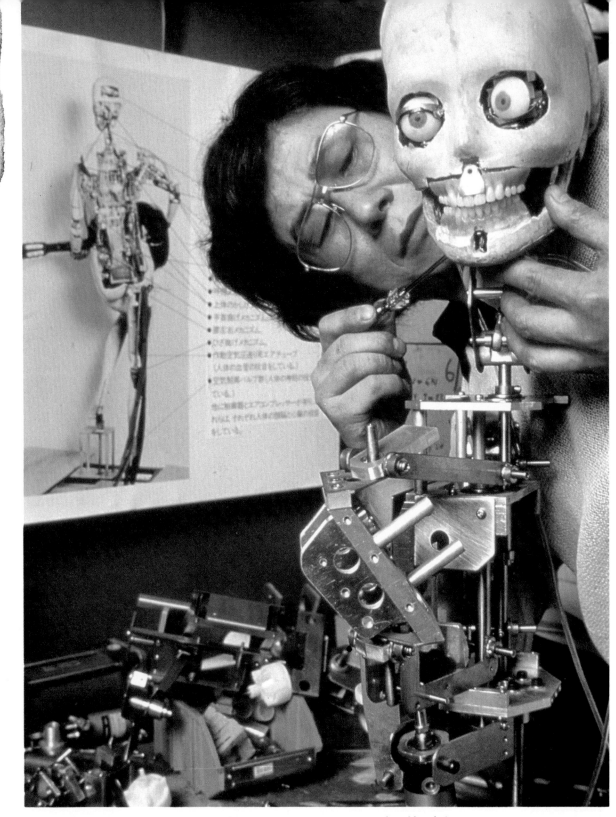

Inventor Shunichi Mizuno, now president of Cybot Corporation in Japan, at work on his robot.

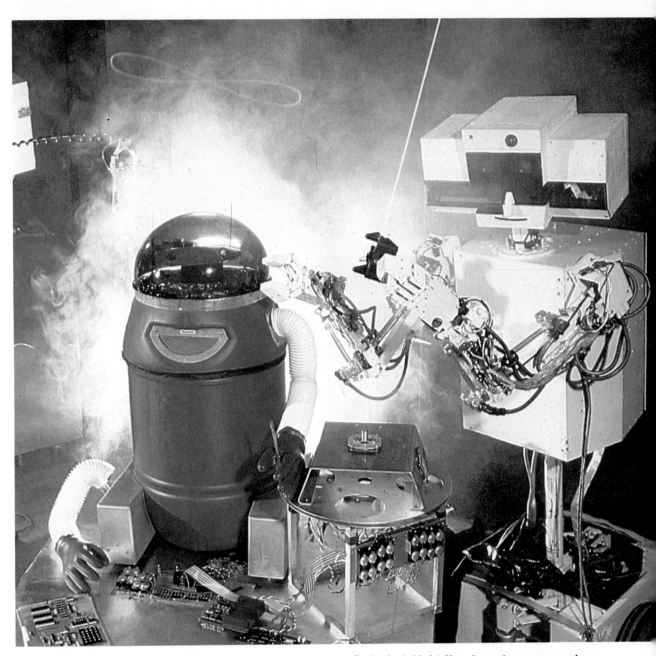

Squirt, by hobbyist Marc Arc and aerospace engineer Tom Caroll, forms a handsome duo with Jim Hill's Charlie. The inventors are members of the U.S. Robotics Foundation, an organization for amateur roboticists.

◄ Jim Hill, who has been building robots since he was fifteen, poses with Charlie, his latest creation. Charlie took four years to build from aluminum and square tubing. The wait was well worth it—Charlie is capable of tasks most humans don't like to do, like dropping garbage into a can, a sequence that ABC-TV's news shot and aired.

B5

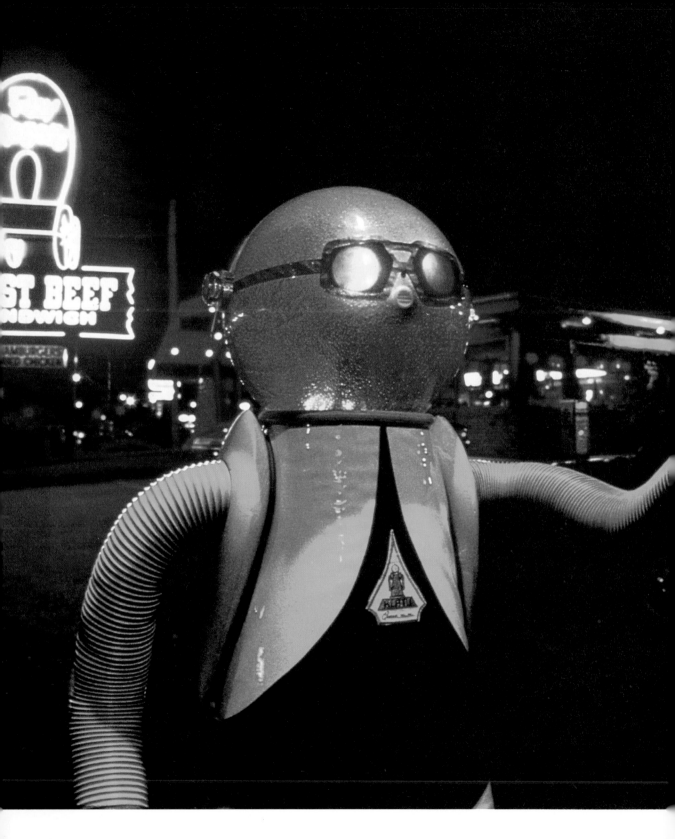

Robots supplied by Renault's ACMA subsidiary, pick gearbox pieces off trolleys and present them to machine tools for assembly operations. The same robots are marketed in the U.S. by the Renault-Ransburg joint venture, Cybotech.

◄ Klatu, an early promotional robot built by Quasar Industries, entertained drivers in the parking lot of a fast-food restaurant in the late 1960s.

Here, at the palletization station, an operator keys in the type of piece that the cart will carry and this information is sent to the machining stations. The cart is behind the computer console and its cargo is an aluminum gearbox cap. Main gearbox casings of cast iron are on a conveyor in the foreground.

◄ The Renault Vehicules Industriels Boutheon factory builds up to 100 truck gearboxes a day. The factory employs an Fr45 million flexible manufacturing system. Electric cables under the floor generate signals that guide the unmanned vehicles.

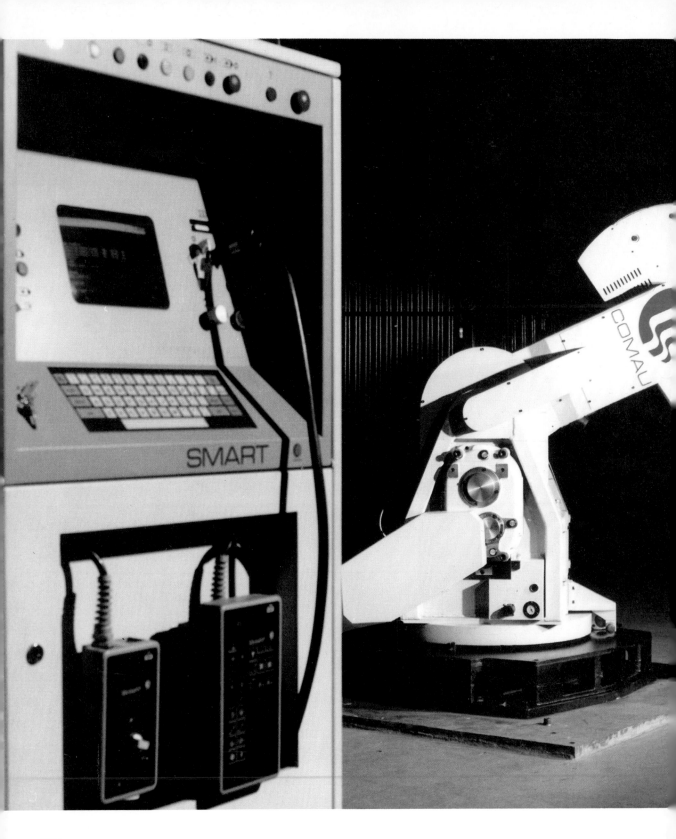

These robots depalletize parts and present them to machine tools. The robot depalletizing the shaft will take it to a lathe for shaping and cutting, for example.

◄ An Italian Smart robot with its control console.

Across the street from the motor manufacturing plant is a factory where Fanuc robots are produced. Completed in 1980, this factory employs about 100 people and has the capacity to produce about 300 robots a month. Like the other plant, it has unmanned carriers but it also has two storage warehouses.

1983 commencement at Anne Arundel Community College in suburban Maryland. Robot Redford's words were delivered by Bakaleinikoff, offstage.

Gutmann's current project is a modular robot he hopes someday to sell as a kit. Most hobbyists build their robots around one frame, box, or cylinder and then add parts, says Gutmann. Later, when they want to change something in the system, they take it apart and start all over again. With a modular design, hobbyists could rebuild sections of their robots without tearing apart the entire project.

Another hobbyist, John J. Gallaher, was hard at work on a personal robot kit during the late 1970s. Unlike Gutmann's, Gallaher's kit grew out of an assignment to design an industrial robot. To market the kit, he founded American Robots in 1978, and he sold the kit for $1,000 all over the world. Gallaher now heads an industrial robotics consulting firm, Gallaher Enterprises, in Winston-Salem, North Carolina.

Gallaher built his first robot when he was fourteen, and completed another robot as a college project. As a custom engineer of soft- and hardware packages for industrial users, he had plenty of opportunities to visit factories. One

Hobbyist William Bakaleinikoff, president of Superior Robots of America, built Robot Redford, which he presents here as "Chairman of the Board—the future young executive of the twenty-first century." But such business-creatures do seem to respect human creativity, for Bakaleinikoff reports that Robot Redford "considers Isaac Asimov his Godfather."

This robot, named "Pulsar," traces its lineage to Klatu, since both were built by teams with members in common. Robert Doornick left Quasar Industries to form International Robotics in New York and build Pulsar. Although Pulsar entertains clients at a Pennsylvania nightclub, other International Robotics creations have cheered hospital patients and even gained the attention of previously unresponsive autistic children.

client in the textile industry had an extremely noisy elastic spinning factory. Because of Occupational Safety and Health Administration (OSHA) rules, the client had to protect the workers who changed elastic spools from the noise. To solve the problem another way, the client asked Gallaher to design a manipulator that could move around the plant floor and change the spools. The result was a robot operated by a worker in a soundproof booth.

OSHA's rules changed, however, and even though the robot worked beautifully, it was no longer needed. Gallaher decided to put his prototype to use, and marketed it as a kit that could be programmed with Radio Shack's TRS-80 personal computer. Gallaher says that the first university exposure to robotics resulted from purchasing his kits. People involved in industrial robot development learned from those kits as well. And American Robots, onetime robot kit manufacturer, is today competing in the industrial robot market.

Another hobbyist, Hobart Everett, Jr., now a lieutenant commander in the navy, built his first robot, Walter, in 1965. Walter is the ancestor of two more Everett creations, Robart I and Robart II, which are sentry robots. Robart I was developed between 1980 and 1982, while Everett was attending the Naval Postgraduate School in Monterey, California. It could sense intruders and detect smoke, fire, toxic gas, earthquakes, and approaching storms. It also recharged its batteries and navigated without bumping into walls and objects.

When Vice Admiral Earl B. Fowler, commander of the Naval Sea System Command, learned of the results, he appointed Everett as special assistant for robotics at the Naval Surface Weapons Center in White Oak, Maryland. Work on a vision system for Robart II is now under way at the center's recently unveiled Robotics Research and Development Laboratory. Directed by Dr. Thomas McKnight, that laboratory also investigates industrial robot applications of particular interest to the navy, such as welding and finishing ship propellers and parts.

There are hobby robotocist societies and clubs in Boston; Washington, D.C.; Atlanta, and Long Beach, California. The organizations bring together individuals with very different approaches to the same activity. In his own group of twenty members, Gutmann sees twelve people going twelve separate ways. One member thinks of his robot as a vehicle for artificial intelligence and programming experiments. Others are interested purely in the appearance of their

Taking advantage of its own road signs in San Ramon, California, this robot, Roboteer, went for a roll.

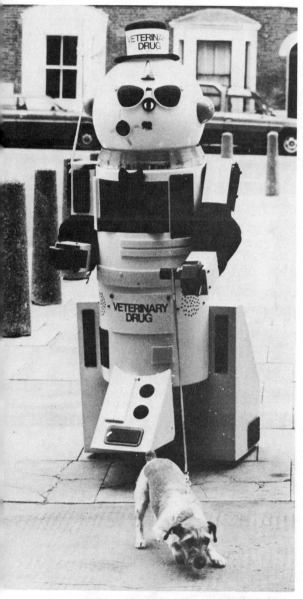

Argon took Penny for a "glide" around the streets of Hammersmith, London, to promote "Pets are Good for People," the largest veterinary congress held in the United Kingdom as of April 1983.

robots. "They have a definite image of what they want their robots to look like, and they'll finish the exterior before attempting to consider artificial intelligence, programming, or what it's going to do," says Gutmann. Still others take a functional approach and are concerned only with control and manipulation of objects. They don't care what the robot looks like.

Hobby robotics societies have come and gone. About four years ago a society, called U.S. Robotics, tried to organize hobbyists, but there were not enough people and interest died. Now interest is peaking again, and hobbyists are organizing Robotic Experimenter Amateur League (REAL) as a network to link members of this geographically dispersed group. A Japanese hobby roboticist has already expressed interest in representing his country.

In April 1984, hobbyists and personal robot manufacturers convened in Albuquerque for the First International Personal Robotics Congress. At seminars, films, and an exposition, personal robot enthusiasts shared their ideas.

Gutmann sees hobbyists as having an important role in bringing down the costs of commercially available robots. Right now he feels robots are too expensive for what they do. In order for personal robotics to take off the way personal computers did, says Gutmann, the first thing they're going to have to do is get parts (such as arms and bases for mobility) down to a lower cost.

Kent Meyers, who runs a robot hobbyist club called "Robig" in the Washington, D.C., area, agrees that hobbyists can help bring down the cost of mass-market personal robots. He also notes that robot hobbyists are not just mechanics who build robots from scratch. "The assumption that the hobbyist has got to have made a robot is quickly passing," he says. "It's like the hobbyist in microcomputers who now is not exactly the guy who put one together ... he's the guy who is running applications, but is doing it in a fun way and for his own interest. It is getting that way with these new robot products. You can buy one and run one without actually having to be a mechanic."

THE WORLD VIEW: JOBS, THE ECONOMY, AND ROBOTS

No country can be fully competitive in new manufacturing industries, including robots, if it falls behind in building the tools needed to be a low-cost manufacturer.

Lester C. Thurow, Professor of Finance and Economic Management, MIT Sloan School of Management (interview, 3/5/84)

Robots and related types of flexible manufacturing may well be the key to the future economic welfare of nations. Where once the level of industrialization dictated the relative power and prosperity of nations, now the level and quality of robotization may spell success or failure for national economies.

Programmable automation began in the United States, which has historically been the technological leader of the world. But there is now a dramatic tug of war between the United States and Japan. Although technological advances are often jealously guarded, no secret remains so forever. Thus, while the Industrial Revolution began in Great Britain and the British tried to keep their textile machinery clandestine, within a century Germany and the United States had surpassed Great Britain.

Information moves faster now, and the dissemination of technology is unavoidable. But while industrial espionage

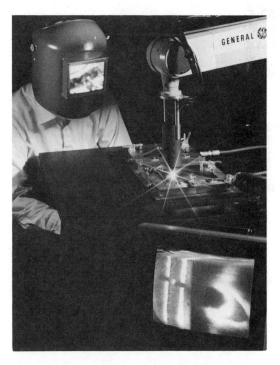

GE unveiled this vision system at Robots VII in 1983. The two vertical lines on the TV screen in the foreground are laser stripes that are beamed across the weld joint. The joint is the dark horizontal line interrupting the two beams. The bright area shaped like a reversed C is part of the welding arc, and the weld puddle trails to the right.

makes headlines, many innovations are transferred legally and reliably through joint ventures, licensing agreements, and sales links between companies based in different countries. These agreements are the key feature of the world industrial robot market today.

Just as economic policies and means of increasing productivity rates are controversial, so too are arrangements leading to technology transfer. These arrangements affect interpretations of world industrial robot sales and installation figures, which are already complicated by different industrial robot definitions. It is clear, however, that Japan is advancing more forcefully and rapidly in robotization than the United States. And some economists suggest that the U.S. is feeling the effects with relative declining productivity.

Productivity, often defined as output per hour worked, is increased through the use of tools, capital, and energy. The *rate* of productivity *growth* is both a contributor to and indicator of a nation's gross national product (GNP) growth, which is a measure of its economic strength.

After World War II and before the current inflationary period, the United States generated an unprecedented yearly average productivity growth of 3.2 percent. Between 1960 and 1977, the United States registered an increase in productivity, but at a much slower rate than its major industrial competitors. U.S. growth in productivity for that period averaged only 2.6 percent, compared with 3.4 percent for the United Kingdom, 4.0 percent for Canada, 5.5 percent for West Germany, 5.7 percent for France, and 8.8 percent for Japan.

In 1976, domestic output per hour worked rose 3.5 percent, but was followed by 1.5 percent in 1977 and 0.5 percent in 1978. During the next two years, the rate declined to negative 1.1 percent in 1979 and negative 3.1 percent in 1980. In light of this trend, several studies analyzed the factors affecting productivity. The best known are a 1979 report by the Brookings Institute's Edward F. Denison, and a 1979 report by J. R. Norsworthy, M. J. Harper and K. Kunze of the Bureau of Labor Statistics.

In his study, *Accounting for Slow Economic Growth: the U.S. in the 1970s,* Denison examined factors affecting a slightly different measure of productivity change—output per person employed. He had showed that from 1948 to 1973, 54.2 percent of productivity growth could be accounted for by "advances in knowledge." Included in this category is tech-

nological knowhow, its implementation into production processes, and knowledge of business organization and management techniques. Improved education and capital accounted for 20.0 percent and 14.6 percent, respectively. When productivity growth rates declined in the late 1970s, so too did advances in knowledge, specifically to negative 0.75 between 1973 and 1976. "This was the dominant development of the period," says Denison.

These findings called into question the prevailing view during the late 1970s that Japanese productivity growth rates were increasing faster than those of the United States because of better labor quality. "The true reason could be greater application of technological breakthroughs (many of which were discovered in the U.S.) and greater commitment of capital to the cost reduction process," suggest Mitchell I. Quain and James B. Townsend in their 1981 report "Factory automation."

The National Bureau of Labor Statistics report, *The Slowdown in Productivity Growth: An Analysis of Some Contributing Factors,* concluded that the slowdown in productivity growth during 1973–78 was due largely to the impact of reduced capital formation. (Capital formation includes plant and equipment spending.) The authors suggested that the sharp rise in energy prices might explain the weakness in capital formation. But Quain suggests that

In 1978, the British government invited English machine-tool builders to participate in its Automated Small-Batch Production program. The 600 Group, a conglomerate, responded with SCAMP (six hundred group computer-aided manufacturing project) Systems Ltd. The new company shares the site of the 600 Group's Colchester Lathe Company, and, not surprisingly, the first SCAMP line unveiled in January 1983 produced lathe parts. Here, a 4 x 4 array of lathe parts on pallets will be unloaded by one of eight Fanuc robots (not shown). Note the loading/unloading pattern on the screen.

the sharp rise in energy prices resulted in an emphasis on greater energy efficiency rather than spurring production efficiency through plant and equipment spending. Ironically, energy cost increases were "one explanation for the relative weakness in productivity growth," he says.

The study showed that while the United States exceeded Japan and Germany in dollars spent on plant and equipment, "real plant equipment spending per manufacturing employee has narrowed significantly relative to those two nations." Twenty years ago, the United States outspent both Japan and West Germany almost four to one in real terms, but "today the gap is closing at an astounding rate," Quain says.[12] A look at machine-tool consumption and plant and equipment spending as shares of gross national product demonstrates this trend. (See Chart 6.1.)

So America's factories have been allowed to age, resulting in a decline in the U.S. manufacturing base. Eli S. Lustgarten of Paine Webber Mitchell Hutchins says, "Two thirds of all U.S. machine tools are over ten years old and one third are more than twenty years old," and "sophisticated numerically controlled (NC) equipment has made only slight inroads into the manufacturing process." In contrast, only 21 percent of Japan's machine tools are over ten years old and 18 percent are over 20 years old. (See Chart 6.2.)

Chart 6.1.

MACHINE-TOOL CONSUMPTION SHARE OF GNP

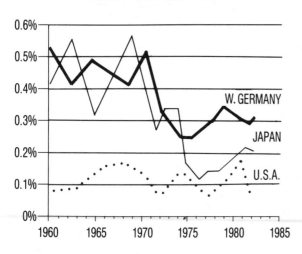

PLANT & EQUIPMENT SPENDING SHARE OF GNP

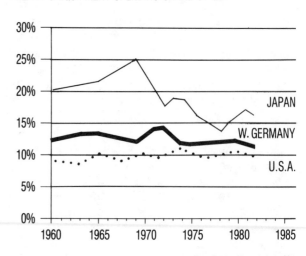

Source: Machine Tool Builders Association 1984.

In describing this state of affairs, Reginald H. Jones, former chairman of General Electric, went so far as to tell the financial community: "The average American factory is an augean stable of antiquated machinery, talent-wasting processes, and tired technology. There is no substitute for research and development and reinvestment, but as a nation we have been trying to do without it, and are now paying the price, like the farmer who had almost taught his horse to live on sawdust when the animal died."[13]

As Quain wryly points out, "These are not the words of a machine-tool company executive or a capital-starved manufacturer who is falling badly behind his competition."

Chart 6.1.—Continued

	GROSS FIXED CAPITAL FORMATION (CF) AND MACHINE TOOL CONSUMPTION (MT) AS A PERCENT OF GNP							PLANT & EQUIPMENT EXPENDITURE AS A PERCENT OF GNP		
YEAR	WG CF/ GNP	US CF/ GNP	JAP CF/ GNP	US MT/ GNP	JAP MT/ GNP	WG MT/ GNP	YEAR	US PE/ GNP	JAP PE/ GNP	WG PE/ GNP
1961	25.2	17.2	33.3	0.10	NA	NA	1961	NA	NA	NA
1962	25.8	17.3	33.7	0.11	NA	NA	1962	NA	NA	NA
1963	25.6	17.7	32.2	0.14	0.26	0.41	1963	9.0	NA	13.9
1964	26.6	17.9	32.5	0.15	NA	NA	1964	NA	NA	NA
1965	26.2	18.6	30.0	0.19	0.32	0.49	1965	10.2	15.3	NA
1966	25.5	18.4	30.5	0.21	NA	NA	1966	NA	NA	NA
1967	23.1	17.7	32.1	0.23	NA	NA	1967	NA	NA	NA
1968	22.4	18.0	33.3	0.19	0.49	0.27	1968	10.1	25.2	NA
1969	23.2	18.1	34.6	0.17	0.53	0.41	1969	10.5	NA	12.8
1970	25.5	17.4	35.6	0.14	0.58	0.48	1970	10.6	21.1	14.5
1971	26.1	17.9	34.3	0.08	0.43	0.55	1971	10.1	19.1	14.8
1972	25.3	18.5	34.1	0.10	0.28	0.39	1972	10.1	17.6	13.8
1973	23.9	18.8	36.4	0.12	0.33	0.31	1973	10.4	18.9	12.8
1974	21.6	18.1	34.9	0.14	0.33	0.27	1974	10.9	18.6	11.3
1975	20.4	16.9	32.5	0.14	0.17	0.24	1975	10.2	16.3	11.2
1976	20.1	17.0	31.3	0.12	0.14	0.24	1976	10.0	15.1	11.3
1977	20.3	18.2	30.5	0.13	0.16	0.26	1977	10.3	14.2	11.6
1978	20.7	19.3	30.8	0.15	0.15	0.30	1978	10.7	14.0	13.1
1979	21.8	19.5	32.1	0.19	0.18	0.34	1979	11.2	15.1	12.0
1980	22.8	18.2	32.0	0.20	0.25	0.31	1980	11.2	15.8	12.3
1981	22.0	17.7	31.1	0.19	0.29	0.29	1981	10.9	15.5	12.0
1982	20.5	16.3	29.6	0.14	0.26	0.31	1982	10.3	14.8	11.3
1983		16.2		0.08						

NA = Not available

WORLD IR INVENTORY

iven this backdrop, how did the world industrial robot market fare during the early 1980s? There are several ways to examine the market. One can look at the number of units manufactured each year and the sales in dollars of those units, for example. One can also examine the number and dollar values of units actually shipped, which is different from sales because there may be a lag between a product's sale and its delivery. Comparing these annual figures allows one to determine the growth or decline of the market. Adding the yearly inventory of units gives the total number of units ever installed. This cumulative figure is known as the installed base.

The Robotic Industries Association (RIA) estimates that 23,800 industrial robots were manufactured worldwide

Chart 6.2.

Machine Tools in Use Are Approaching Obsolescence*

	% OF TOTAL MACHINES IN USE	YEARS IN USE UNDER 10 YEARS	YEARS IN USE 10–20 YEARS	YEARS IN USE OVER 20 YEARS	NUMERICALLY CONTROLLED
UNITED STATES		31.0%	35.0%	34.0%	2.0%
Transportation equipment	13.7%	23.8	33.0	43.2	2.1
Motor vehicles	6.7	23.8	31.4	44.8	0.6
Aircraft and parts	5.3				
Non-electrical machinery	36.5	32.8	35.1	32.1	3.1
Electrical machinery	12.9	33.0	41.7	25.3	1.4
Fabricated metal	24.0	27.4	35.2	37.4	0.9
Precision Instrument	5.0	38.0	36.8	25.1	1.9
WEST GERMANY		37.0	37.0	26.0	NA
UNITED KINGDOM		39.0	37.0	24.0	NA
JAPAN		61.0	21.0	18.0	NA
FRANCE		37.0	33.0	30.0	NA
ITALY		42.0	30.0	28.0	NA
CANADA		47.0	35.0	18.0	NA

*Data based on 1976-78, except for Japan, France, and Italy where the data is based on a 1973-75 survey.

Source: American Machinist: 12th American Machinery Inventory of Metal Working Equipment 1976-78; Verein Deutscher Werkzeugmaschinenfabrik e. V.; NMTBA Statistical Handtools. As reprinted in Eli S. Lustgarten's "Robotics and Factory Automation," December 15, 1981.

in 1983. Of these, 16,200 (68.1 percent) were Japanese and 2,400 (10.1 percent) were American. (See Chart 6.3.) The total 1983 monetary value, in 1982 U.S. dollars, was estimated at $997.7 million, but excludes Italy because a dollar figure was not available. Japan's dollar figure was $550.0 million and the United States' was $230.0 million.

RIA's figures have been challenged because it collects statistics from foreign countries' industrial robot trade associations whose industrial robot definitions are broader than RIA's. But RIA maintains that the 1982 reported figures now include only industrial robots as it defines them—except for France, which includes variable sequenced manipulators in its statistics.

The industrial robot installed base by the end of 1982 totaled 48,427 units, according to RIA, with 31,900 (65 percent) in Japan; 6,300 (13 percent) in the United States; 4,300 (9 percent) in West Germany, and 1,450 (3 percent) in Sweden. (See Charts 6.4 and 6.6.) Walter Weisel, RIA president and president of Prab Robots, calls Japan's figures "staggering." Figures collected by the Japan Industrial Robot Association (JIRA), the U.S. International Trade Commission, and Paul H. Aron, executive director of Daiwa Securities in New York and an expert on Japan's robot industry, show slightly different numbers, but reflect essentially the same distribution. (See Chart 6.5.)

But several authorities question these figures. Joseph Engelberger estimates instead that Japan has 16,000 to 17,000; the United States 6,000, and western Europe approximately 9,000. He says that trade associations pump up their figures to get people excited about the industry. His figures are more in line with those released by Tech Tran Corporation, which showed a total of 35,000 and attributed 18,000 (51 percent) robots to Japan, and Asia, 6,200 (18 percent) to the United States, and 7,200 to western Europe (20 percent). Unlike the other two reports, Tech Tran's includes the USSR and eastern Europe, but the USSR 3,000-unit estimate dates back to 1981, and other sources suggest that the figure could be 7,000. (See Charts 6.7 and 6.8.)

Thomas E. Brock, director of the British Robot Association, also says that the Japanese and French counts distort the overall picture to such an extent that the statistics are meaningless. He goes so far as to say that JIRA's broad definition, which results in a count of 100,000 to 150,000, is irresponsible and has caused the first rumblings of Japanese workers' resistance to robots.

Chart 6.3.
1983 Estimated Industrial Robots Manufactured, by Nation

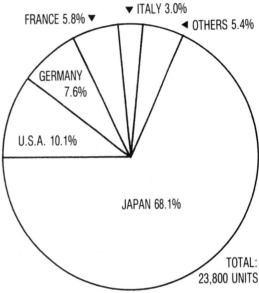

FRANCE 5.8% ▼ ▼ ITALY 3.0% ◄ OTHERS 5.4%

GERMANY 7.6%

U.S.A. 10.1%

JAPAN 68.1%

TOTAL: 23,800 UNITS

Estimated Industrial Robot Units to Be Manufactured in 1983, 1984, 1985, and 1990, by Nation

	1983	1984	1985	1990
AUSTRIA	80	130	150	NA
CANADA	130	180	280	630
CZECHOSLOVAKIA	220	54	800	1,800
FRANCE	1,380	1,580	1,820	4,540
GERMANY	1,800	2,000	2,300	3,500
ITALY	700	900	1,200	5,000
JAPAN	16,200	17,500	18,800	34,600
NETHERLANDS	100	150	250	NA
SWEDEN	470	600	750	2,400
UNITED KINGDOM	320	500	550	1,500
UNITED STATES	2,400	3,400	4,500	24,000
TOTALS	23,800	26,994	31,400	77,970

NA = Not available

Source: "Worldwide Robotics Survey and Directory" (RIA, Nov. 83).

Chart 6.4.

World Industrial Robot Installed Base, End of 1982

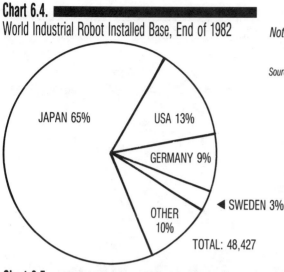

JAPAN 65%

USA 13%

GERMANY 9%

◀ SWEDEN 3%

OTHER 10%

TOTAL: 48,427

Note: Percents have been taken from 48,427, not 57,427, the total in "World Industrial Robot Installed Base, by Application, End of 1982."

Source: Worldwide Robotics Survey and Directory, original chart titled "World Robot Population Chart," (November 1983).

Chart 6.5.

World Robot Installed Base, 1978–1982*

	IN UNITS				
COUNTRY	1978	1979	1980	1981	1982
JAPAN	10,095	11,533	14,246	21,684	31,900
UNITED STATES	2.831	3,340	3,849	4,700	7,232
WEST GERMANY	450	†	823	2,301	3,500
SWEDEN	800	†	1,133	1,700	†
FRANCE	†	†	200	620	993
UNITED KINGDOM	125	†	371	713	977
BELGIUM	†	†	†	44	305
CANADA	†	†	†	214	273
ITALY	†	†	400	450	600
FINLAND	†	†	40	†	75
AUSTRIA	†	†	†	†	70
NORWAY	†	†	†	†	20
SWITZERLAND	†	†	†	†	200
TAIWAN	†	†	†	†	11
ALL OTHER	†	†	†	†	‡2,000
TOTAL †	16,000	19,000	24,000	35,000	50,000

*Excluding Communist countries.

†Information or estimates are not available.

‡Estimated by the staff of the U.S. International Trade Commission.

Source: Japan Industrial Robot Association, responses from questionnaires of the U.S. International Trade Commission, and Paul H. Aron, *The Robot Scene in Japan: An Update* (September 7, 1983). As reprinted in "Competitive Position of U.S. Producers of Robotics in Domestic and World Markets," original chart titled "World Robot Population 1978–82," (International Trade Commission, December 1983).

Chart 6.6.

World Industrial Robot Installed Base, by Application, End of 1982

	WELDING	PAINTING & FINISHING	ASSEMBLY	CASTING	MATERIAL HANDLING	MACHINE LOADING UNLOADING	OTHER	TOTAL
AUSTRIA	20			5	5	20		50
BELGIUM	219	22	4	2	10	34	14	305
CANADA	88	40	43	39	43	17	3	273
CZECHOSLOVAKIA	12	6	12	10	30	60	24	154
DENMARK	12	13	8	20	0	8	2	63
FINLAND	30	29	0	11	9	14	5	98
FRANCE	*605	106	*3,000	300	*4,000	*500	*1,482	**9,993
GERMANY	1,916	417	122	120	587	193	945	4,300
ITALY	492	97	111	0	100	102	198	1,100
JAPAN	8,052	1,071	6,099	557	6,797	2,578	6,746	31,900
KOREA	0	0	0	0	2	8	0	10
NETHERLANDS	23	23	5	0	1	8	11	71
POLAND	40	133	20	10	0	20	62	285
SINGAPORE	4	6	0	0	5	10	0	25
SWEDEN	260	245	15	190	130	580	30	1,450
SWITZERLAND	25	0	26	0	0	20	2	73
UNITED KINGDOM	400	155	18	54	85	94	171	977
UNITED STATES	2,453	490	72	875	1,300	1,060	50	6,300
TOTAL	*14,651	2,853	*9,555	2,193	*13,104	*5,326	*9,745	**57,427

*Includes variable sequenced manipulators
**Includes 9,000 variable sequenced manipulators

Source: Worldwide Robotics Survey and Directory, original chart titled "Estimate of Robot Population within Each of the Following Applications by the End of 1982" (RIA, November 1983).

Chart 6.7. ▬▬▬▬▬
World Robot Installed Base, End of 1982

	NUMBER	PERCENT
JAPAN, ASIA	18,000	51
U.S.A.	6,200	18
WESTERN EUROPE		
West Germany	2,800	8
Sweden	1,600	5
United Kingdom	800	2
France	700	2
Italy	500	1
Norway	400	1
Other	400	1
Total	7,200	20
U.S.S.R	3,000	9
EASTERN EUROPE	600	2
TOTAL WORLD POPULATION	35,000	100

Source: Industrial Robots: A Summary and Forecast, 2nd ed. (Tech Tran Corp., March 1983).

Chart 6.8. ▬▬▬▬▬
World Industrial Robot Installed Base, End of 1981

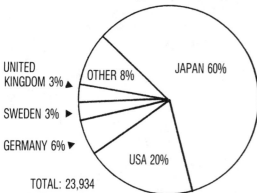

UNITED KINGDOM 3% ▲
OTHER 8%
JAPAN 60%
SWEDEN 3% ▶
GERMANY 6% ▶
USA 20%

TOTAL: 23,934

Note: Percents have been taken from 23,934, a total that excludes the Soviet Union's 3,000 robots so that 1981 and 1982 data can be compared. RIA included 1980 figures for Italy in its original chart. That information is included in the "Other" section above.

Source: Worldwide Robotics Survey and Directory, from chart compiled in response to the request, "Estimate the robot population in your country" (RIA, mid-1982).

The total world installed base seems to have tripled in the years 1978 to 1982: Japan's installed base has tripled, the United States' has increased by a factor of about 2.5, and West Germany's has increased by a factor of about 4.4. Between 1981 and 1982, Japan's share of the world installed base increased from 60 percent to 65 percent and the United States' share decreased from 20 percent to 13 percent. Japan's installed base at the end of 1982 was at least two-and-a-half or as much as five times that of the United States, depending on whose figures you accept.

What are the world's robots being used for? Almost 25 percent of industrial robots are used for welding. Material-handling robots make up almost another quarter, but this figure is distorted by France's variable sequenced manipulators. The next largest application is assembly, followed by machine loading and unloading, painting and finishing, and casting. (See Chart 6.6.)

Both Japan and the United States use their robots mainly for welding and material handling, but the distributions of these and other operations differ. The United States uses more of its robots for welding than does Japan—almost 40 percent of America's robots weld whereas only about one quarter weld in Japan. Material-handling robots are about one fifth for both countries. But Japan's third largest application, assembly, also takes up about one fifth of its pie, dwarfing the U.S. assembly slice. America's third largest application is machine loading and unloading—Japan's fifth largest. Another difference is Japan's "Other" category, which represents a fifth of Japan's robots. The same category for the U.S. accounts for a tiny fraction of its robots. (See Chart 6.9.)

THE UNITED STATES IR MARKET

In 1980, sales of U.S.-based robot companies were about $90 million, less than four one thousandths of one percent of the $2.6 trillion GNP, according to Laura Conigliaro, a vice president at Prudential-Bache Securities. In 1982, U.S.-based sales totaled approximately $190 million, still a fraction of a percent of that year's $3.1 trillion GNP.

The number shipped to American users was smaller,

Chart 6.9. ▬▬▬▬▬▬▬▬▬▬▬▬▬▬▬▬▬▬▬▬▬▬▬▬▬▬▬
World's Two Largest Industrial Robot Users, by Application, 1982

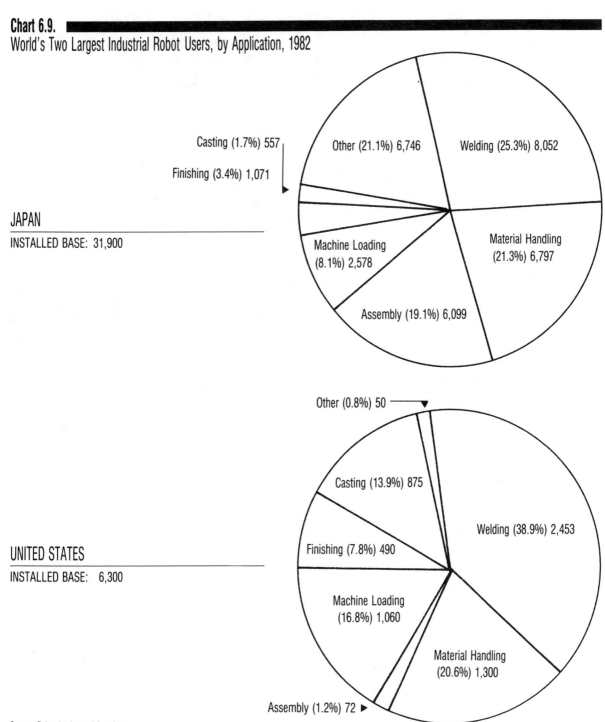

Casting (1.7%) 557

Finishing (3.4%) 1,071

Other (21.1%) 6,746

Welding (25.3%) 8,052

Machine Loading
(8.1%) 2,578

Material Handling
(21.3%) 6,797

Assembly (19.1%) 6,099

JAPAN

INSTALLED BASE: 31,900

Other (0.8%) 50

Casting (13.9%) 875

Welding (38.9%) 2,453

Finishing (7.8%) 490

Machine Loading
(16.8%) 1,060

Material Handling
(20.6%) 1,300

Assembly (1.2%) 72 ▶

UNITED STATES

INSTALLED BASE: 6,300

Source: Robot Institute of America

At Japan's annual New Year calligraphy competition in Tokyo, a robot showed off its calligraphic skills before thousands of young human entrants. Here the robot draws the Chinese character for "path" or "road," which is often associated with spiritual and moral enlightenment.

Opposite page: Cincinnati Milacron's T³-726 robot used vision and voice synthesis to act as dealer in games of Twenty-one at the 1983 Robots VII show in Chicago. Two visitors at a time could try their luck against the robot, which used its multiplication and division capabilities to keep track of its winning percentage.

however, because U.S.-based sales include robots shipped abroad. According to a U.S. International Trade Commission's 1983 report,[14] American manufacturers shipped $123 million worth of robots in 1982 and 86 percent, or $106 million, went to domestic customers.

The United States robot industry is still in its infancy. The general failure to upgrade and retool factories is one reason why the technology has not been implemented here. There are also other reasons, unique to industrial robots, that are responsible for industry's hesitation to roboticize in the United States.

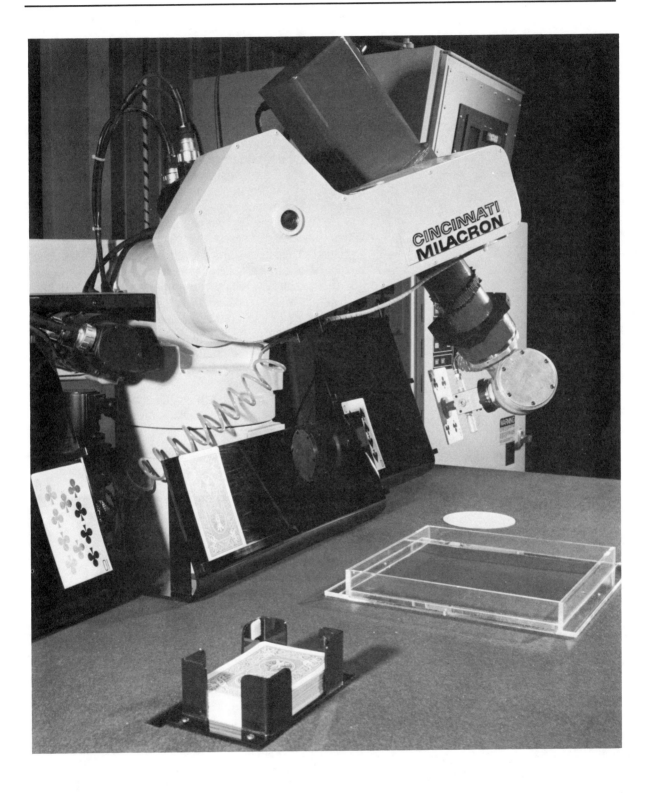

While the rise in sales from $90 million to $190 million in two years was quite a jump, Wall Street's robot industry analysts expected far better results. There was tremendous enthusiasm as a result of Robots VI, a Robot Institute of America/Society of Manufacturing Engineers (RIA/SME) trade show that took place in spring 1982. "It was thought that the industry would go on to fabulous heights in 1982 and thereafter, and just ignore what was happening throughout the economy," says Conigliaro. Instead, estimates for 1983 lingered at a mere $163 million in sales and domestic shipments of $135 million.

Still, an industry that had been partly overlooked suddenly underwent microscopic inspection. Robots painting pictures, handing visitors souvenirs, and taking bows contributed to "an atmosphere of tremendous euphoria," Conigliaro says. But few robots were shown performing manufacturing applications—potential customers had to walk around and look at serious equipment and make connections between the colorful tasks and manufacturing applications. "The users had to be able to say, 'Oh, if the robot can lift a bowling ball, that means that it can also lift this casting,'" Conigliaro explains.

There were many new companies exhibiting at the show and hoping to carve a niche in the market. In 1980, Unimation, Cincinnati Milacron, Prab Robots, DeVilbiss,

Chart 6.10.
Estimated Market Shares of Original Robot Companies (1980–1983)

	UNIMATION $	%	CINCINNATI MILACRON $	%	PRAB ROBOTS, INC. $	%	DEVILBISS $	%
1980	39,960,000	44.4	28,980,000	32.2	5,490,000	6.1	4,950,000	5.5
1981	68,200,000	44.0	50,065,000	32.3	8,215,000	5.3	6,510,000	4.2
1982	62,510,000	32.9	31,730,000	16.7	12,350,000	6.5	23,560,000	12.4
1983E	43,500,000	17.4	34,000,000	13.6	16,250,000	6.5	21,750,000	8.7

	ASEA, INC. $	%	COPPERWELD ROBOTICS $	%	TOTAL, "BIG 6" $	%	OTHER COMPANIES $	%	TOTAL MARKET $
1980	2,520,000	2.8	2,970,000	3.3	84,870,000	94.3	5,130,000	5.7	90,000,000
1981	8,990,000	5.8	3,565,000	2.3	145,545,000	93.9	945,500	6.1	155,000,000
1982	9,500,000	5.0	1,900,000	1.0	141,550,000	74.5	4,845,000	25.5	190,000,000
1983E	13,750,000	5.5	3,500,000	1.4	132,500,000	53.0	117,500,000	47.0	250,000,000

NOTE: Each company's dollar figures were determined by taking its percent of the total market figure.

Source: Prudential-Bache Securities, Inc.

Chart 6.11.

Changes in Market Share Composition (1980–1983)

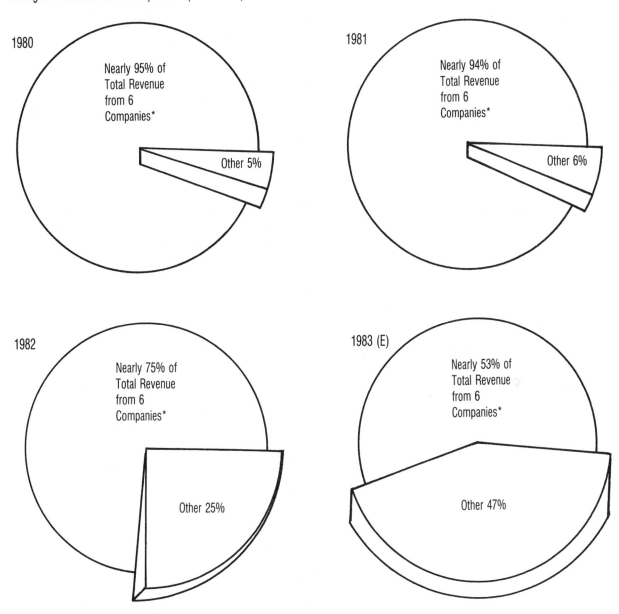

1980

Nearly 95% of
Total Revenue
from 6
Companies*

Other 5%

1981

Nearly 94% of
Total Revenue
from 6
Companies*

Other 6%

1982

Nearly 75% of
Total Revenue
from 6
Companies*

Other 25%

1983 (E)

Nearly 53% of
Total Revenue
from 6
Companies*

Other 47%

*Unimation, Cincinnati Milacron, Devilbiss, ASEA Inc., Prab Robots, Inc., Copperweld Robotics.

Source: Prudential-Bache Securities, Inc.

ASEA, and Copperweld had 94.3 percent of the U.S. market share. But by 1982, their share declined to 74.5 percent with the remaining 25.5 percent going to new entrants. (See Charts 6.10, 6.11, 6.12.) And while there were 106 exhibitors from all over the world at the 1982 show, as many as 205 offered their wares the following year at Robots VII.

Many new entrants were small start-up ventures, either offering robots, vision systems for robots, or support for the industry such as software, distribution, customization, servicing, and consulting. Some were under the leadership of Unimation alumni—former Unimation executive vice president Paul Allegretto joined Advanced Robotics, and Victor Scheinman teamed up with Automatix, for example.

While both shows reflected the trend of more new entrants, there was a major difference between Robots VI and VII. Because of the recession during the intervening years, potential robot customers had less money to spend. The few users who had recognized the need to upgrade the technology in their factories with robots became even fewer. And those who still could afford to buy robots had to be very selective, and far more demanding, of equipment they could buy.

In response to this situation, manufacturers put together an applications-oriented show. They exhibited industrial robots as they would be used on the production floor, integrated with other equipment in order to get jobs done. IR cells and systems, rather than stand-alone IRs, stole the show. IBM, for example, showed IRs integrated with Computer-Aided-Design (CAD) links. An IBM robot inserted components onto circuit boards and shared data with a computer used to create circuit-board blueprints. When the operator changed a part's location on the blueprint displayed on the computer screen, the robot automatically "knew" to insert the actual part on the real circuit board.

There were few technological innovations at the show, but one surprise was a new spray-finishing IR developed in Mölndal, Sweden, by Spine Robotics. The robot arm is modeled after the human spine and is so flexible that it can reach practically anywhere. The company would not reveal how many joints the arm has and cloaked it with a black accordionlike cover. "We almost didn't come to the show, but at the last minute we decided to look for a joint venture," quipped one Spine official.

Joint ventures between large corporations and corporate takeovers of small robot firms did, in fact, characterize

Chart 6.12.

Market Share: U.S.-Based Robot Vendors* (1980–1983)

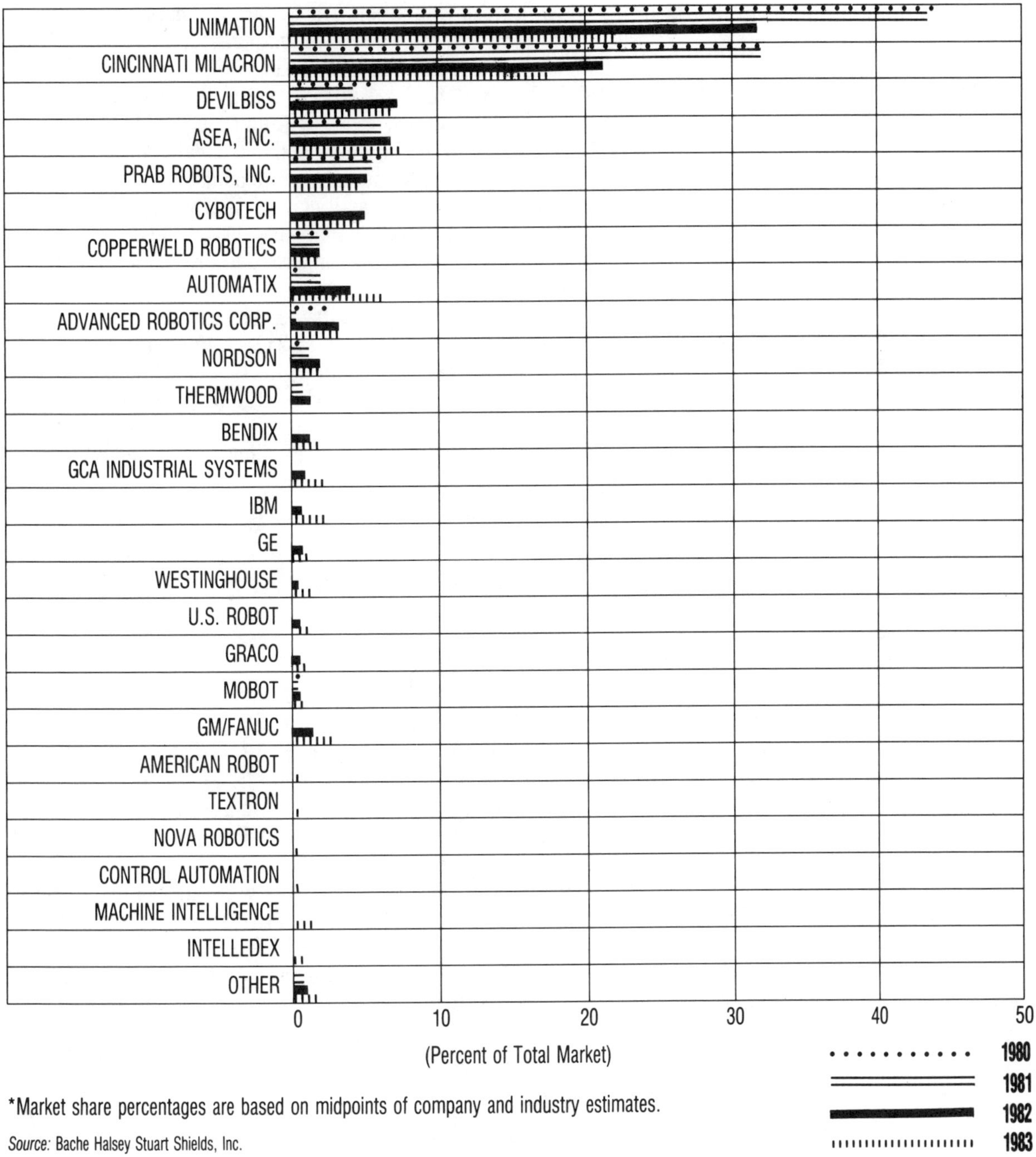

UNIMATION	
CINCINNATI MILACRON	
DEVILBISS	
ASEA, INC.	
PRAB ROBOTS, INC.	
CYBOTECH	
COPPERWELD ROBOTICS	
AUTOMATIX	
ADVANCED ROBOTICS CORP.	
NORDSON	
THERMWOOD	
BENDIX	
GCA INDUSTRIAL SYSTEMS	
IBM	
GE	
WESTINGHOUSE	
U.S. ROBOT	
GRACO	
MOBOT	
GM/FANUC	
AMERICAN ROBOT	
TEXTRON	
NOVA ROBOTICS	
CONTROL AUTOMATION	
MACHINE INTELLIGENCE	
INTELLEDEX	
OTHER	

(Percent of Total Market)

0   10   20   30   40   50

· · · · · · · · · · · 1980
═══════════════ 1981
▬▬▬▬▬▬ 1982
| | | | | | | | | | | | | | | | | | 1983

*Market share percentages are based on midpoints of company and industry estimates.

Source: Bache Halsey Stuart Shields, Inc.

Chart 6.13. ▬▬▬▬▬▬▬
International Agreements

Licensing Agreements

	Licensor	Licensee
U.S.–Japan	Unimation (Westinghouse)	Kawasaki[1]
	Prab	Murata Machinery
Japan–U.S.	Dainichi Kiko	GCA
	Hitachi	Automatix
	Hitachi	GE
	Hirata	Automatix
	Komatsu	Westinghouse
	Mitsubishi	Westinghouse
	Nachi Fujikoshi	Advanced Robotics
	Sankyo Seiki	IBM
	Yaskawa	Hobart Brothers
	Yaskawa	Machine Intelligence[2] (Vision)
	Yaskawa	Bendix (part of Allied)
U.S.–Norway	Trallfa	Devilbiss
U.S.–Finland	Unimation	Nokia
U.S.–Great Britain	American Robots	Rediffusion Simulation (Vision)
France–U.S.	Sciaky	Allegheny International
Italy–U.S.	Basfer	Nordson[3]
	DEA	GE
	Olivetti	Westinghouse
West Germany–U.S.	Niko	United Technologies
	Volkswagen	GE
	Jungheinrich	Automatix

Joint Ventures

Japan–U.S.	Fanuc[4]	GM
	Ransburg	Tokico[5]
France–U.S.	Renault	Ransburg
Italy–U.S.	Fiat-Comau	Bendix[6]

(Continued on facing page)

the year between the shows. General Motors, the world's largest industrial robot user, announced GMF Robotics, a joint venture with Japan's Fanuc. Besides Westinghouse's purchase of Unimation, The Square D Company, an electrical and electronic equipment manufacturer in Palatine, Illinois, acquired U.S. Robots in King of Prussia, Pennsylvania. Such corporate Pac-Man behavior is not new—in 1979, Copperweld Robotics snapped up Auto-Place and Schlumberger acquired Fairchild Camera and Instrument Corporation, the world's first commercial semiconductor manufacturer, which now conducts artificial intelligence research. Other takeovers continue—in January 1984, Allied Corporation sold its Bendix Automation Group to Cross and Trecker for $65 million.

Nevertheless, industry experts expect a shakeout. In 1983, Kulicke and Soffa Industries of Horsham, Pennsylvania, abandoned its robotics effort after investing several million dollars. And in early 1984, Nordson Corporation of Amherst, Ohio, announced that it was leaving the robotics arena, and Copperweld sold its robotics division to Rimrock Corporation of Columbus, Ohio.

LICENSING, JOINT VENTURES, AND SALES LINKS

Although RIA/SME robot shows are traditionally international events, Robots VII seemed to be an American IR manufacturers event. Some American IR manufacturers even placed American flags in their robots' "hands." A closer look, however, revealed many foreign-built but American-packaged IRs. The familiar logos of Fortune 500 firms like IBM, GE, and Bendix were affixed to Japanese, West German, and Italian-built IRs, so packaged as a result of licensing agreements. (See Charts 6.13 and 6.14.)

These and other arrangements are not surprising, because the IR market promises large future profits and because the cost of developing a prototype robot alone is upward of $1 million, and the full cost of market entry is $15 million to $20 million.[15]

Through licensing agreements between Japanese and Western companies, the best of two different worlds can be captured, says Laura Conigliaro. "Licensing captures the strategic approach and culture of Japan—the ability to turn out a high-quality, low-cost product in volume—and the best of the strategy and culture of the United States—the ability to take those products and add value to them and use computer and software knowledge to increase the potential of the product." To some extent, the overall products are considered improvements. The consensus regarding Japanese IRs, for example, is that their arms are mechanically superior, but that they are enhanced by superior American controls, software, and servicing.

However, licensing agreements have both advantages and disadvantages for manufacturers, as Joseph Engelberger points out. In response to the question "Are the Japanese much better at manufacturing than we are?" he says: "...We have a robot design licensed to Kawasaki in Japan. They get an order from Toyota for 720—the biggest order we've ever had is for 120. The customer commits himself to three years production into the future. Do they know what they're going to do with those robots in the future? No, they don't know. They just say, "Dammit, we're going to use them. And you know what we're going to do? We're going to tell you six months before we want them which model we want and what articulations they should have." That's all the lead our licensee needs. Then the customer gets the damn robots for 60 percent of what American customers could buy them for. These guys come to me and cry, "Goddamn, look how cheap the Japanese robots are." I say, "Hey, you want to give me an order for 720, 25 a month for the next three years, and tell me even only six months ahead what the model is—and you've got it. You've got it 10-15 percent cheaper than Japanese prices."[16]

While the Japanese will not hesitate to buy many robots even if they are uncertain where they will use them, Americans will not risk a large order. As a result, an American manufacturer looking for other markets may become a licensor. The licensor then receives royalties on every robot produced according to its design, but sometimes the licensee can outdo the licensor. Licensors and licensees vie for users' favor as they wait for a young technology to prove itself.

When Kawasaki Heavy Industries took out a license from Unimation to produce Unimates, that meant that for a fee Kawasaki (the licensee) could produce robots according to Unimation's (the patent holder, and licensor) design. Unimation, in turn, gained rights to all of Kawasaki's own

Chart 6.13.—Continued

Subsidiaries

U.S.–Great Britain	Unimation	Unimation
Sweden–U.S.	ASEA	ASEA

Manufacturing and/or Marketing

	From	To
U.S.–Belgium	Prab	Fabrique Nationale
U.S.–Canada	Prab	Canadian English
Japan–U.S.	Dainichi Kiko	GCA
	Dainichi Kiko	Cincinnati Milacron
	Hitachi	Automatix
Japan–Germany	Fanuc	Siemens

Private Label Agreements

U.S.–U.S.	Thermwood	Binks
	Thermwood	Cyclomatic

Original Equipment Manufacturers (OEMs)

U.S.–U.S.	American Robots	Cyclomatic
	Thermwood	Didde Graphics

[1]This agreement is being renegotiated.
[2]Yaskawa will provide Machine Intelligence with robots; Machine Intelligence will provide Yaskawa with vision sensory devices.
[3]Nordson announced in January 1984 that it was leaving the robotics business.
[4]Fanuc is a subsidiary of Fujitsu, Ltd., a telecommunications company.
[5]Hitachi owns 40 percent of Tokico. Tokico owns 33.5 percent of Ransburg Japan.
[6]Bendix was taken over by Allied in 1983.

Note: This chart does not represent all international agreements. It is only a sample.

Sources: Prudential-Bache Securities, Inc., RIA, International Trade Commission, Daiwa Securities America, and information gathered by the authors.

IBM entered the industrial robot market with the SCARA-type robot in 1982. Built by Sankyo Seiki of Tokyo, the robot can be programmed with IBM's personal computer using a special version of IBM's robotics language, AML (a manufacturing language).

technology without charge. But a *Forbes* article in March 1983 accused Unimation of giving away its pioneering robot technology "for a song" in a "fateful deal." Unimation gained rights to all of Kawasaki's technology, benefited from immediate entry into Japan's IR market, and was protected from copycats through Kawasaki's enforcement of its patents in Japan. But Kawasaki never developed robots that were attractive to Unimation, so the two-way deal seemed to have deteriorated into a one-way technology transfer in Japan's direction, *Forbes* writer John A. Byrne wrote.

But Engelberger replies that the agreement has not really deteriorated. Although he admits that Kawasaki started with no robotics expertise and got the technology from Unimation, since the original agreement Kawasaki has built up a "very competent team." It has developed industrial robots, such as Kawasaki's spray-painting 9700 model, which Unimation does not make, but now sells in the U.S. and Europe. "There is a shining example of the Japanese developing a technology we use," he says. In addition, the two companies jointly developed vision systems for welding. Kawasaki contributed to a design team that worked in America with Unimation's people, And while Unimation developed the largest PUMA, the 760, Kawasaki built the mechanical structure and Unimation built the computer control. These are examples of "hands across the ocean," Engelberger says.

If there is one matter about which Engelberger and Devol disagree, it is holding hands with the Japanese. "I wouldn't have licensed the Japs on anything," says Devol, who did not have a say in the Kawasaki agreement. Although he notes that by being competitive the Japanese have indirectly helped push the U.S. and other countries toward automatic manufacturing systems, he points to such incidents as IBM's lawsuit alleging that Hitachi bribed IBM officials to disclose valuable computer secrets. Besides distrusting the Japanese, he asks, "Why create a competitor? I just don't think it is good business and I think sooner or later it's going to boomerang."

If the number and kind of licenses from Japanese companies to American firms is a measure of a boomerang effect, it is happening sooner than later. The Japanese generally offer nonexclusive licensing agreements so that they can tap the distribution resources of several companies. This trend is very distressing, says Engelberger. "They

Chart 6.14.
General Robotics Agreements (1982)

| T—TECHNICAL LINKS | S—SALES LINKS | JV—JOINT VENTURE |

U.S. FIRMS — JAPANESE FIRMS — OTHER COUNTRIES' FIRMS ....COUNTRY

DAIDO STEEL ——— T —— S ——— HAWKER SIDDELY ....UNITED KINGDOM

- SYKES GROUP ....UNITED KINGDOM
- SAMSUNG PRECISION ....KOREA
- CHARTERED ....SINGAPORE
- ROBOT TECHNOLOGY SYSTEM — NETHERLANDS
- ARITMOS................................SWEDEN

WAMAC MACHINERY ——— S
GCA ——— T ——— DAINICHIKIKO
CINCINNATI MILACRON ——— JV

- FENWICK ....FRANCE
- BUISCAR ....NETHERLANDS
- PERSONER...............................SWEDEN
- RUSSEL & SONS..........................UNITED KINGDOM
- VEGA ....ITALY
- SIN SIN ....TAIWAN
- WAMAC MACHINERY ....SWEDEN
- BARTEL ....WEST GERMANY

GMF ——— T / JV ——— FANUC ——— T
ADVANCED ROBOTICS ——— S ——— NACHI-FUJIKOSHI ——— S
COPPERWELD ——— S ——— T

- SIEMENS ....WEST GERMANY
- THE 600 GROUP ....UNITED KINGDOM
- MANURHIN.............................FRANCE
- KUKA ....WEST GERMANY
- VW ....WEST GERMANY

GE ——— T
AUTOMATIX ——— S
AMADA ——— S
HITACHI ——— S

- DEA ....ITALY
- LANSING ....UNITED KINGDOM
- ZEPPELIN-METALLWERKE ....WEST GERMANY
- NAUDER...............................FRANCE
- OERLICON ....SWITZERLAND
- GEC ....UNITED KINGDOM

UNIMATION ——— T S
——— T ——— HIRATA / KAWASAKI
WESTINGHOUSE ——— S
——— KOMATSU

- OLIVETTI ....ITALY

——— MITSUBISHI ELEC
KOBE STEEL ——— T S
MITSUBISHI HI ——— T

- TRALLFA ....NORWAY
- VOEST ALPINE ....AUSTRIA

PRAB ROBOTS ——— T S ——— MURATA
IBM ——— S ——— SANKYO ——— S
GENERAC ——— T ——— SHIN MEIWA ——— S

- CGMS.................................FRANCE
- BLUNDY AND PARTNER....................UNITED KINGDOM
- COMMERCI ....FRANCE

PRAT SACO ROYAL ——— T ——— OKAMURA
SHOKU ——— T S
ROBOTICS ——— T ——— TAIYO
TOKICO ——— S
MACHINE INTELLIGENCE ——— JV ——— YASKAWA ——— S

- VFW ....WEST GERMANY
- KOPPER SCHMIDT ....WEST GERMANY
- MESSER GRIESHEIM.....................WEST GERMANY
- GKN ELECTRIC ....UNITED KINGDOM

ADMIRAL ——— S
HOBART BROTHERS
FARED ROBOT SYSTEMS
NORDSON
BENDIX

- AUTOM ARCOS..........................ITALY
- BALLOWS ENGG. ....S. AFRICA
- ANI PERKINS..........................AUSTRALIA
- TORSTEKNIK ....SWEDEN
- CEM ....FRANCE

VSI AUTOMATION ——— S ——— NITTO-SEIKO
PENTEL ——— S

- BADALEX..............................UNITED KINGDOM

Note: This chart shows the directions of international agreements and the very complicated industrial robotic marketing web.

Source: Japan Industrial Robot Association (revised by Daiwa Securities America). As reprinted in *Worldwide Robotics Survey and Directory* (RIA, 1983).

have gone and made deals all over the world—not real tight licensing deals, but distribution deals, short-term licensing deals. Every one of those Japanese machines is like a Trojan horse." With several nonexclusive agreements they buy market position, he says. "Hitachi hadn't had their license for two years with General Electric before they opened up their own shop with full-page ads in *Business Week*. They came to me and said, 'Oh, you know, the company isn't aggressive enough. We have to help them.'"

Walter Weisel describes the phenomenon this way: "They attempt to go in and find large companies that will support a selling effort and then they demand that they buy a quantity of machines, which first gets a commitment for shipments as well as hopefully installation of the part. But what the Japanese lack is the input into our factories. In other words, you can land a robot for practically nothing, but without the applications engineering and without the interfacing and hand tooling and so on that goes into getting a robot installed, that robot's worthless. The Japanese are not good at walking around our factories and figuring out how to interface their machines with our controllers and so on. So the strategy is you sign up as many people as you can, get them to do all the leg work—all the front end work for applications and hand tooling—and you ship them cheap robots."[17]

The arrangement that Weisel is most alarmed about is not a licensing agreement, but a joint venture—GMF Robotics. "It's going to change the entire complexion of the industry," he says, since, as a robot customer, GM will represent 30 percent of the projected industrial robot market. GMF could take away 30 percent of the U.S. market from U.S. robot manufacturers. Orders like GM's for one thousand GMF robots in 1983 "devastate the U.S. industrial robots industry," he says.

According to Eric Mittelstadt, GMF Robotics president and chief executive officer, GM's decision to team up with Fanuc was motivated by the need to improve productivity by robotizing its plants. GM wanted 14,000 robots in its plants by the end of the 1980s. "To do that it thought it had to commercialize (its own robot products, particularly the NC painter), but GM also felt it needed a broader product line," he says. About ten American and European companies were approached, he says, but they either did not have broad enough lines, having only highly sophisticated robots, for example, were interested in the overall factory of the future,

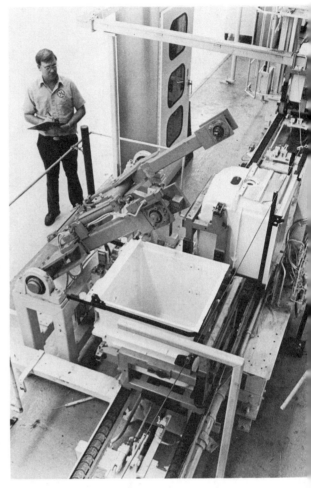

A dishwasher tub at a turnover station.

Opposite page: *In April 1983, GE unveiled a new automated dishwasher manufacturing system, an investment that cost $38 million. Called "Project C," the system occupies the same building in Appliance Park, Louisville, Kentucky, where appliances have been built for thirty years using traditional methods. To cut production costs, new dishwashers were specially designed for automated assembly. As many as 400 parts were eliminated. Here, dishwasher door liners move on a conveyor, having been assembled by robots in a thirteen-step process. Dishwasher tubs are made of plastic by injection-molding machines. When they emerge, they are delivered by conveyor to the tub structure area where robots and automated equipment perform a twenty-one-step assembly process.*

or did not want to be swallowed by GM. The giant auto maker was attracted to Fanuc's mechanical hardware and the company had robots in use throughout the world. Fanuc was looking for a way to sell its robots in the States and was attracted to GM's applications and software expertise. According to Mittelstadt, "That may be an unbeatable combination for what GM is trying to do, which is to robotize its plants with the best possible robots at the least possible cost and best possible reliability. It's hard to imagine why that's bad for America."

Weisel's contention that an order for one thousand GMF robots devastates the U.S. IR industry "is a supposition that American companies would have gotten all that business if not for GMF," says Mittelstadt. That's highly questionable since in the past those companies had problems handling orders from GM and other customers, he says. GMF expects orders for 1,300 units and sales of over $90 million in 1984.

While not saying that they want protectionism, American manufacturers do want to help potential customers learn how to use robots and to have incentives to do so. They testified to that effect at Federal Trade Commission and Department of Commerce hearings during 1983. As much as 30 percent of a robot's cost of sale in the United States goes for marketing expenses—twice the amount spent marketing for machine tools, says Weisel. "There are companies that are being totally eaten up by their marketing expenses."

No matter whose robot you buy, you will increase production 20 to 30 percent, "and there aren't too many things that companies can invest in that will give that kind of return in productive output," Weisel says. Unless Americans are educated about robotics and encouraged to use it as do the Japanese, the U.S. industry will lose more of its world market share. Right now, the Japanese dominate the Japanese market, the Europeans dominate European markets, and the Americans are "nowhere in either one of them."

Looking at the International Trade Commission statistics, it seems that of the 1,670 robots imported by the U.S. between 1979 and 1983, 1,295 units (78 percent) were Japanese. If the installed base is about 7,232 units, then one seventh to one eighth has already been supplied by the Japanese. That represents $35.1 million, or 56 percent of the $62.6 million U.S. import total.[18] And Weisel says that exports are all but closed to the U.S. industry now: "If we don't get sharp and learn how to use them and make the U.S. a

dominant factor in this technology, we'll always be bringing it in from overseas."

Commenting on American mega-corporations entering the robotics industry, Bernard Roth, a Stanford University professor of mechanical engineering, once asked Engelberger, "What do GM, IBM, GE, and Westinghouse have in common? They've all decided it's better to buy manipulator systems from Japan rather than to develop their own." Engelberger says Roth is right to "decry the fact that these centers of excellence couldn't produce their own products in the field." The Japanese are going after the U.S. market. And as Walter Weisel puts it, "We are under serious attack by the Japanese."

Every day 1,000 complete dishwashers arrive at the end of the line. At key points along the way they are computer checked, and thirty are selected at random for visual inspection and operational testing by humans.

JAPAN

he rise of robotics in Japan in the 1970s grew out of economic, social, and demographic upheavals that continue today. After the 1973–74 oil crisis, Japanese industrial production fell 14.5 percent and corporate incomes fell 30.7 percent. But because of their management codes of honor, corporations did not fire workers. As a result, labor costs as a percentage of total production soared, and to compensate, management trimmed labor forces by encouraging early retirement and cutting back on new hiring.

Even after economic recovery, "labor-stingy" policies continued. Managers looking for alternatives to human labor, as the manufacturing labor work force aged and skilled workers became scarce, found a solution in robots. Japan first encountered sophisticated IRs in 1967, when Tokyo Machinery Trading Company imported AMF's Versatran robot. A year later, it was installed in a Toyota Automobile Group plant.

As managers modified their strategies, the Japanese government arm, Japanese Ministry of Trade and Industry (MITI), also recognized the need for robots and encouraged their implementation. The Electric Machinery Law of 1971 defined an *IR* as "an all-purpose machine, equipped with a memory device, and a terminal device (for holding things) and capable of rotation and of replacing human labor by automatic performance of movements." Later, JIRA further defined industrial robots.

In 1975, MITI announced that robotics was one of several industries Japan intended to dominate by the late 1980s. In 1978, MITI promulgated the special Machine Information Industry Promotion Extraordinary Measures Act. This act officially designated the IR as an "experimental research promotion product" and as a "rationalization promotion product." This meant that the government regarded IRs as having a great future in automating and rationalizing production. A year later, IR terminology was standardized under the Japanese Industrial Standards, so that there would be uniform ways to describe and calibrate (tune up) IRs throughout the industry.

As reported by Aron, another MITI measure of encouragement was establishing a robot leasing company, Japan

Robot Lease (JAROL) in 1980. Jointly owned by 70 percent of JIRA's thirty-seven members and 30 percent owned by ten non-life insurance companies, JAROL's aim is to support small- and medium-scale manufacturers who want to install robots to increase their productivity. Sixty percent of JAROL's operating funds are financed by the low-cost loans from the government's Japan Development Bank, and the remaining 40 percent comes from the Long-Term Credit Bank, Industrial Bank of Japan, and city banks. So JAROL can lease IRs under more advantageous conditions than ordinary leasing companies.

To allow for capital formation, direct low-interest government loans through the Small Business Finance Corporation, a government finance agency, are also available for robot manufacturers. Tax incentives, such as extra depreciations, can be taken in addition to regular depreciations, upon capital improvement. Extra depreciation in Japan for robot installers has allowed them to depreciate 13 percent, and currently allows 10 percent, from the initial purchase price. This is in addition to regular depreciation, which has been as high as 50 percent. Extra depreciation must be paid back in six years in five equal installments. This encourages installers because it helps their cash flow from pretax income and because by the last three years or so, the robot has already made profits for the installer.

Unlike American firms, most Japanese companies initially developed robots for their own needs. Firms like Yamaha Motor in Iwata, Nippon Denso in Kariya, and Honda in Shibuyaku did not offer their robots publicly. Hitachi in Chiyoda-ku, Tokyo; Matsushita Electric Industrial in Kadoma, Osaka; Nippon Electric in Minato-ku, Tokyo, and Toshiba Seiki in Ebina, Kanagawa, developed robots specifically for welding and assembly within their own companies. They were not originally machine-tool firms that wanted to expand their product lines, as were some early U.S. robot manufacturers.

Japanese companies are developing IRs to protect and extend their product lines—Fanuc in Hino, Tokyo, Japan's major manufacturer of numerical control equipment, has developed robots to work in conjunction with its machine tools. To protect themselves from Fanuc, machine-tool makers like Ikegai Tekkou in Minato-ku, Tokyo, and Ohkuma Tekkousho in Nagoya, Aichi, and Aida Engineering in Sagamihara, Kanagawa, and Komatsu in Minato-ku, Tokyo, have begun developing loading and unloading IRs.

One of two Hitachi process robots that toil together in a workcell welds a steel tubular motor frame. The robot's teammate, not shown, has picked up cooling fans, support braces, and the conduit box mounting support, and positioned them on the frame one at a time. After these have been spot- and seam-welded to the frame, a conveyor removes the completed motor frame and brings the next tube.

Unlike the situation in the United States, where five firms have more than half the market share, Japan's robot market is splintered among two hundred and fifty firms and the leader changes every year, says Aron. Kawasaki Heavy Industries in Minato-ku, Tokyo, a diversified manufacturer with shipping, aircraft, construction, engineering, motorcycle, and machinery divisions, was Japan's largest robot manufacturer until 1981. But it had only 7 percent of Japan's market share then, having sold 650 units. Yaskawa Electric Manufacturing in Chiyoda-ku, Tokyo, an electrical equipment manufacturer, outdid Kawasaki in 1981 with 835 robots sold, thereby capturing 10.8 percent of the market.

Another difference in industry behavior, according to Aron, is that Japanese managers do not have the opportunity of corporate takeovers. There are no "unfriendly takeovers" in Japan, unlike in the United States. In Japan, mergers and takeovers are possible only with the approval of the board of directors of the company to be taken over. Since the board in Japan consists almost entirely of active senior management, only the threat of imminent bankruptcy will compel the board to accept a takeover. As a result of this absence of takeover strategies and the need to maintain employment, Japanese managers have had to seek new ways to employ their human and machine assets through internal expansion. But in the U.S., acquiring another firm's profitable assets, which often are the fruits yielded by years of research and development, is regarded as less expensive.

Japanese, American, and European IR manufacturers also differ in their respective engineering philosophies. Western engineers have concentrated on developing innovative and sophisticated robots, a practice that has resulted in some overengineered products. Furthermore, American engineers often want to establish a small company and make an important breakthrough. Poised at technology's leading edge, the engineer more often than not hopes and expects a huge conglomerate to snap up his firm.

The Japanese take a more minimalist approach. Their IRs were gradually developed from unsophisticated manual manipulators to more complex systems that incorporate "intelligence." Since the Japanese engineer expects to remain employed by his company for life, his creativity is directed toward his company's benefit.

Because robotics integrates several technologies, different specialists within a company often collaborate, says Professor Toshio Sata, of the University of Tokyo Department of Engineering. Collaboration can even occur between specialists at different companies, he says. This sharing contrasts sharply with America, where research and development is often jealously guarded and perhaps, therefore, needlessly duplicated.

WESTERN EUROPE

Sweden's ASEA shared a significant part of the world IR pie in 1983 with about $13.7 million in sales by its U.S. operation. Since the Swedish robot market is small, ASEA exports most of its robots or manufactures them in countries where there is a market. In 1981, ASEA's worldwide sales were $40 million and its worldwide installed base was two thousand. The company bought Electrolux in early 1982 and became the largest robot manufacturer in western Europe.

Renault Vehicules Industriels facilitated gearbox production in its Bouthéon factory by adding a Fr45 million flexible manufacturing system in 1982. Today the system builds up to 100 truck gearboxes a day. Machining centers for drilling, boring, polishing, and inspecting receive rough castings of gearbox parts that are transferred from a palletizing station by automatic carts. Electric cables under the floor generate signals that guide the unmanned vehicles as they journey through the factory.

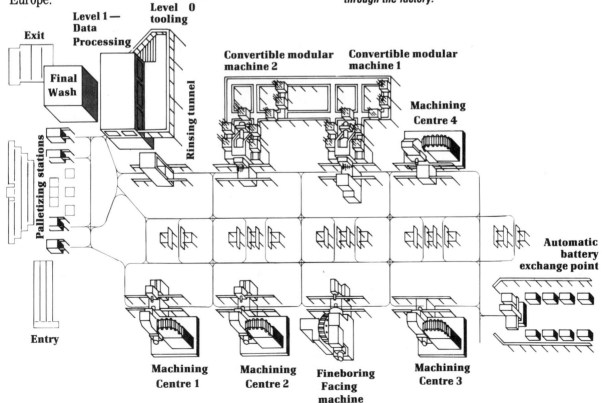

Norway's Trallfa, which licenses the DeVilbiss Company, a division of Champion Spark Plug, exports about 95 percent of the robots it produces. In 1982, the firm's production of robots was valued at $12 million. DeVilbiss had about 8.7 percent of the U.S. market in 1983.

France's first IR was imported in 1971 by Sciaky S.A. in Vitry-sur-Seine. A past supplier of transfer machines to Renault Industries, Sciaky bought a Unimate and delivered it to Renault's Paris headquarters. The Unimate was installed in Renault's R-5 plant, which manufactures Le Car. Since then, French engineers have developed remarkable ideas for robots, but have lacked the machine-tool industry to build them in large quantities. Consequently, about 60 percent of the robots operating in France are imports. Renault and the Ransburg Corporation in Indianapolis, Indiana, have created a very successful joint venture, Cybotech, also in Indianapolis, Indiana, in 1980. Renault says it had two thousand IRs installed worldwide in 1982 and is the leading supplier of spot-welding IRs in Europe. Sciaky follows West Germany's Volkswagen A.G., of Wolfsburg, in integrating spot-welding IRs in Europe.

Until recently, West Germany had developed and used few robots since manufacturers there do more mass production than small-batch production, even though West Germany has an excellent machine-tool industry and manufactures many automobiles. But car companies such as Mercedes and Porsche use custom machinery for one-of-a-kind-type production. So a segment of the automobile industry cannot be considered potential robot users. In contrast, Volkswagen does less custom design, uses industrial robots for automobile production, and is Germany's largest IR manufacturer. The company is entering the U.S. market through its license and marketing agreement with General Electric. I.W.K.A. Kuka in Augsburg, distributes robots in the United States through Expert Automation in Sterling Heights, Michigan.

The German government has financially supported firms since the 1970s, when it recognized a technology gap between Germany and other industrialized countries. Today about fifty firms produce robots, with five accounting for 70 percent and ten accounting for 90 percent of production. In 1982, they built sixteen hundred robots valued at $108 million.

Italian technology, like Japan's, was spurred by the oil crisis. Italy is extremely dependent on imported petroleum and natural gas to fuel its industries, provide feedstocks for its chemical plants, and heat its homes, according to Stephen Kindel and Rosemary Brady of *Forbes*. One reason for Italy's foreign oil thirst, say these writers, is that the nation's industrial base was developed long after the coal age and that the Italian government kept oil prices artificially low. This caused oil companies to pull out of Italy and created a need for foreign currency.

A KUKA robot automatically mounts a wheel onto a vehicle being transferred by an overhead conveyor. The robot's vision system recognizes the orientation of the hub bolt hole so that the robot can properly align the wheel.

To produce its Uno automobile, Fiat spent $700 million. A large portion of that went into flexible automation—$46 million was spent on sophisticated painting equipment at Fiat's Mirafiori plant, for example. That plant and the Rivalta plant, produce 2,200 units daily, the largest ever for a single Fiat model. The Uno, so named because it is Fiat's first car to be produced by almost entirely automated assembly, is built in one third less time than the Fiat 127. Its body has 172 parts, 35 percent fewer than the 267 parts making up the Fiat 127. The Uno therefore has fewer weld points—2,700 compared to 4,280. Of those welds only 30 are made by humans, the rest are made by 200 welding robots.

To increase overseas business and capture foreign currency, Italian companies have looked to high-technology markets for income. With this motivation, Italian automation has made tremendous strides and robot systems like Fiat-Comau's Robogate line are now considered state of the art. In Turin, Fiat S.p.A., the car manufacturer, is Italy's largest privately held company and Comau S.p.A. in Turin is its machine-tool division. Fiat's flexible manufacturing system has boosted productivity by 20 percent and the company is spending more than $1 billion to improve design, according to *Forbes*.[19] That money is not being spent on U.S. or Japanese technology, but on "homegrown advances in automation." In fact, U.S. and Japanese auto industries have lately been going to Italy to see how cars ought to be manufactured, and they have been returning with Robogate, *Forbes* reports. Bendix, now part of Allied Corporation, has a joint venture with Comau—Bendix-Comau Production Sys-

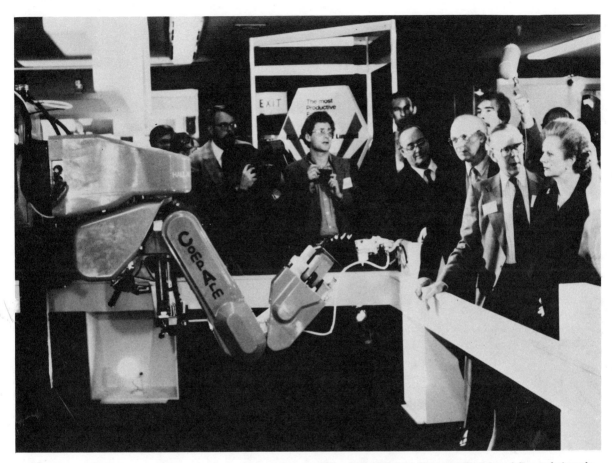

Prime Minister Margaret Thatcher visits a robot made by Hall Automation, a small British manufacturer that was bought by GEC, Britain's equivalent of General Electric.

tems. Comau is particularly strong in its software capabilities and it first built robots in 1976. Ironically, its designs were created specifically to compete with Kearney and Trecker, which owns Cross and Trecker, and with Cincinnati Milacron.

As Comau became the largest automated-systems supplier in Europe, other Italian companies started to compete. Digital Electronic Automation (DEA) in Turin, and Olivetti in Ivrea are making their mark as well. Another American company that recognized and hailed Italian technology early on was Nordson in Amherst, Ohio. It bought the design, manufacture, and marketing rights of Basfer S.R.L., a Milanese robot manufacturer, in 1978, but announced that it was leaving robotics in January 1984.

Robots in Great Britain have come in, out, and returned to favor during the past two decades. According to Thomas E. Brock, director of the British Robot Association,

This robot, also designed at the University of Notting-ham in the early 1970s, was called "SIRCH," for semi-intelligent robot for component handling. It had a binary vision system and three grippers. Says Wilfred B. Heginbotham, "I could still show a film of this ma-chine working today and it would be looked on as quite up to date."

Britain was at the forefront of robot use during the late 1960s and early 1970s. Throughout the 1970s, however, Britain had a low-wage economy and it was hard to justify expensive robots with payback periods of three years.

In the mid-seventies, however, companies recognized that unless they automated, they would be unable to compete. "If you don't automate, if you don't increase your manufacturing capabilities, you won't be in business in five years' time at all. This has been supported by the government and our Prime Minister, and this has caused a change in attitude," says Brock. It was also found that large automotive companies, such as Ford, were more likely to give contracts to British suppliers that used robots because Ford had confidence that they would deliver on time.

The British government set up several schemes in the late 1970s to encourage the production and use of British robots and discourage imports. When a British company develops a robot, the government shares half the cost. Then the government places the first four or five prototypes, free of charge, in potential users' plants. If the user is satisfied, he then pays the market value of the equipment to the government. If the user is not satisfied, the government offers the equipment to someone else. The government guarantees that it will get the prototypes into industry.

Equally concerned with new applications for robotics, the British government will pay one third of a robot system cost, even if the system has foreign-made robots, as long as the system does not involve an established application. In the eighteen months since it began, the scheme has approved 120 to 150 projects at a cost of £10 million to £15 million.

A similar scheme exists for flexible manufacturing systems (FMSs), which were first developed in Great Britain. In 1967, D.T.N. Williamson of Molins Machine in London described System 24, a sophisticated system of machine tools having separate but complementary functions. Together, "they make possible the manufacture of a wide variety of machined components from simple to complex with the minimum of human intervention, but still preserving great flexibility and freedom of change," he said. The system did not catch on, but according to Professor Wilfred B. Heginbotham, director general of the Production Engineering Research Association of Great Britain, the Japanese bow to the ground when System 24 is mentioned. To revitalize interest in FMSs, the government has earmarked £14 million for such projects.

In response to a massive upturn in the aerospace industry, Rolls-Royce began planning sixteen flexible manufacturing systems in 1978. The company hopes these lines will reduce inventory by 50 percent and produce small batches cheaply. The first installation is being made at the 1906 machine shop where Henry Royce built his first Silver Ghost motor car. The $8 million AIMS (automated integrated manufacturing system) will manufacture turbine disks and compressor wheels for jet engines. Robots on this automated grinding line load turbine blades from the transfer conveyor to machining cells.

7 CELL AUTOMATED GRINDING LINE

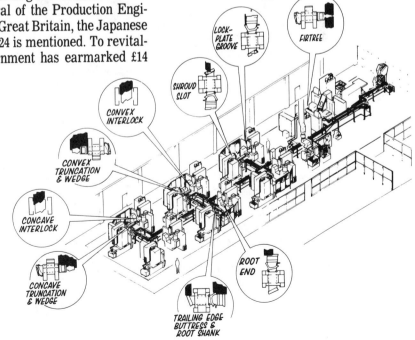

This prototype assembly robot called "Minitran," was developed during the mid-sixties by J. R. Ashley, Wilfred B. Heginbotham, and A. Pugh at the University of Nottingham. Designed for small-batch, light assembly, Minitran could handle parts weighing up to 4 ounces and no wider than 2 inches. The width of the robot frame itself was merely 6 inches so that several could work in close groups along a conveyor. The device was sequentially controlled, and so had mechanical stops, and its power was pneumatic.

According to the 1983 International Trade Commission report, Taiwan is beginning to produce robots with government aid. Sixteen organizations and institutes have developed eleven prototypes. Five of these are assembly robots that were developed at the Industrial Research Institute, which is funded by the government. These were transferred to five of Taiwan's eight robot firms in 1982. They plan to produce 60 robots annually, beginning in 1984, to serve local markets. Local demand for robots was expected to be 200 in 1983 and forecasts for 1986 and 1990 are 2,000 and 10,000 units, respectively.

THE SOVIET UNION AND EASTERN EUROPE

A GE technician surveys the control console, which is linked to twenty-four computers at critical points on the 850,000-square-foot factory floor. He or she can monitor the condition of all automatic equipment and track inventory status.

Reports vary on robotics manufacturing in the USSR and Soviet Bloc countries. Professor Del Tesar, director of the Center for Intelligent Machines and Robotics at the University of Florida, visited the Soviet Union in June 1981. On the invitation of the Moscow Machine Science Institute's director, he toured ten robotics research facilities. While robot patents are held by these institutes, it is not yet known who manufactures them. In December 1981 the West German daily, *Frankfurter Allgmeine*, reported that East Germany was to "cooperate closely with the USSR in developing robot technology." But a spokesman for the East German embassy in Washington indicated only that there might be a "specialization agreement," whereby East German manufacturers would produce Soviet-designed robots.

Tesar estimates that 3,000 robots were operating in the Soviet Union in 1979. But a *Business Week* report in August 1981 said that between 6,000 and 7,000 robots were in place. Paul Aron suggests that these figures are far too conservative. He quotes three Russian books showing that the USSR is quite advanced in robot technology.

At the 26th Congress of the Communist Party, Leonid Brezhnev announced the mobilization of twenty-two ministries to build 40,000 robots over a five-year period. *Business Week* described the plan as "a relatively quick fix for two agonizing problems: a shortage of manpower and the lowest labor productivity in the industrialized world."

Reports on the sophistication of these installed robots are also varied. RIA's 1979 data showed that there were between one hundred and two hundred robots similar to Unimation's PUMA and Cincinnati Milacron's Model T³. The report also said that Soviet robot technology is ten years behind that of the United States and Japan.

Since Russia's massive Kama River truck plant ordered twenty welding robots in 1981 from Unimation, and the Fiat-designed auto plant at Togliatti used KUKA robots from West Germany, it seems that the Russians want, or need, to learn from the West. But *Business Week* quoted Yuri G. Kozarev, head of the Machine Building Ministry's Metalworking Research Institute's robot department, as saying with a huff, "Two thirds of the equipment at Kama and Togliatti is Soviet."

FANUC: A MODEL FOR THE FUTURE

hat will the factory of the future be like? Articles in newspapers and magazines headlined "Flexible Systems Invade the Factory" and "Era of Flexible Manufacturing System Arrives" already describe plants with few human workers and many integrated machine-tool and robotic stations.

Here we offer a glimpse of some of the world's most sophisticated factories, FMSs. The future factory will be today's FMS on a larger scale perhaps, with fewer human workers and probably equipped with more sensing robots.

The world leader in FMSs in place is Japan. One industrial giant, Toyoda Machine Tool, had over thirty FMSs

Fanuc's Mount Fuji motor manufacturing factory has two floors. Parts are machined on the first floor and are then stored in an automatic warehouse between floors. These parts are gradually sent out from the warehouse according to the needs of assembly operations done on the second floor.

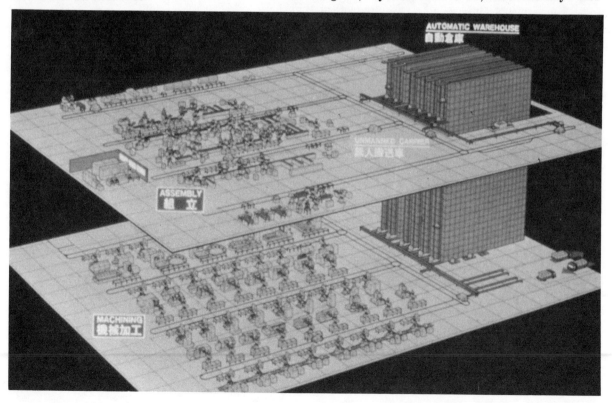

The automatic warehouse.

as of January 1983, while the United States had only thirty nationwide, according to *Fortune*.[20] European countries also appear to be installing more FMSs than the United States. The differences in American and Japanese engineering philosophies described in chapter 2 also account for the Japanese lead in FMSs.

One particularly interesting FMS is the Fanuc plant near Mount Fuji. (Fanuc is GMF Robotics' Japanese parent.) The plant, which cost $30 million and has 101 machine-loading, assembly, unmanned carrier robots, and 60 human workers, turns out 10,000 motors a month. True to the term *flexibility*, the system produces over forty different electric motors.

Machining of parts for these motors is done twenty-four hours a day on the first floor of the yellow, two-story building. Unmanned carts bring parts, on pallets capable of holding up to one thousand pieces, to sixty machining cells. Fifty-two robots make it possible for these cells to function properly by loading and unloading parts to and from turning, grinding, tapping, drilling, boring, and facing machines.

Robots 1 through 8 load motor shafts to finish grinders, for example. Robots 15 and 16 load shafts to a machine that inserts a part called a "key way" into the shafts and then drills holes at the ends of the shaft. Twenty humans work on this floor.

After the parts are machined, they are loaded onto pallets and taken to an automatic warehouse until they are assembled on the second floor. The second floor consists of four assembly lines, made up of twenty-five cells. Forty-nine robots work with the cells, which are positioned on both sides of an unmanned carrier path. When an unmanned carrier arrives with parts, such as magnets and pole shoes, that it has automatically retrieved from the warehouse, robots A and B unload them onto a cell where they are glued. This partial assembly is then fed to the next cell, where robot C takes a motor shell through a cleaning-and-heating operation and then places it over the magnets for more bonding. Robot D unloads that subassembly onto a pallet, from which robot J picks it up and places it over a rotor. The rotor has been handled by robots E, F, G, H, and I in the meantime.

Unlike the machining sequence, which operates three shifts a day, the assembly sequence operates only one, eight-hour shift a day. This is because it takes one third the time to assemble parts as it does to machine them. Certain assembly tasks, like wiring and installing detectors and inspection are done by twenty human workers. Twenty other human workers are involved in administration tasks.

The plant's operations are monitored by one central computer in a control room. A display board shows the status of each machine and assembly cell and a colored graphics terminal shows machine running time, and daily and monthly production rates. The system can also monitor how many parts are stored in the automatic warehouse so that when a particular motor is to be assembled, the plant operators know whether they have parts available. Three TV screens attached to cameras offer different views of the factory floors.

The forty human workers involved in machining and assembly are also involved in maintenance. But in describing his parent company's plant, Douglas F. Urbaniak of GMF Robotics says, "They have designed and built such a high-quality product that maintenance is almost minimal. They are strong believers in preventive maintenance programs and do appropriate inspections, repairs, and mainte-

The Rolls Royce FMS. Each of the six cells, three on either side of the conveyor, consists of a robot for turbine-blade handling, two creep-feed grinders for blade machining, plus cleaning and inspection facilities.

nance at appropriate intervals, which gives them a high degree of uptime."

Fanuc says that its new plant has increased productivity threefold. Before it built the facility, 32 robots and 108 people manufactured 6,000 motors a month.

In the U.S., examples of FMSs include GE's locomotive manufacturing plant in Erie, Pennsylvania, John Deere's transmission cases manufacturing system, and Hughes Aircraft's system for producing aluminum frames for weapons aiming devices. *High Technology* reports that these companies as well as Avco Lycoming, Lockheed, Sundstrand (all aerospace companies), and agricultural and con-

In this close shot of a cell, one ASEA robot (at the end of the L-shaped conveyor) services two creep-feed grinders (to the left and right of the conveyor).

struction companies such as Caterpillar Tractor, Allis-Chalmers, and International Harvester, installed FMSs as a result of foreign competition.[21]

More and more, it would seem, factories are liable to come to resemble "black boxes" into which new parts are inserted and out of which finished products emerge. Thanks to robots, the internal portions will proceed automatically. One would almost expect that human interference will be as little desired as in the case of the day-to-day workings of the interior of a television set.

MAKING ROBOTS SMART: RESEARCH AND DEVELOPMENT

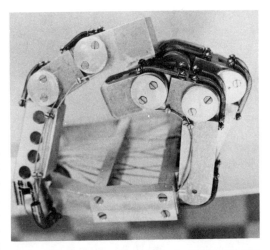

Movement of this five-fingered hand, developed by M. Caporali and Mohsen Shahinpoor at Clarkson College of Technology, is controlled by springs and cables wrapped around pulleys that are fixed to each finger joint. The hand is twice the size of a human hand.

aking robots smart involves the efforts of researchers from a multitude of disciplines. In a robotics laboratory, one will find mechanical, electrical, and software engineers. But their laboratory is probably a division of an artificial intelligence (AI) laboratory or department where more researchers approach machine intelligence through neuroanatomy, physics, psychophysics, linguistics, and the psychology of learning. This potpourri of researchers often results in shared ideas and collaborations, as efforts proceed to formulate a theory of machine intelligence and to construct intelligent machines.

These endeavors—theorizing and building—occur simultaneously in AI research. Many researchers hope to arrive at a better understanding of intelligence while trying to achieve intelligent machines.

Since AI is a young science, researchers are still wrestling with the formidable task of defining machine intelligence or thinking. One direction AI has taken is toward robots that have the ability to perceive their surroundings. In their quest for perceptive robots, researchers confront the question of biological duplication—should sensor systems for robots be modeled after human sensing systems? Some researchers argue that robot sensor systems should be modeled on what we know of human systems. If the results fall short, analyzing what is lacking and why can offer insight into biological systems. Other researchers take the evolutionary approach that machine sensor systems should first be modeled on more primitive natural systems. They reason that once less complex systems are understood and robots are endowed with those capabilities, research can then focus on more sophisticated systems. Still others question biological duplication altogether, asking why bother to anthropomorphize, if we can develop systems bearing little or no resemblance to biological structures and yet achieve the same functions? They argue that too little is known about biological visual and tactile systems to emulate them. Instead, they suggest directing research toward duplicating the *function* of the sense, rather than its biological structure and form.

Regardless of the approach taken, endowing robots with senses is enormously challenging. To understand the difficulties involved, we will first examine why state-of-the-art robots are not adequate to a task known as the bin-picking problem. We will then look at examples of sensor research directed toward making robots capable of this type of task. It will become clear that adding sensing capabilities is both a hardware and a software matter, as are improving walking machines and remote manipulators. Finally, we will discuss what many consider the ultimate challenge in making robots smart—getting them to learn.

Much has been written recently about expert systems, which are software packages that some consider applied AI. An expert system emulates human expert reasoning. It contains a "knowledge base" and an "inference engine" that programmers have created on the basis of interviews with human experts. The knowledge base contains several hundred rules, stated in "if-then" terms. The inference engine asks for information and then simulates decision making according to the knowledge base rules. One early expert system, for example, asks for symptoms data and laboratory test results, which are fed in by an operator. It then sifts through its knowledge base rules and prioritizes information according to the strength of each rule, thereby arriving at a medical diagnosis and emulating a doctor's reasoning.

Some "knowledge engineers," as those who develop expert systems are called, were trained in robotics labs and they may confront questions similar to those of robotics researchers. But knowledge engineering has not yet been used in robots. Robotics engineers are exploring other methods of making robots smart.

THE BIN-PICKING PROBLEM

icking parts out of a bin, a task easily accomplished by humans, is enormously difficult for robots. This task is important because parts in factories are most often found jumbled in bins. Breaking down the task into smaller problems will show why a PUMA robot, which was described in chapter 4, cannot solve those problems.

Imagine that a bin of wrenches arrives within the reach of a PUMA. What will the robot "see" when it looks into the bin? If one wrench was lying at the bottom, the bin bottom was dark, the wrench was shiny, and a light was shining directly down, the robot would be in luck. With the image of a wrench stored in its memory, it could recognize the actual wrench's silhouette. If there were several wrenches at the bottom and none touched or overlapped, the robot would probably still recognize them, since it is designed to recognize parts similarly arranged, and lit on a conveyor belt.

But what if the lighting failed to provide enough contrast or the bin's edges cast shadows on the wrench or wrenches? The robot would not "know" that it was seeing part of a wrench and that the other part was hidden. It could not compare the visible wrench section with the complete wrench image, so it could not determine the real wrench's orientation.

What if the bin were half-filled with overlapping wrenches? Lacking depth perception, the robot would fail to distinguish a wrench on top from those underneath. Without three-dimensional vision, the robot could not recognize a wrench among wrenches or know how far to reach. A 3-D vision system would have to be very accurate to indicate the precise distance between the gripper and the wrench.

Suppose the robot did reach a wrench. It would not know that it had touched one. If its gripper picked it up with a certain force and the wrench began to slip, how would the robot "know" that and "decide" to apply more force?

Suppose the robot was trying to pick up soft chocolate candies instead of wrenches. How would it know what force would squash the candy when its gripper picked it out of the bin? Suppose some candies were softer than others. How would the robot know to lessen the force?

Scientists at Japan's Ministry of International Trade and Industry built this battery-run "seeing-eye robot." The computer-controlled device detects obstacles and warns of other dangers.

Take one or any combination of these conditions, and you've got a dumbfounded robot. To some extent, mechanical devices such as bowl feeders and shakers that sort parts and place them on a conveyor belt can be used to circumvent the bin-picking problem. These devices remove uncertainties from the environment so that when a part is presented to a robot, its *internal* arm position sensors—optical encoders and potentiometers—are all the sensors it needs. But this approach requires designing costly special-purpose equipment for each application, and much of the robot's flexibility is wasted since it can only work with such dedicated equipment.

Because *external* sensors would enable robots to perform with uncertainties in the environment, researchers at university and industry laboratories are seeking solutions in vision and touch sensors. Since sensed information must be processed and controlled, the solutions require hardware and software research.

 # GETTING ROBOTS TO SEE

ision researchers are pursuing three main tracks to enable robots to see: gray-scale processing, stereo or binocular systems, and structured light. They are also improving two-dimensional vision by refining binary systems.

Gray-scale, stereo, and structured light approaches can yield information about an object's surface and orientation, as well as its distance from the robot. Like the human visual system, gray-scale and stereo are passive—they do not require interaction with an object in order to sense it. Structured light, however, is active because it senses an object using special light shone and reflected off the object. Of all the approaches, stereo is the closest to human vision because it uses two cameras as its "eyes." Some aspects of all the approaches may eventually be combined, so that a structured light system uses two cameras, for example. But excepting current stereo research systems, other systems remain Cyclopes.

Like binary vision, gray-scale systems create digitized images. (See Fig. 7.1.) These images are composites of little

Fig. 7.1.
Example of Gray-Scale Digitized Image

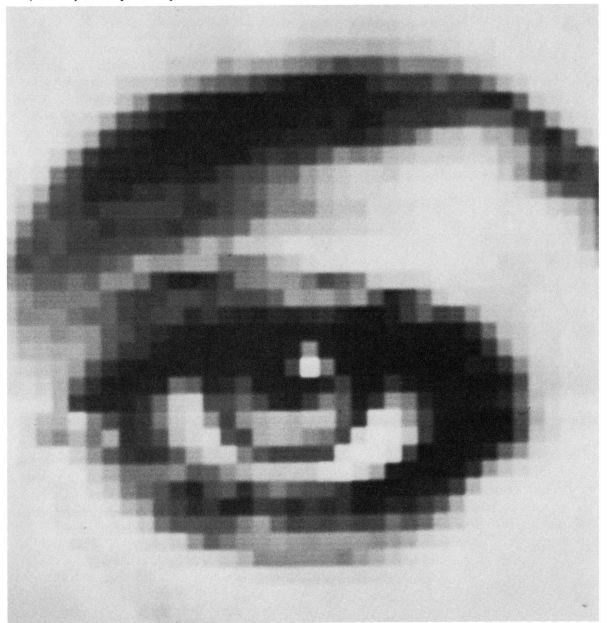

To arrive at this gray-scale digitized image of an eye, each pixel—or "picture element" of the overall picture—was assigned one of sixty-four gray levels. The system is built by Cognex Corporation, a Boston vision company.

Source: Cognex Corporation

squares, called "pixels," from the words *picture* and *element*. Whereas binary assigns each pixel either a 0 or 1 for black and white, gray-scale can assign values up to 16, 64, and 256. Several shades of gray are apparent because the system processes *variations* in light intensity, or brightness, picked up by the camera. Brightness results from the way a surface reflects light, so digitizing brightness variations provides the computer with information about the object's texture, for example. Complex images formed by overlapping parts can be analyzed because they no longer look like one new silhouette.

Early gray-scale vision research was conducted at the University of Rhode Island robotics laboratory under the direction of John Birk and Robert Kelley. In 1981, they and their associates demonstrated a PUMA picking connecting-rod castings from a bin, solving several bin-picking problems. Their prototype became the basis for a commercial system, called "i-bot," now manufactured by Object Recognition Systems of Princeton, New Jersey. The i-bot system locates those parts in a bin that seem to be in the best position for picking and guides the arm toward them. The arm's parallel jaw grippers know when a part is between them because the part interrupts an infrared light beam shining across the jaws. The jaws also have tactile and collision sensors so that they can gently handle a part. While the system does offer the equivalent of hand-eye coordination, its processing speed is thirty-six parts per minute, too slow for many operations.

Other commercial gray-scale systems are available—Applied Intelligent Systems in Ann Arbor, Michigan; Automatix in Burlington, Massachusetts; Cognex in Boston; International Robomation/Intelligence in Carlsbad, California; Octek in Burlington, Massachusetts, and Robotic Vision Systems in Melville, New York.

But current gray-scale systems are limited because they require much more data processing than do binary systems. Even today's fast computers take a relatively long time to process the information. Let's look at the data processing involved for a system in which each pixel can have up to 256 gray values. For a computer to store a value, it must have two memory locations—one for a "yes" and one for a "no." This information unit is called a "binary digit," or "bit" for short. The 256 possible pixel values can therefore be expressed as 2^8 memory locations, or 8 bits.

But this is only the memory needed for *one* pixel of an

entire image. Suppose that the solid-state video camera used divides the image into 65,536 pixels—256 columns × 256 rows. The total becomes 65,536 × 8 bits, or, since one byte equals 8 bits, 65,536 bytes. This figure may look more familiar expressed as 64K, the entire memory capacity of many personal computers. (K equals 1024, so 65,536 divided by 1024 equals 64K.) This amount of memory is needed to process *one* image *once.*

Since for practical applications from thirty to sixty image frames must be processed per second, the memory requirements are enormous. While mainframes are perfectly capable of handling this amount of data, they may not be able to do so quickly enough to keep up with the required flow of parts. That is, the computer may not be able to process in "real time"—at the speed required, given the *actual* time allocated for a task. A 256 × 256 pixel image of one part generally takes one second to process. But many operations require recognizing fifteen parts per second.

Researchers are trying to develop programs that process data images in real time without reducing the number of pixels or pixel values—the more there are, the better the resolution and detail of the image. In fact, researchers would like to use cameras with 512 × 512 or 1,024 × 1,024 pixels for better resolution because that would improve edge detection, for example. The solution to the data-processing problem lies in limiting the amount of processing by selecting only the relevant data.

Programmers are investigating one data selection approach called "windowing" for both gray-scale and binary systems. Instead of processing the entire image, the program processes a region within which a part is expected to appear. Only selected groups of pixels, or even just one pixel, need to be processed. Pixels covering regions of no interest are not processed and so do not take up computer memory and time.

Robert C. Bolles of SRI International developed such a system, called "local feature focus." The system uses a model of a part to focus on key features. Then it uses the key features' locations to find secondary features. First, interesting features like holes, corners, protrusions, and intrusions are grouped together if they are similar. Then nearby secondary features are used to uniquely identify each key feature, its orientation, and position. When key features have thus been defined, the part's position and orientation are also determined. Automatically selecting for key and

Fig. 7.2.
Stereo (or Binocular) Vision

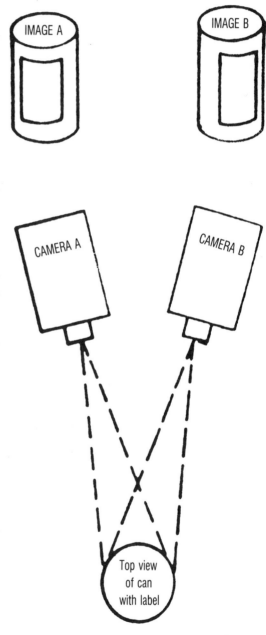

Source: *Machine Vision Systems: A Summary and Forecast* (Tech Tran Corp., 1983).

secondary features saves image processing time. This kind of "model-based" approach is becoming more popular.

Another timesaving approach uses several microprocessors—each processing one window of an image. The microprocessors can operate independently, or communicate with one another and function cooperatively. Algorithms for such systems are being developed at several laboratories, including IBM, Carnegie-Mellon University, and AT&T Bell Laboratories.

One such distributed vision system, developed by Peter G. Selfridge of AT&T Bell Laboratories, uses microprocessors to process regions at low and high resolutions. Varying resolutions is similar to varying the focus of a camera—when sharply focused, more details are apparent, when less focused, details blur. So at high resolutions more details must be processed and at low resolutions fewer details must be processed. In the distributed system, a "master" microprocessor examines the entire image at low resolution and identifies windows to be examined. Then the master directs "slave" microprocessors to examine those windows at a high resolution and keeps track of what each slave reports.

By selecting areas for high-resolution processing, the system saves processing time and is considerably cheaper than mainframe processing. The sum of several small, less powerful, inexpensive processors affords greater speed than does a large, more powerful, more expensive processor.

 STEREO VISION SYSTEMS

tereo vision systems, with their two cameras mimicking human visual systems, are attractive to researchers, but also currently present major programming challenges. When a human looks at an object, the two eyes see it from slightly different angles. This difference creates a disparity between what each eye sees—the right eye sees an object as if the object were rotated slightly compared to the object position observed by the left eye, and vice versa. The closer the eyes are to the object, the greater the difference in rotation. Similarly, the farther the eyes are from the object, the smaller the difference in rotation. (See Fig. 7.2.) This difference, known as parallax, gives humans perspective—somehow, information from right and left eyes results in depth cues.

It is extremely difficult for a computer to use digitized information from two cameras and arrive at our equivalent of a depth cue. Researchers are writing algorithms to compute shift due to parallax, known as the correspondence problem. Calculating the correspondence between two object images and their features would yield information about the actual object's distance from the cameras. The two cameras and the processor would send this information to a bin-picking robot, to return to our example, so that it would then know how far to reach.

But when two cameras receive two slightly different wrench images, the wrenches and their features appear at different coordinates. Similarly, features of these wrench images such as edges would be displaced. But the computer does not know which edge of wrench B's image matches which edge of wrench A's image because there are other wrench edges (or shadows) at the corresponding coordinates. These other wrench edges can be mistaken for the corresponding edge.

One approach to the correspondence problem is somewhat like the high- and low-resolution examinations described for distributed vision. To compute depth, researchers at MIT attempt to match edges of two images at multiple resolutions. Once an image has been matched in two low resolutions this guides and makes matching easier at higher resolutions. Filters are used to vary resolution, so that at a fine resolution many edges are apparent, and at a coarser resolution some of these edges combine to appear as fewer larger edges. Left and right image matching is easier when fewer edges are visible, so once an edge has been matched at low resolutions, the procedure to do so guides and makes matching easier at higher resolutions.

This approach to the correspondence problem is part of a more general theory of vision developed by the late David Marr at MIT's AI lab, which is headed by Patrick Winston. The theory involves multiple processing steps that lead to maps of edges, dimensional representation of the object's surface. (See Fig. 7.3.) The necessary programming is so complex that the emphasis is on creating the appropriate algorithms and not so much on their speed. This technique continues to be researched by Marr's colleagues

Fig. 7.3.
Left and Right Image Matching

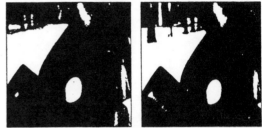

PHOTO OF HENRY MOORE SCULPTURE

"PRIMAL SKETCHES"

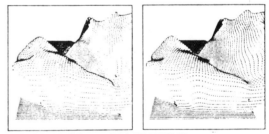

THREE-DIMENSIONAL MAPS OF SURFACE

Source: High Technology, Paul Kinnucan, "How Smart Robots Are Becoming Smarter" (September–October 1981).

Fig. 7.4.
Triangulation

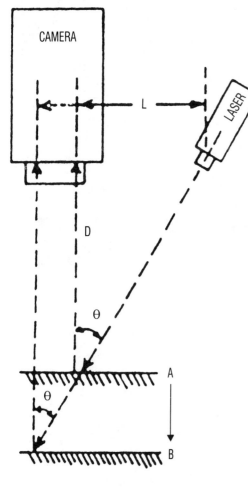

Source: *Machine Vision Systems: A Summary and Forecast* (Tech Tran Corp., 1983).

Thomaso Poggio, W. Eric L. Grimson, Ellen C. Hildreth, and H. Keith Nishihara, and other members of the MIT team.

STRUCTURED LIGHT

A third approach to robot vision is structured light. One type of structured light, triangulation, can give very accurate information about an object's location, orientation, and surface characteristics. Triangulation uses the object, one camera, and a light source (usually a laser beam or a slit of light) placed at the vertices of right triangles. (See Fig. 7.4.) The light source, a laser in this case, shines on the object at a known angle theta, or "θ." This line of light is the triangle's hypotenuse. When the object reflects the light toward the camera, that line of light forms the triangle's base. The length of the base is the object's distance from the camera—the unknown. The triangle's third leg is the distance from the camera to the laser, which is measured.

If one angle and one leg length of a right triangle are known, the other leg lengths can be calculated. In triangulation, we want to calculate the length of the base, so we use the trigonometric function tangent.

$$\text{tangent } \theta = \frac{\text{distance from laser to camera}}{\text{distance from object to camera [the base]}}$$

Rearranging the equation yields:

$$\text{distance from object to camera} = \frac{\text{distance from laser to camera}}{\text{tangent } \theta}$$

This straightforward calculation can be done without a computer—many of us learned to solve such problems with just trigonometric tables. A computer becomes necessary, however, if the object moves from point A to point B in Fig. 7.4. The same calculation for the newly created triangle must be done as quickly as possible, so that triangulation can "tell" a robot arm an object's location and orientation as a conveyor moves it away from the camera.

In this laboratory setup of CONSIGHT, GM's triangulation system, two light sources on the supporting structure shine down on a connecting rod placed on a conveyor by computer scientist Steve Holland. Because the connecting rod has height, it separates the light. The camera, also on the supporting structure and in between the light sources, sends an image of the line break to the computer, which "tells" the robot arm, on the left, where the connecting rod is and how far to reach for it.

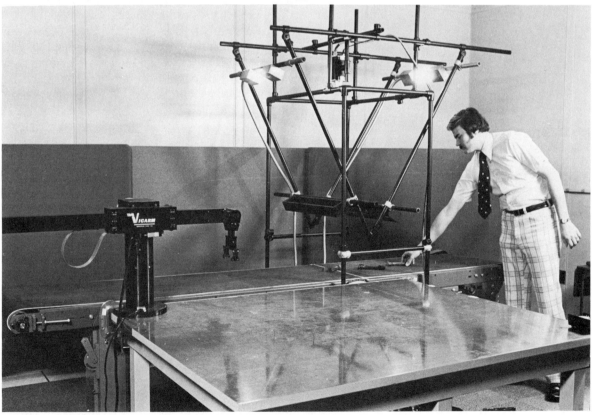

Structured light can also be used to deduce an object's shape by studying the deviation of a slit of light as it strikes the object's surface. When the light falls on a convex surface, like a ball, the bar of light is curved. When the light falls on a cube, however, the bar of light zig-zags.

Several variations of triangulation are under study at the National Bureau of Standards (NBS), NASA's Jet Propulsion Laboratory (JPL), GM, GMF Robotics, and SRI International. One system, designed by NBS chief of Industrial Systems Division James S. Albus, uses a slit of light and a camera mounted on a robot's wrist. The system sorts cylinders and blocks into an array. It can also measure the shape of a casting, find the edge of a window frame, detect the crack between a pair of bricks, and measure the angle between two pieces of steel.

Another system, called "CONSIGHT," was developed by GM with the guidance of Lothar Rossol, now GMF Robotics vice president of research and development. This system combines some triangulation principles and adds others. CONSIGHT uses two light beams to determine part position and orientation on a conveyor. These beams converge at a vertex on the conveyor surface. (See Fig. 7.5.) When a moving part arrives under the system's camera, the height of the part displaces the beams. They reach the surface as two beams shifted relative to the single beam formed at the conveyor's surface. This displacement is calculated as the part moves, so that a sequence of images builds a two-dimensional object image.

At SRI International's robotics laboratory, headed by David Nitzan, researchers are using triangulation to create a lighting system so that robots can "see" what they arc-weld. The prototype creates three-dimensional images of the object and the joint to be welded. The robot, a Cincinnati Milacron T³, carries a camera mounted alongside the welding gun. When first built, the system welded 15 inches per minute, and with improved hardware and software, it now welds 30 inches per minute. The researchers believe their approach to arc-welding vision systems will lead to truly flexible and easily programmed welding robots that see. Such systems could greatly benefit ship and heavy earthmoving equipment fabrication, industries that cannot use current robots that blindly weld.

One shortcoming of structured lighting is that the light path and the camera view may be accidentally blocked, or a shadow may be cast on the target object. Also, certain shapes require extremely precise triangulation. Suppose, for example, that an object has a hole that must be measured. If the hole is deep, the triangle must be very slim so that the hypotenuse and the base light beams are not interrupted by the hole's edges. Each angle must be precisely measured for the system to function with such extreme accuracy.

In addition to requiring extreme accuracy, structured light systems put constraints on the object's environment. The special lighting requirements demand that the operation must be separate from operations in normal lighting environments, which is not always possible or advantageous in factories. On the other hand, structured light systems calculate part geometry and surface characteristics *directly,* a distinct advantage over gray-scale systems, which must *infer* part geometry and surface characteristics from brightness variations. For these reasons, Lothar Rossol says that structured light systems have great promise, but notes their dissimilarity to biological systems may render them less appealing than other systems mimicking the human visual system.

Fig. 7.5.
GM Consight System Used on Metal Casting Conveyor Belt

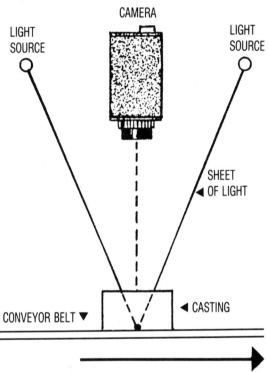

A. Side view, showing placement of light sources and camera

B. Top view from camera, showing displacement of light lines on casting surface

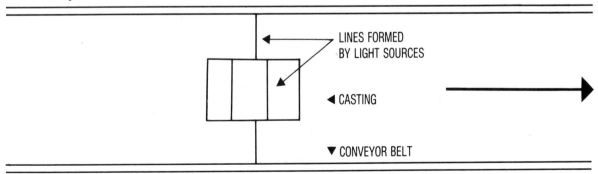

Source: *Machine Vision Systems: A Summary and Forecast* (Tech Tran Corp., 1983).

GETTING ROBOTS TO FEEL

The question of biological duplication arises again over strategies to improve gripper dexterity and tactile sensing. At a 1982 MIT workshop on the design and control of dexterous hands, two researchers expressed the classic opposing views. Stanford University's Bernard Roth argued that rather than duplicate the human hand, different artificial hands should be designed to accomplish particular tasks. Literally arguing on the other hand, Steven Jacobson, of the University of Utah, said that the biological system has much to teach us. It is worthwhile to use our understanding of that system to construct artificial hands, even if results differ substantially from the biological system, he said.

Besides reflecting the differing approaches of researchers in bioengineering, prosthetics, and robotics, the hand dichotomy has an economic element. Special-purpose hands can often cost as much as an entire arm. They would be expensive, and also reduce the robot's flexibility. As MIT computer scientist Tomas Lozano-Perez has put it, "One of the primary advantages of robots is their generality and programmability. When an associated mechanism is not general or reprogrammable, much of the advantage is lost." And even if hands were interchanged when needed, a battery of special-purpose hands could then become prohibitively expensive.

One reason for building a general-purpose, multifingered, and dexterous hand with sensors is that tactile and visual information are, to a large extent, analogous. Just as a highly sensitive visual system could eliminate other dedicated equipment, so too could a sophisticated hand. As MIT psychology professor and AI collaborator John M. Hollerbach wrote in his workshop report, both tactile and visual information "are attempting to ascertain some of the same information such as surface shape, texture, and material."

Citing research of the late 1970s, Hollerbach reports: "Single tactile images from a single finger can yield local information about surface shape and texture. More global shape information can be obtained by moving the finger along the surface." Moreover, "When tactile information is combined with a knowledge of finger position, objects may be located precisely. Sensor position readings from multiple

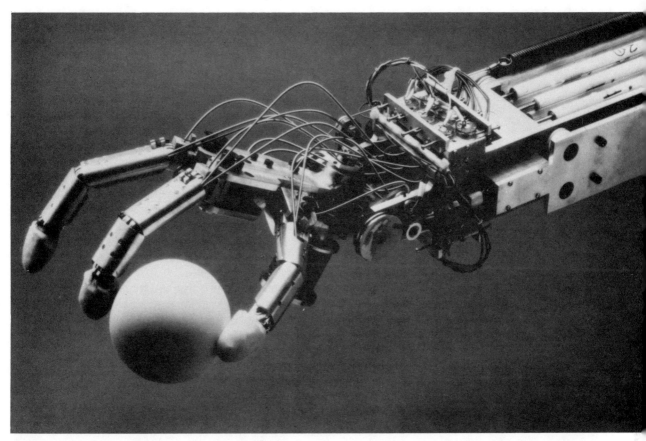

fingers yield shape and position information on a larger scale." It also seems that for those capabilities yielding information not quite analogous to visual information, like feeling slippage and the stability of a grasped object, more fingertips are better.

One kind of contact sensor that could be used to make artificial fingers feel is a small array of microswitches to measure the deformation of some material, like rubber, when an object is encountered. In 1981, W. Daniel Hillis of MIT developed a prototype sensor that fitted on the tip of a mechanical finger. With 256×256 microswitches per square centimeter underneath an electrically conductive rubber sheath, the sensor had a resolution comparable to the human forefinger. The current flow was measured when the rubber sheath was pressed, made contact with the microswitches, and the microswitch wires sent signals to a printed circuit board. This generated an image with 16×16 tactile elements, the highest resolution achieved.

Hitachi scientists Yoshiyuki Nakano, Masakatsu Fujie, and Yuji Hosada used shape-memory alloy to create a three-fingered hand. For wrist and finger movement, nickel and titanium wires are pulled and stretched by springs, but the wires "remember" their original lengths after electrical current passes through. This way, few actuators are needed and the hand and fore-arm remain small—measuring about 27.5 inches.

The system recognized screws, pins, and washers by detecting whether they were round or long. The force the finger had to apply in order to roll the part along a tabletop was another clue to recognizing a part. The system also detected local features, such as holes or bumps. Like earlier tactile research efforts, Hillis used vision processing techniques as direct prototypes for his tactile data-processing system. The vocabularies are similar—a sensor may be described as having high or low resolution, and its image is divided into tactile elements. Hillis has argued that vision techniques might have a better chance of working for tactile sensing since even at high resolutions less data would have to be analyzed. Consequently, complex tactile processing would be easier to perform in real time. He also noted that data collection is more readily controlled and, using reasoning parallel to Rossol's, data are directly collected rather than inferred.

It is not so surprising that tactile researchers have looked to visual research for models. Unlike vision, tactile perception is not supported by a large body of neurophysiology and psychophysics to guide model development, and there have been relatively few efforts. The same is true of multifingered, dexterous hands. In 1965, an aluminum five-fingered prosthetic hand was developed at the University of Belgrade, Yugoslavia, by Rajko Tomovic. But hand research seems to have plateaued, and as recently as 1977, researchers F. R. E. Crossley and F. G. Umholtz complained that most robots used grippers with dexterities comparable to a car mechanic using only pliers to execute all repairs. The parallel jaws, essentially two numb, jointless fingers, restrict manipulation as would using a pair of pliers to hold a screwdriver. These and other researchers, notably Frank F. Skinner, began building three-fingered hands, the simplest arrangement allowing arbitrary grasping. Also, three fingers are the minimum for a hand to act on an object while holding it—two can grasp it while the third performs. And unlike jaw grippers, three fingers can pick up asymmetrical objects.

Examples of three-fingered hands being developed today are J. Kenneth Salisbury's hand at MIT and the Stanford/JPL hand, a combined effort between NASA's Jet Propulsion Laboratory in Pasadena, California, and Stanford University. The JPL team is headed by Carl Ruoff, and John Craig is developing the controller at Stanford. Alfa Romeo S.p.A. of Milan, Italy, received a 1982 U.S. patent for

C4

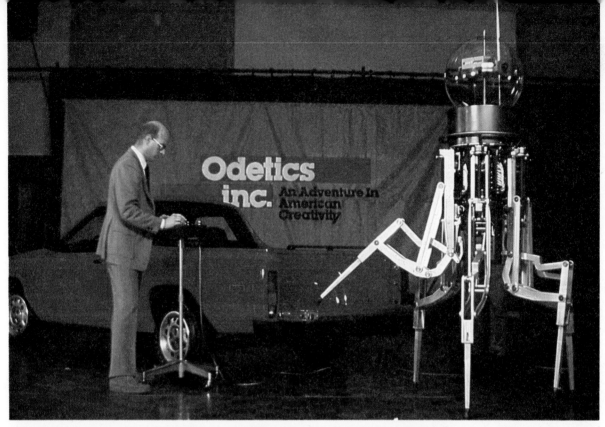

The six-legged "functionoid" called "Odex 1" climbs into and out of the back of a pickup truck.

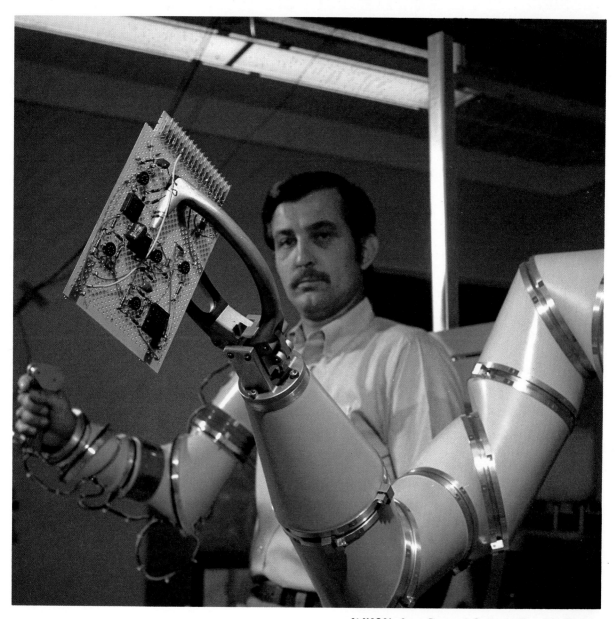

At NASA's Ames Research Center in Mountain View, California, researchers have developed an exoskeletal arm that they hope will one day be used as a therapeutic aid to the neurologically handicapped. It might be useful for patients undergoing physical therapy for muscle atrophy, and if several such arms were preprogrammed by computer, one physical therapist could help patients simultaneously. In another application, the irregular arm motions of patients suffering from cerebral palsy, could be eliminated electronically so that patients could feed themselves, for example.

◄ NASA's remote manipulator arm was first tested in space on the Space Shuttle Columbia. This on-board photo, taken from an aft window of the cabin, shows the 50-foot arm's gripper and a remotely operated television camera at its elbow.

This most recent version of an ACM, reported in 1981, is called "Oblix"—for its oblique axis mechanism. The mechanism gives it a snakelike swivel action allowing it to roll on flat surfaces and inclines.

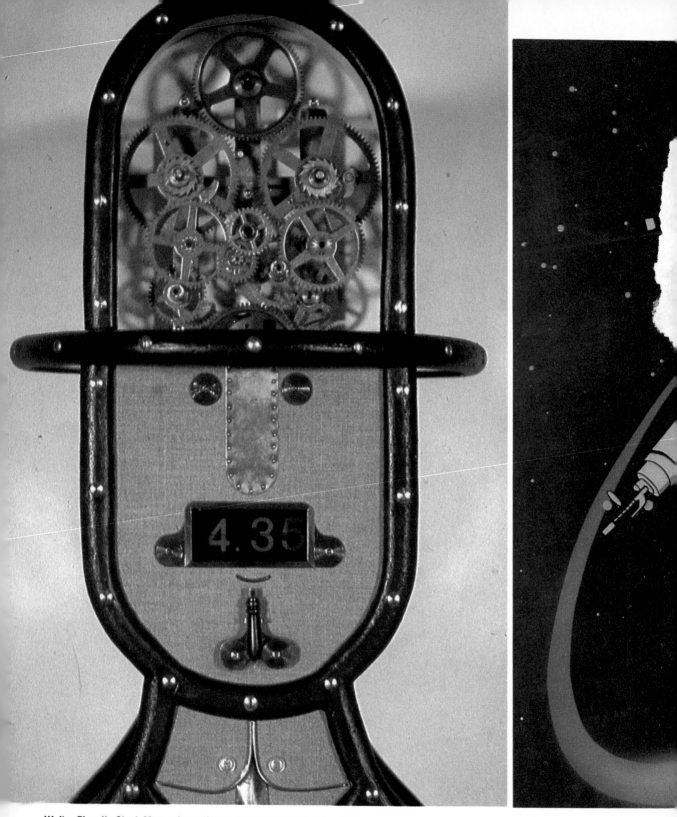

Walter Einsel's Clock Man, whose "gears turn, simulating thought."

C8

Japanese cartoonist Osamu Tezuka created the character Astro-Boy in 1951. Here Astro-Boy soars through space, in search of adventure.

In his later work, Phoenix 2772, Tezuka's scientists used this robot for the research and development of "magma energy."

◄*Soldier robots from* Phoenix 2772.

Artist Toby Buonagurio created a mobile robot out of ceramic with glass, acrylic paint, flocking, and glitter, 1979.

C12

Military interest in walking machines resulted in a British proposal in 1940 to construct a thousand-ton walking tank, and the U.S. Army sponsored research on the mechanics of walking vehicles in the late 1950s and early 1960s. "The need for military legged vehicles is due to the fact that legs are still the fastest way to cross rough country where battles are usually fought. While airplanes can fly faster than birds and ships can swim faster than fish, no ground vehicle has yet been built which can move over broken terrain as fast as a horse," reports Professor Ali Seireg of the University of Wisconsin in Madison.[22]

In the late 1960s, General Electric built an experimental four-legged truck for the army in the hope that such trucks could transport troops ashore from ships or wade into mud and push out a mired Jeep. The program proved unsuccessful and was discontinued after the first prototype.

The moon exploration program also precipitated interest in walking machines because the moon's surface was

In 1980, Shigeo Hirose and Yoji Umetani, of the Tokyo Institute of Technology, built this four-legged walking machine, "Perambulating Vehicle Mark II," or PV II for short. The walker has eight tactile sensors, is electrically powered, and tethered to a microcomputer.

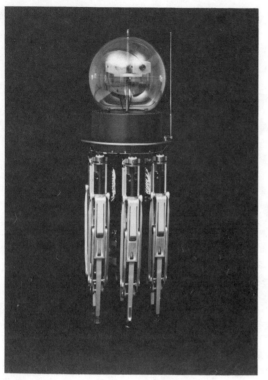

Odex 1.

believed to be covered with soft, light dust that would not support wheeled exploration vehicles. A series of lunar vehicles were proposed in the early 1970s.

In 1975, Professor Ali Seireg and R. M. Peterson reported the successful completion of a three-legged walker that was powered by compressed air. Concurrently, Seireg was developing an exoskeletal walking machine to provide paraplegics with locomotion. Other research in this area was being conducted at the Institute for Automation and Telecommunications in Belgrade, Yugoslavia, by M. Vukobratovic, and at Waseda University in Tokyo, Japan, by I. Kato. Tokyo University researchers also have developed a series of walkers, including a four-legged device that can climb stairs.

Research on six-legged walkers in the United States is currently under way at Carnegie-Mellon University's Robotics Institute in Pittsburgh, Pennsylvania, and at Ohio State University in Columbus, Ohio, and Odetics, Inc., in Anaheim, California.

At Carnegie-Mellon, Visiting Professor Ivan Sutherland, the father of computer graphics and co-founder of Evans and Sutherland, built a hydraulically actuated walking machine. To construct the walker, the researcher asked such questions as "Why do most animals have two and four legs and not three?" and "Why does six seem to be such a special number for insects?" Study of the coordination of six-legged insects showed that at least three legs are always on the ground for stabilization. After much study, they produced a sixteen-hundred-pound, gasoline-powered walking machine that can carry a human.

At Ohio State University, Robert McGee and associates have also been building a six-legged walker that adjusts the height of its legs to keep its body level when traversing an irregular terrain. The researchers consulted ethologist Robert Franklin of the University of Oregon, who found that daddy longlegs use their longest pair of legs as feelers to judge their gait. Sweeping the ground ahead, the longer legs seem to make eyes less essential for navigation than previously thought. To keep itself level while walking over bumps, the walker, called the "Ohio State University Hexapod," has a vertical gyroscope and pendulums. The feet have force-sensing devices so that they can conform to the terrain. Algorithms are being developed to combine information from both types of sensing and coordinate several kinds of gaits. The computer-controlled OSU Hexapod is four feet,

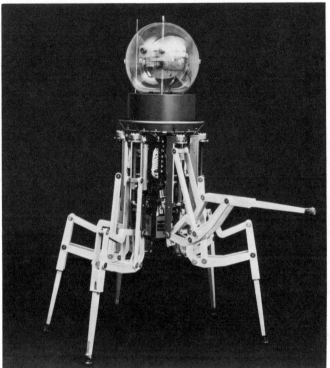

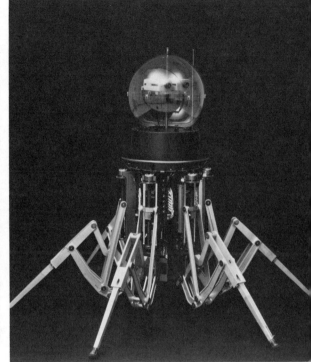

Two different profiles of Odex 1.

ten inches long, stands three feet tall, and weighs about 285 pounds. The legs are mounted on an aluminum frame and each has three joints, powered by electric motors.

The problems these researchers confront make such projects very long term. Work at Ohio State, which is funded by the National Science Foundation, was ridiculed by Senator William Proxmire, Democrat of Wisconsin. He gave them a Golden Fleece Award for what he considered wasteful government spending. If progress has been slow, it is because the problems of balance and multilimb coordination are formidable. According to Professor David Orin, of Ohio State, there are 40 million possible sequences of leg movements or gaits for a six-legged machine.[23]

In the Soviet Union, the government supports work on a six-legged walker. Though little is known about the effort, at Moscow State University of Mechanics, it is reportedly more advanced than the one at Ohio State.

When Odetics of Anaheim, California, unveiled a six-legged walker called "Odex 1" on March 22, 1983, many considered it an engineering feat (although the *Wall Street Journal* ridiculed it). Odetics is the world's leading manufacturer of space-borne magnetic tape recorders, which are used in satellites. Odex 1 was the company's first effort in robotics.

In describing stages in the functionoid's development, Odetics chairman of the board Joel Slutzky surpasses the enthusiasm of a father awaiting his toddler's first step. "At least a dozen times there was just absolute elation," he says. The first step was so momentous that Slutzky says: "I was in a meeting with customers when a note from the engineering manager was delivered. The note read 'It lifted.' I couldn't even finish the meeting, I was so excited. I had to explain the note, leave the meeting, and go over there. I *had* to see it." It was the zenith of a project conceived eight years earlier. Odetics says the functionoid is a feasibility model and that other configurations to suit specified applications will follow.

The Odex 1 can travel over any terrain, at about two miles per hour and, when stationary, can lift up to six times its own weight of 370 pounds. Each leg is controlled by one microprocessor, which receives information from sensors on leg joints about the location of the leg. A total of six microprocessors report this information to a seventh, central microprocessor. A human operator commands the functionoid via radio link to go in a certain direction at a certain speed, and from that point on, the microprocessors take over, coordinating its gait.

To make Odex 1 lift and climb, however, the operator has to switch into another mode that allows him to control legs individually. For example, when Odex 1 climbs into the back of a pickup truck, the operator must position two legs on the truck bed. The other legs then complete the climb on their own. In this mode, the operator participates in the functionoid's feedback loop. He is the man-in-the-loop because he has used his eyes and brain to give the functionoid information about the environment.

The functionoid's jointed legs can assume several "profiles" that enhance its agility in certain environs. In the "narrow" profile, it has a width of 21 inches and so can walk through doorways, hallways and other narrow openings. To take a step in this profile, Odex 1 first moves three legs forward simultaneously and then three hind legs simultaneously, so that it looks something like a moving inchworm. In the "tuck" profile, its legs are drawn up close to the body. When in its "tall" and "low" profiles, the functionoid stands 78 and 36 inches high, respectively. In the "narrow articu-

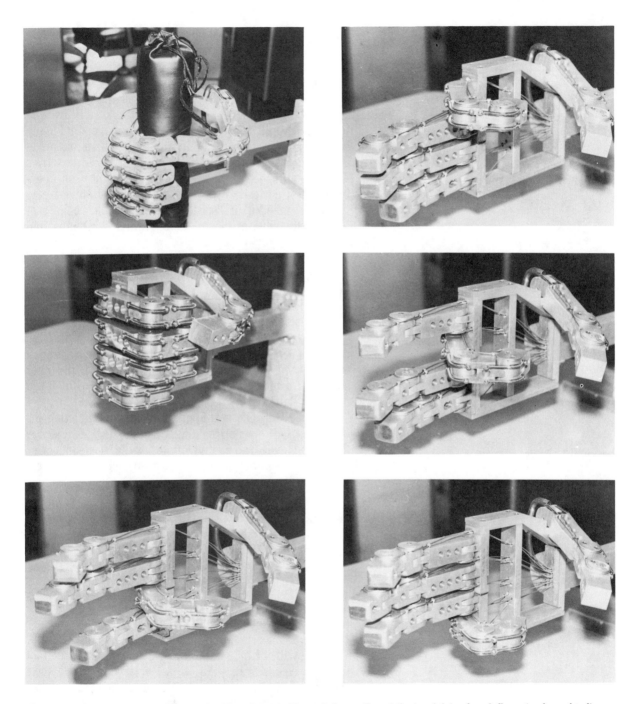

Stepper motors control the pulleys and cables connected to each finger. To get the two joints of each finger to close simultaneously, the linear velocity of the second joint's cable had to be twice as fast as that of the first joint. Here, each finger and the thumb are shown closed and, finally, the hand grips an object.

lated'' and "wide articulated" profiles, Odex 1 stands on five legs and uses the sixth as a manipulator, to push open a door, for example. Odex 1 lifts objects by raising itself from the squat position.

According to Slutzky, 50 percent of the earth's land surface is inaccessible to wheeled or track vehicles, and therefore man has not had a chance to explore it. Many areas are thought to be rich in minerals, others are worth exploring because they might help Third World countries gain self-sufficiency, and still others we might wish to explore out of curiosity. Odex 1 could be used to investigate Antarctica; the Yukon Territory in Canada; the Gobi desert in Mongolia, Siberia; the jungles of Surinam in Guiana, and the great Australian outback.

Besides mining and exploring, Slutzky envisions wartime applications, particularly for troop support. A functionoid could assist in carrying the wounded from battlefields or handling munitions and other hazardous materials. He suggests that the functionoid could be useful in tactics to confuse the enemy and cause diversion. "We may have the day when robots are fighting robots or facing robots, and in one sense that's a grim thing to think about and in the other sense it's a lot better than men fighting men. But it's a reality," Slutzky says.

In other peacetime applications, future functionoids could be used to repair satellites, act as sentries and fire fighters, handle radioactive materials in nuclear power plants and linear accelerators, and even participate in deep-sea exploration.

GETTING ROBOTS TO THINK

In 1949, British brain surgeon, Sir Geoffrey Jefferson said, "Not until a machine can write a sonnet or compose a concerto because of thoughts and emotions felt, and not by the chance fall of symbols, could we agree that machine equals brain—that is, not only write it but know that it had written it. No mechanism could feel (and not merely artificially signal, an easy contrivance) pleasure at its successes, grief when its valves fuse, be warmed by flattery, be made miserable by its mistakes, be charmed by

sex, be angry or miserable when it cannot get what it wants."[24]

Alan Turing, a mathematician, had a different opinion. He replied: "[Solving mathematical problems] is only a foretaste of what is to come, and only the shadow of what is going to be. We have to have some experience with the machine before we really know its capabilities. It may take years before we settle down to the new possibilities, but I do not see why it should not enter any one of the fields normally covered by the human intellect, and eventually compete on equal terms. I do not think you can even draw the line about sonnets, though the comparison is perhaps a little bit unfair because a sonnet written by a machine will be better appreciated by another machine."[25]

Whether or not machines think has been debated through the ages, but only in the latter part of this century has it seemed possible to create thinking machines and so test the proposition. Never before have we been so close to intelligent machines. But for some computer scientists and AI researchers, machines will not be intelligent until they can learn from experiences in their environments. For others, perception is itself a subcategory of intelligence.

If a computer's intelligence is thought of as mainly a

In an effort to transfer robotics technology to medicine and agriculture, Shigeo Hirose of the Tokyo Institute of Technology has conducted research on grippers that can gently conform to objects of any shape. A series of active cord mechanisms (ACMs), begun in 1976, resulted from studying flexible structures in nature, such as snake spinal cords, elephant trunks, and octopus tentacles.

software matter, testing its intelligence would, to a large extent, mean running some estimation of an intelligent program and then characterizing subsequent behavior. And since a robot is nothing without a computer, one could approach questions regarding robot intelligence the same way.

If hardware and perception are included in this consideration, then, as we have seen, it is still true that even if camera "eyes" and mechanical robot "hands" were perfected today, no one would know how to write programs for them. The levels of sophistication of software and hardware are not quite in synch. So testing for intelligence would be premature.

Debate over the question "Can machines think?" is swayed, as in the past, by the availability and capabilities of both software and hardware.

For Descartes, who theorized about a hypothetical automaton's ability to reason, machine intelligence was far removed from testability. In *Discourse on Method* he wrote, "It is *in practice* [author's emphasis] impossible to conceive of enough diversity of behavior in a machine to make it act in all the circumstances of life in the way in which our reason makes us act."[26]

But with the design of the Analytical Engine in the 1840s, it seemed that the answer to machine intelligence would come soon, perhaps even when such a machine was built. Ada, the countess of Lovelace, and Lord Byron's daughter, imagined that the issue, at least as far as the Analytical Engine was concerned, would be settled with experience. A talented mathematician considered by some to have been the first programmer, she collaborated with Babbage but never had the chance to run her programs on his machine. Her "software" efforts, including a scheme for a tic-tac-toe–playing machine, were based on drawings of the Analytical Engine "hardware." In her 1842 memoirs, the countess discussed the engine's capabilities, calling it the "executive right-hand of abstract algebra" and distinguishing it from the Difference Engine and earlier calculating devices. She wrote:

"The bounds of *arithmetic* were, however, outstepped the moment the idea of applying the cards had occurred; and the Analytical Engine does not occupy common ground with mere "calculating machines." It holds a position wholly its own; and the considerations it suggests are most interesting in nature. In enabling mechanism to combine together *general* symbols, in successions of unlimited variety and extent, a uniting link is established between the operations of matter and the abstract mental processes of the *most abstract* branch of mathematical science. A new vast language is developed for the future use of analysis, in which to wield its truths so that these may become of more speedy and accurate practical application for the purpose of mankind than the means hitherto in our possession have rendered possible. Thus not only the mental and the material, but the theoretical and the practical in the mathematical world, are brought into more intimate and effective connexion with each other. We are not aware of its being on record that anything partaking of the nature of what is so well designated the *Analytical* Engine has been hitherto proposed, or even thought of, as a practical possibility, any more than the idea of a thinking or of a reasoning machine."[27]

Besides being the "uniting link" between "operations of matter" and "the most abstract branch of mathematical science," the Analytical Engine was capable of both synthesis and analysis. But the "*analysing* process must have been gone through by a human mind in order to obtain data upon which the engine then *synthetically* builds its results."[28] Cautioning that it is easy to overrate the new and remarkable, yet not wishing to undervalue the Analytical Engine, the countess concluded that "the Analytical Engine has no pretensions whatever to *originate* anything. It can do *whatever we know how to order it* to perform. It can *follow* analysis; but it has no power of *anticipating* any analytical relations or truths. Its province is to assist us in making *available* what we are already acquainted with. . . ."[29]

If originating is akin to thinking, then according to Ada, the engine was not a thinking machine. But she reserved the final answer regarding the engine's ability to "*really* even be able to *follow* analysis in its whole extent," for a later time when the "actual existence of the engine" would yield "actual experience of its practical results."

A century later, analog and digital computers were up and running. They were further refined during World War II and practical results changed the course of history. When British Intelligence captured a German cipher machine, dubbed "Enigma," with which the Nazi High Command transmitted military messages, authorities tried to crack the German code with methods used during World War I. Failing, they drew up a list of the best minds in England and set up a recruiting program to train cryptanalysts. One

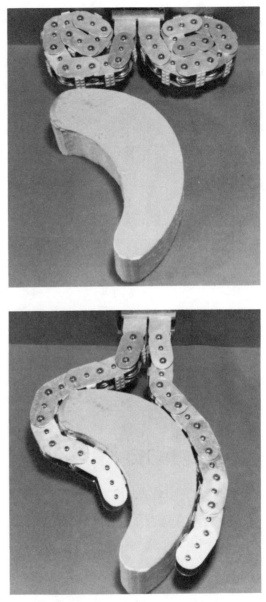

Here a later ACM wraps around a curved object. Its ability to carefully exert uniform pressure makes turning patients in hospital beds and picking easily damaged fruits possible future applications.

This unusual-looking robot, also designed at Tokyo Institute of Technology, creeps from pipe to pipe and checks for cracks. It is hoped that the robot will be used to inspect pipes in nuclear power plants.

recruit was Alan Turing, who played a pivotal role in designing the computer that decoded Enigma. Decoded messages were sent directly to Winston Churchill and were crucial to the strategy and success of the Allies.

In 1937, Turing had made his mark by proposing an abstract machine that helped characterize what kinds of problems could be computed. The machine, later called the "Universal Turing Machine," also helped define algorithms, the step-by-step instructions for solving problems that are the basis for computer programs today. The Turing machine was an important contribution to the emerging field of computer science. Turing's vision of intelligent computers, as expressed after the war, suggested research goals for the next three decades.

The post-war era was rich with researchers in and outside of computer science, asking what thinking is. Those approaching the question through neuroscience, cybernetics, and information theory, spun a complicated web of interaction. Turing, Norbert Weiner, famous for feedback theory and cybernetics, and John von Neumann, a mathematician at Princeton University's Institute for Advanced Studies credited with conceiving the idea of the stored program, all knew each other.

Weiner and von Neumann were influenced by Warren McCulloch and Walter Pitts, who proposed in 1943 that the behavior of neurons, and therefore intelligent behavior, could be described using mathematical models. The on-off behavior of neurons, they thought, corresponded to the on-off switches of computers. This theory has since proved incorrect—neurons also exhibit intermediate signals that do not fit into either "on" or "off."

With the publication of Weiner's *Cybernetics*, debate over the supposed structural analogy between neurons and switches extended to debate over a functional analogy between brain and computer. The brain surgeon Sir Geoffrey Jefferson led the opposition. Weiner, von Neumann, and Turing each argued for a functional analogy, to differing degrees.

As researchers everywhere investigated and debated the relationship between the brain and the new "electronic brain," lines between scientific disciplines blurred and the debate seemed to enter the realm of philosophy of mind. The nature of thinking and knowing, believing and feeling, are the topics of epistemology. So, although Turing was not a philosopher, his seminal essay "Computing Machinery and

Intelligence," appeared in a 1950 issue of the philosophy journal *Mind*. In this essay he proposed a test to determine whether machines think.

Turing realized that the question "Can machines think?" was fraught with emotional connotations and approached it instead by asking what it would take to convince an ordinary person that a machine thinks. So he presented the problem in the form of a game in which an interrogator communicates via Teletype with a man and a woman in separate rooms. The interrogator must determine which one is the woman. But his task is complicated by the rule that the woman must try to aid the interrogator and the man must try to confuse the interrogator by responding the way he thinks the woman would. So if, in this "Imitation Game," the interrogator types "Describe the length of your hair," both the man and the woman type back descriptions of a woman's hairstyle. After a series of questions the interrogator must decide who is female and who is the imitator.

Turing asked whether the interrogator would be fooled as often if a machine took the part of the man. A machine that played as successfully as a man could be said to think, Turing concluded. Therefore machines would pass Turing's test for intelligence if they were successful in the Imitation Game.

After describing this game, Turing refuted nine objections to the proposal that machines think. Although too extensive to summarize here, these arguments showed that Turing believed there was a functional analogy between the brain and the computer. Both were information processors, and insight into the organization of one would give insight into the organization of the other, as Pamela McCorduck reports in her book *Machines Who Think*.[30]

Turing also described the relationship between machine thinking and learning. This paragraph is extraordinary, for it touches on the core issue that researchers now tackle in their efforts to make computers, and thus robots, smart:

"[A learning machine] might still be getting results of the type desired when the machine was first set up, but in a much more efficient manner. In such a case one would have to admit that the progress of the machine had not been foreseen when its original instructions were put in. It would be like a pupil who had learnt much from his master, but had added much more by his own work. When this happens I feel that one is obliged to regard the machine as showing intelli-

This photo, taken by a camera on board the satellite **SPAS-01**, *shows the Space Shuttle* Challenger *and its remote manipulator arm. Also visible is the* **Challeng-**er's *cargo bay, which holds protective cradles for retrieved satellites. During this June 1983 expedition, as-tronauts used the manipulator to retrieve the* **SPAS** *and stowed it in the cargo bay for the return to Earth.*

gence. As soon as one can provide a reasonably large memory capacity it should be possible to begin to experiment on these lines. The memory capacity of the human brain is of the order of ten thousand million binary digits. But most of this is probably used in remembering visual impressions, and other comparatively wasteful ways. One might reasonably hope to be able to make some real progress with a few million digits, especially if one confined one's investigation to some rather limited field such as the game of chess."[31]

For Turing, an intelligent machine had to be able to learn. Learning meant modifying the initial program, or programs, with which it had been endowed by man.

Although Turing did not live to see it, "experimentation on these lines" began in the late 1950s, with increased computer memories. Much early AI work did in fact focus on chess programs, because chess is the game we associate most with human intellect and because chess strategy closely resembles a logic tree. Claude E. Shannon, a Bell Telephone Laboratories mathematician known for his statistical theory of information, began the effort in early 1950 by proposing a hypothetical chess-playing machine in *Scientific American,* which Turing had doubtless read.

Although Turing mentioned vision in the context of memory, other more specific vision research was undertaken by neurophysiologists and computer scientists in the fifties, as both groups attempted to understand the same gestalt. Although they took different approaches, advances in one discipline often meant advances in the other, as Turing predicted they would.

Research in pattern-recognition software resulted in a program, reported in 1955, containing a principle so fundamental that it not only altered approaches to software design in general, it also influenced the inquiry of neurophysiology vision researchers. The principle of that program, created by Oliver G. Selfridge, Weiner's former assistant, and G. P. Dinneen, both of MIT's Lincoln Laboratories, was that many simple subprocesses could produce a system that behaved in complex ways. The program recognized patterns because it computed characteristics of capital letters—its subprocess was to pick out several features, assign values, and, in a sense, reconstruct the whole letter from the selected characteristics. We have seen how some of today's vision and tactile research programs incorporate this method. The Selfridge-Dinneen program could learn, to some extent, because it chose some characteristics and eliminated others.

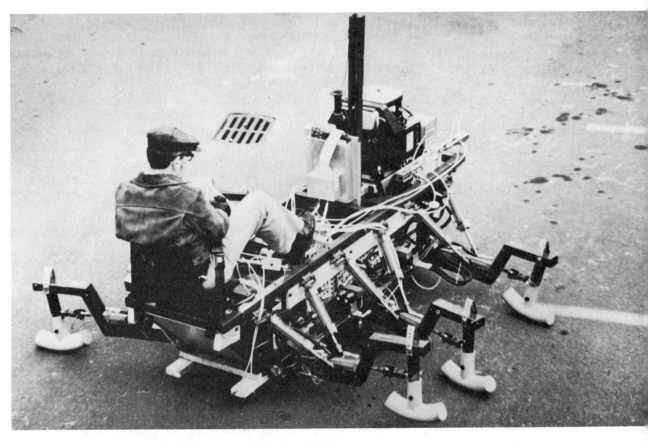

Ivan Sutherland's walking machine.

Scientists at Rand Corporation soon constructed a chess program applying the same principle. The principle also showed up in a 1959 breakthrough vision paper, resulting from research on frog eyes, which showed that the optic nerve acts as a data processor because it sends specific kinds of information to corresponding parts of the brain. Such data reduction by simple, specific processors culminates in a complex, but interpretable whole image. The findings are one of the early accomplishments of artificial intelligence research.

More was heard from Rand's chess programmers at a special summer workshop that was held at Dartmouth College in Hanover, New Hampshire, during the summer of 1956. Conceived by Dartmouth Associate Professor of Mathematics John McCarthy, it was called the "Dartmouth Summer Research Project on Artificial Intelligence," and so McCarthy is credited with coining the phrase "artificial intelligence."

Assembled at this event were many of the men who would later found university and industry artificial intelligence laboratories throughout the United States. Organizing the project with McCarthy were Marvin L. Minsky, then a Harvard Fellow in Mathematics and Neurology; Nathaniel Rochester, IBM manager of information research, and Claude E. Shannon of Bell Telephone Laboratories. Other attending scientists included Selfridge; Ray Solomonoff, also of MIT, and Arthur Samuel of IBM. Those who came for short visits included Alex Bernstein of IBM and Allen Newell and Herbert A. Simon, both of Carnegie Institute of Technology (now Carnegie-Mellon University) and the Rand Corporation.

The goals expressed in the workshop grant request to the Rockefeller Foundation reflect the enormous ambitions of enthusiastic scientists about to embark on a new mode of scientific inquiry. The proposal read: "The study is to proceed on the basis of the conjecture that every aspect of learning or any other feature of intelligence can in principle be so precisely described that a machine can be made to simulate it. An attempt will be made to find how to make machines use language, form abstractions and concepts, solve kinds of problems now reserved for humans, and improve themselves. We think that a significant advance can be made in one or more of these problems if a carefully selected group of scientists work on it together for a summer." In an internal memo, foundation officials had suggested that "the theory of brain function as related to mathematics of computation is still in the pre-Newtonian or pre-Einsteinian phase where what may be needed is some brilliant insight rather than group discussion." But in the end, half the requested funds were granted.

Most participants now recognize that they were naïve to expect to achieve the goals outlined in a few months. But Simon and Newell did give a pivotal presentation—perhaps more so than it seemed at the time, according to McCorduck. These researchers arrived at the workshop with printouts of a program called "Logic Theorist." That program, developed simultaneously with the chess-playing program mentioned earlier, and with the help of a third Rand researcher, J. C. Shaw, turned out proofs of mathematical theorems in Alfred North Whitehead and Bertrand Russell's *Principia Mathematica*. It even discovered a shorter and more satisfying proof to a particular theorem, and Simon communicated the news to Lord Russell, as McCorduck reports. Although

Russell was delighted, *The Journal of Symbolic Logic* declined to publish the proof, which was presented as an article co-authored by Logic Theorist. And yet, by coming up with a superior proof, the program had fulfilled the Countess of Lovelace's requirement that an intelligent machine "originate" and the program had gotten "results of the type desired... but in a more efficient manner," and so would very likely have satisfied Turing.

Still, the hoped-for "significant advance" was not achieved that summer. Instead, the workshop clarified research goals that the participants would pursue for much of their professional lives. And their interpretations of the meaning of artificial intelligence and what a true learning program must do, dictate the direction of AI labs today.

McCarthy and Minsky went on to found the first AI laboratory in 1957 at MIT. McCarthy left MIT in 1963 to found Stanford University's AI lab, which he now directs. Herbert Simon, who has a Ph.D. in political science and is a 1978 Nobel laureate in economics, and Allen Newell, built Carnegie-Mellon's AI department. In 1980, this was expanded to the Robotics Institute, now under D. Raj Reddy.

McCarthy's approach to AI is quite philosophical. He originated the computer language called "LISP" for computing with symbolic expressions that is used by many AI researchers. And he pioneered using mathematical logic to prove the correctness of computer programs. But McCarthy's primary interest is in what he calls "commonsense knowledge," which would allow computers to combine general knowledge about the world with facts about a particular situation in order to make decisions. Part of the agenda for AI research, he says, is to identify what knowledge and reasoning methods are required for common sense and what AI tasks require these. "While many impressive and useful artificial programs don't have or need much common sense," McCarthy says, "general intelligence requires it, and so do many important AI programs. Moreover, until programs have some general common sense, a human will have to use his common sense to determine whether a program is usable in a given situation."

McCarthy explained the need for representing commonsense knowledge, using an example involving robots, at the April 1983 Computer Culture symposium in New York City sponsored by the New York Academy of Sciences. "If I wave a glass of water around," McCarthy told the audience, "people in the front row might feel threatened but those in

NASA's Jet Propulsion Laboratory in Pasadena, California, and the Veterans Administration teamed up to develop a voice-controlled mechanical arm and wheelchair. Michael Condon, a quadraplegic, demonstrated the prototype chair before the Committee on Science and Technology in the House of Representatives in January 1976. The arm and wheelchair respond to thirty-five one-word commands.

the third row would not. The guy next to me might jump, but that would not be because he has set up equations for hydrodynamics, mechanical equations, etcetera. He has common-sense physical knowledge." To predict the behavior of an object, however, one cannot get information about its position, the velocity of all the molecules it contains, etcetera. And even if one had this information, which can be used to derive the Laws of Motion and the Laws of Gases, one could not use it without applying common sense. But there is, as yet, no way "to represent the initial conditions [for common sense] in a robot in the third row of the audience so that it sits still and in a robot in the first row so that it gets out of the way."

Besides his other work, McCarthy has been examining the components of common sense since 1958. Some components allow for changes in situations and changes in word meanings depending on context, for example. Ways to teach a computer this sort of "ambiguity tolerance" are needed so that simple modifications of behavior can take place. Not enough work is being done in this area today, he says, although it is the first prerequisite for machine learning.

If McCarthy's approach leans toward the philosophical, Minsky's leans toward the psychoanalytic. An admirer of Freud, Minsky would like to see AI programs contain inhibited processes akin to unconscious censors and the Super Ego. In 1979 he published a memory theory called "K-lines" based on the assumption that at any moment there are many mental processes going on in the mind. "Maybe [there are] a million little machines lying around in your brain and when you solve a problem you might be using a certain thousand of them and the other ones are off," he explains. You are using a list of programs or agents or processes to solve that problem. Such a list, a K-line, could be turned on for a computer to solve a problem. He says: "Suppose you have a big shop and you fix a bicycle and then when you're fixing the bicycle you need this size wrench, and that kind of clamp, and so forth and you paint them green whenever you use them. After you finish bicycle fixing, you put them all back and then some other time you fix the toaster and when you fix the toaster you paint the tools red. And these colors are the K-lines. Then some day another bicycle comes in and so without thinking, you just go and get all the green tools. Then you'll be in a good state to fix the thing, you won't get all these tools for fixing toasters. . . . So a K-line is just a set of ideas you use for solving a problem."

Minsky advocates developing programs that make machines learn by analogy. Such a machine would "see a new situation and have various ways of remembering old situations and then see which [situations] have a lot of features in common." MIT AI lab director Patrick Winston, Minsky's former graduate student, is now working on learning by analogy.

Minsky is working on what he calls layers of learning that occur simultaneously in humans. "I suspect that what we do is, when we notice something we also think of some use for it or some purpose. Everything has purposes," he says. At his company, Thinking Machines in Cambridge, Massachusetts, he is building an enormous parallel processor, invented by Daniel Hillis and called the Connection Machine, so that he can experiment with such a program and other K-line-type programs.

Although he thinks that most programs are "purposeless," and "flounder a lot," he admires one written by Douglas Lenat that runs continuously on a computer at Stanford University. Minsky calls it a "living program" that learns and remembers what it learns. Its three accomplishments are discovering prime numbers, square roots, and—most recently—figuring out a new kind of transistor. It displays its discoveries by listing things it considers interesting and things it considers boring, Minsky explains.

Although Minsky may use anthropomorphic terms to describe a computer or a program, he does not, by any means, insist that machine learning or intelligence emulate the human brain or mind. "If you think about AI as theoretical psychology," he says, "there may be other ways to think that aren't exactly how the brain does it. You might find other ways. If we find a way to make a pretty smart machine and it turns out that the brain doesn't work that way, that's terrific. So we'll have another way." The statement that theories of thinking might not be biologically confirmed does not disturb him. "Eventually the biologists will figure out how [the brain] works and then there'll be two [ways of being smart]."

On the other hand, Minsky says, "Thinking is a matter of degree. I think you say something thinks when you don't know how it works. And the more you understand and make these programs, they get better and better at learning and figuring things out. But there isn't any point at which they think. That's just a sort of social word for a certain quality of performance. It's not clear that people think, too."

Professor Tomas Lozano-Perez, of MIT's artificial intelligence laboratory, and a group of visiting students program an IBM computer so that it instructs a robot arm to pick up blocks.

Like McCarthy, Minsky does not believe there are enough researchers working on theoretical issues—progress has been quite slow. But Minsky is not sure that it would necessarily be better to speed things up. "I have mixed feelings about whether society could tolerate intelligent machines. It was three hundred years from Newton to Einstein, and mechanics developed very nicely.... If artificial intelligence came in ten years, it might be an intolerable thing for most people."

He likens the state of the art in AI not to pre-Newtonian or pre-Einsteinian physics, as did the Rockefeller officials, but to late eighteenth-century chemistry. That science was on solid footing for the first time when Lavoisier understood the conservation of mass in chemistry and he and Priestly discovered that gases were chemicals. It took over two hundred years for the specifics to be sorted out. The situation in AI is similar, Minsky says. "It seems to me that what's happened is that the right ideas about what minds are, are now around. But nobody knows much of the details."

But dangers do not have to be physical. Since robots are designed to do the same tasks over and over again without change, and cannot become bored, they can make it unnecessary for human beings to spend much of their lives in boredom and stultification. As many as 10 million American workers are, in the absence of robots, compelled to work at such repetitive labors.

And yet the advent of robotization has its disadvantages, although even if there were no disadvantages at all, there might still be resistance to the advent of robots.

Human beings tend to be uncomfortable with change, even hostile to it, and generally this tendency increases with age. Writings of the past abound with statements concerning the manner in which things grow steadily worse with the years. Socrates complained that the youngsters of his day lacked the respect and manners that were prevalent when *he* was young. From generation to generation, elders feel that manners decay, traditions are flouted, respect and decency disappear while materialism and selfishness rise, and everything just deteriorates.

From our vantage point in the present, we may well believe that people in the past were unduly pessimistic in such matters since it is obvious, as we look at the development of society that time has *not* caused a one-way degeneration of the quality of life. Granted, we face unprecedented problems of overpopulation, pollution, potential shortages of resources and, above all, the danger of nuclear war. But the fact remains that the human species and the society it builds has largely become better off with succeeding generations. Most of us are more secure and comfortable now, and less hungry and fearful than we would have been in any previous century.

Especially if we are over forty, we may well feel that *this* generation has degenerated compared with its forebears, that conditions today are a good notch below what they were when we were young, that young people today are horrible compared to the rather angelic characters we were in our own day, and what's more, we can all remember aspects of our youthful world that have been utterly spoiled. "They don't write music (publish books, make movies, manufacture candy bars, and so on) like they used to." All these feelings arise out of our discomfort with change. Whatever was, was right. What we grew accustomed to in our teenage years was cosmic law; whatever changes occur thereafter are examples of society going to the dogs.

CREATING THE FUTURE: ROBOTS AND SOCIETY

Science-fiction robots could be nonhumanoid—simple geometry—multiple legs and eyes—tentacles in place of arms.

The development of the microchip made possible for the first time machines that were truly entitled to the name robot. But in order to make these robot machines more broadly useful, we now need other advances—mobility; hands as dexterous as those of human beings; various senses such as vision, hearing, and touch, and something like reasoning power. These are neither easy nor flatly impossible achievements. There is hope that, with sufficient ingenuity, such qualities may be developed.

However, technological challenges are only some of the barriers that keep society from making full use of robots. In fact, it is just conceivable that the more advanced, versatile, and able robots become, the *less* likely they will be to take their place among us. There remains another barrier, after all, that may be higher and more formidable than any merely technological difficulty—and that is people's attitudes toward robots.

It seems odd for people to feel hostility toward the advent of robots, in view of the undoubted benefits they can confer on society. Robots can help produce more goods more cheaply than can be achieved without them. Robots can help produce goods more reliably, with fewer mistakes and shortcomings than is possible without them. Even from a nationalistic viewpoint, robots can help the United States maintain its competitive edge against other nations that might charge ahead with robotic technology.

From the human standpoint, robots can do dangerous

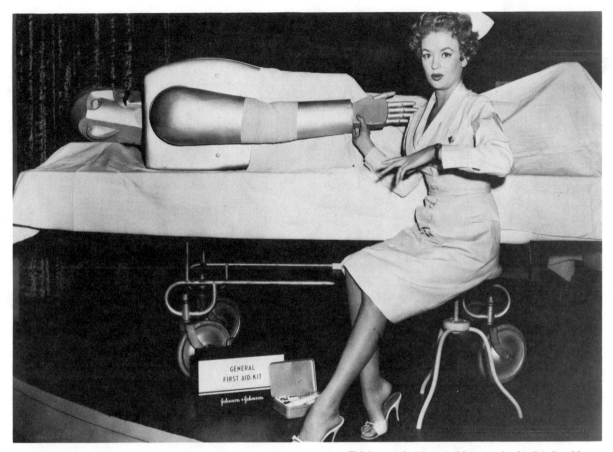

Thinko, a robot invented by a mad scientist, has his pulse checked in Sex Kittens Go to College, *1960.*

It is no wonder, then, that the more drastic and all-pervasive a change, the more our uneasiness grows. Nothing introduces change more drastically than some startling technological advance. For perspective, consider how the advent of the automobile, or of television, changed American society, and how quickly. Therefore, nothing should arouse suspicion like some dramatic technological advance. In other words, our morbid fear of anything new—"neophobia"—is particularly exaggerated by anything technologically new and becomes "technophobia."

Still, feeling the fear and acting upon it are two different things. There is no question that the sight of robots at work in industry may arouse uneasiness in many people simply because they are unfamiliar sights. There is also no question that the uneasiness would grow if robots looked more human than they do now. But would this feeling in itself prevent robots from being accepted?

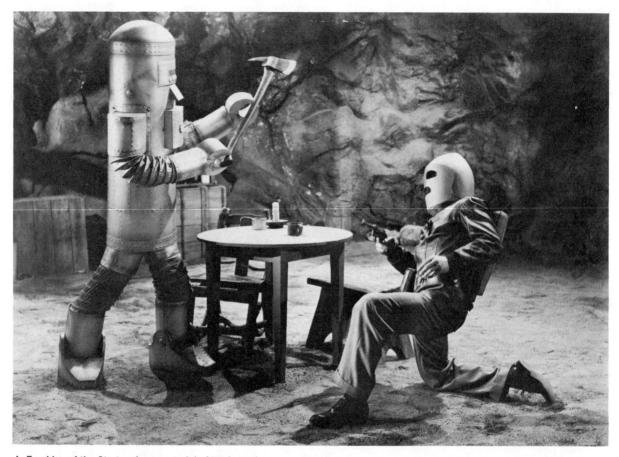

In Zombies of the Stratosphere, *a serial of twelve episodes, robots from outer space planned to blow up the Earth.*

We live in a period of rapid change; we have been living in one ever since the Industrial Revolution two centuries ago. The portion of humanity that has lived in those regions affected by the Industrial Revolution felt changes directly at the emergence of the steam engine, the electrical generator, the internal-combustion engine, the vacuum tube, and the transistor. The portion of humanity that lived outside the reach of the new technologies nevertheless felt change indirectly since the industrialized nations could dominate, colonialize, impoverish, and sometimes advance them.

It is fair to say, then, that we have grown used to change; or that, at any rate, we should have grown used to it. Futhermore, even if we have remained uneasy with change despite all that has taken place, and have *not* grown used to it, history shows that we haven't stopped it. Opposition has not been entirely absent, but it has seldom taken militant form, and then only weakly. Nor has that opposition ever succeeded in stopping the change, or even in slowing its coming very much. In the end, change has been accepted, however sullenly.

There were times, in fact, when technological change was not only accepted, but was accepted with enthusiasm. To use examples already cited, the automobile fascinated Americans from the start, and every technological advance that made it easier to operate, more comfortable, and faster, made it more acceptable. The love affair between the American and the automobile survives fifty thousand deaths a year, hundreds of thousands of lesser injuries, pollution of the atmosphere, and cacophony on the streets. Yet solving these problems by abandoning the automobile is unthinkable.

Television was accepted far more quickly still, and even more enthusiastically. Some glumly forecast the death of conversation (as if conversation among most people were anything more than a trite mumble). And while no one forecast the death of newspapers and magazines, it wouldn't have mattered if anyone had. Television was a change people wanted and they got it as soon as they could.

Might it not be that people would be just as enthusiastic about robots, and accept them into their lives and into the social fabric just as quickly as they did television, in view of the advantages that robots would bring with them?

There's a difference!

An automobile does things a human being desperately wants to do but can't on his own. A human being can't travel at fifty-five miles an hour for eight hours, and it is terribly convenient to be able to do so, if you want to go from New York to Cleveland in a day. Nor is the automobile a threat to you, since *your* hand is on the wheel, your foot on the gas, your eyes on the road. The automobile is merely a mechanical slave absolutely responsive to your will, as long as it is in good working order.

And so it is with television and all the other devices that have met with instant favor. Television brings entertainment or instruction into the home—something most of us want—and it is your hand on the control knobs that starts it, stops it, dictates the channel, and even modifies sound, color, brightness, and so on.

There is a functional difference in the case of the computer, however, that stands out even more sharply in the case of that computerized device we call a robot, and that

Above and opposite page: *In Stanley Kubrick and Arthur C. Clarke's film* 2001: A Space Odyssey, *the spaceship* Aries *becomes a deranged robot when the HAL computer malfunctions.*

will stand out ever more sharply the more closely the robot approximates human appearance. The robot, even a simple one, may be "only" a machine, and this may be demonstrable. Nevertheless, it performs functions which, until now, no machine could, so that the robot gives the illusion of possessing human ability, or even intelligence. A human being cannot help but feel vaguely threatened as he or she feels uniqueness totter. For that reason alone, we are not likely to embrace the robot the way we took the automobile and the television set to our bosoms. In fact, so outrageous does the production of a mechanical quasi-human being seem, that the feeling arises not only of personal violation, but possibly of an invasion of the prerogative of the Creator, who (we are taught in the Bible) created human beings in His own image.

These feelings are both exemplified and reinforced by such influential legendary and literary creations as the Golem, Frankenstein's Monster, and Capek's *R.U.R.* robots. All were attempts at illustrating the dangers of human efforts to overstep the boundary of natural life. Whether or not there is an inherent danger in artificial life and intelligence, and whether or not an angry deity strikes back, in these stories the result is the same—disaster.

The vague emotional turmoil over the robot, when people think of such a creation as a Frankenstein's Monster, would, however, surely not be enough to stop the advance of robotics. It hasn't so far, although resistance may stiffen in the future. After all, there is more to that resistance than just vague neophobia. There are definite and palpable disadvantages to the introduction of robots to our society, and these could reinforce such resistance enormously.

To use anything really new, one must go through the process of learning how to use it, and that may mean unlearning what one already knows.

Virtually all humans learn how to handle numerous complicated devices in their lifetimes, even if it is only the language of their parents and their society. The learning is not always easy, but once the complications *are* learned—and if they are learned properly—that learning is permanent and the use of the device becomes automatic. There is bound to be an enormous relief, if a person stops to think about it once in a while, that the learning process *is* over, and that use *has* become automatic.

If the thought arises that the use of the device must be unlearned, and that another form of learning must be taken up, carried through, and mastered, there is bound to be resistance. To have to go through the process again, when one has thought oneself to be done with it, is unbearable. This is particularly so for mature people, since, by and large, learning becomes more difficult as one grows older. As children, we learn our language perfectly and without an accent—or at least with precisely the accent of those around us. Learn a new language as an adult, however, and you will rarely be able to speak it without somehow giving away the fact that you are a foreigner.

We have a number of examples of the reluctance to unlearn and relearn, even when to do so is quite necessary. The system of common measures in the United States— inches, feet, yards, miles, ounces, pounds, pints, quarts, and gallons—is an incredibly complicated and nonsensical farrago of units that we are taught endlessly in school and that few of us ever remember beyond twelve inches to a foot and three feet to a yard. The rest of the world almost without exception uses the metric system which, in comparison, is simplicity itself. Using the metric system would save us endless hours of educational procedure that would be better spent on other things, that would benefit our trade and industry, and that would remove a terrible burden that the United States suffers when it competes for trade with the rest of the world. There would be the initial expense of

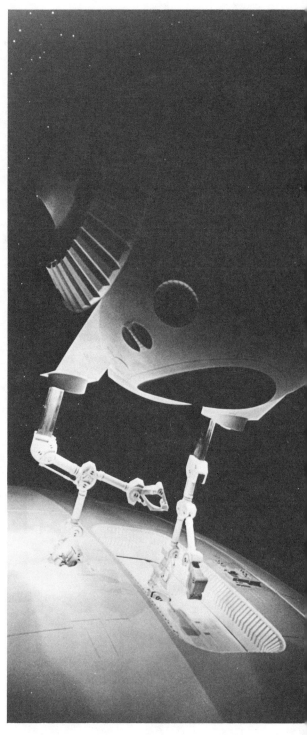

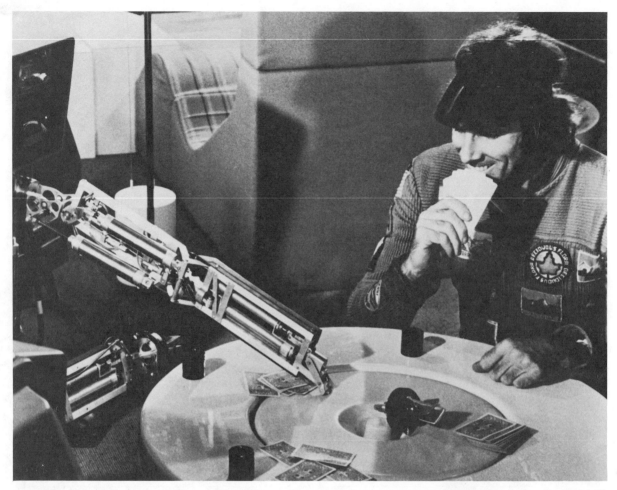

The botanist Lowell Freemant, played by Bruce Dern, has only robotic companionship in **Silent Running,** *a 1971 film.*

conversion, to be sure, but that would eventually be paid back by the savings that would ensue. (The initial expense would have been comparatively nominal if we had done it nearly two centuries ago when Thomas Jefferson had suggested we should.)

Why didn't we? Why haven't we since? Why don't we now? The American public fears the metric system and, if it had its way, would cling to the present system forever. Not because we know our present system, because we don't. We merely *think* we know it, because the words are familiar—"I love you a bushel and a peck" even though virtually no one knows how many pecks to a bushel, or what those units measure—and the mere *thought* that we know it is enough. We don't want to have to unlearn and relearn.

The same dread keeps the world from adopting a

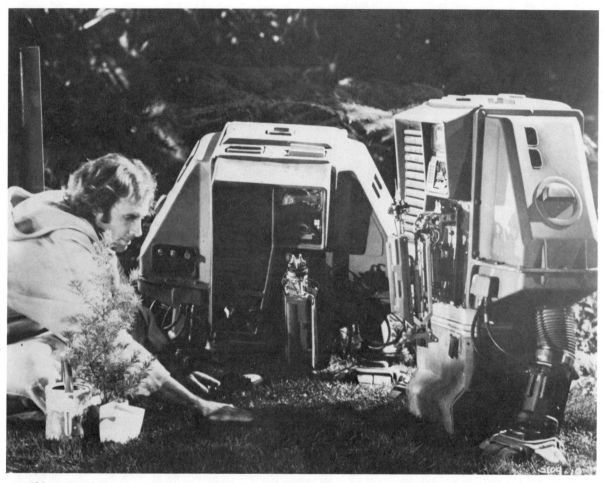

Here, Lowell Freemant teaches a robot to plant trees at the space station where he was trying to keep Earth plants alive.

sensible calendar in place of the incredibly inconvenient one we now have, and from simplifying the spelling of English words. We insist on only twenty-eight days for February, and in spelling "nite" with a "gh" that we don't pronounce, simply because we *already know* the nonsense, and we would have to *learn* the sense.

Nor is this fear confined to the unsophisticated and the less intelligent. If anything, the reverse is true. Capable people, who are thoroughly educated and highly intelligent, would surely be more prone to fear reeducation than would others. In reeducation, you tend to start from scratch, and the more educated you are, the more baggage you must dispose of. The greater the contrast between what you were and what you must become to relearn, the greater the humiliation that would result from putting yourself on a par, even if only initially, with those whom you thought you had permanently surpassed. Furthermore, you might fear that this second time around you might not do as well, or qualify for so high a position, as the first time.

Does all this apply to the matter of robots?

Of course it does. Installing robots means that managers must unlearn the techniques they have developed for handling human beings they had worked with for years, and that they must learn a totally different set of techniques for handling robots. It is no use saying that robots are "only" automatic machines. Of course they are, but they mimic actions we associate with human beings so that it is very difficult not to associate them with humanity. It will become steadily more difficult to avoid that association as they continue to approximate human behavior, abilities, and appearances more closely. Switching from handling human beings to handling robots is liable to be as traumatic as switching measuring systems, calendars, or spelling conventions.

Furthermore, replacing human beings with robots introduces a more subtle psychological difficulty. Since time immemorial, the social status of an executive has been judged by the number of human beings to whom he or she can give orders. This has not changed with the introduction of machinery. The tendency has been for executives to interpose underlings between themselves and machinery, even when the whole point of machinery is to make underlings unnecessary.

For instance, the telephone makes it unnecessary to send a messenger or write a letter. It is necessary only to lift a receiver, dial a number, and then talk directly. There is absolutely nothing to the task, and the highest executive can do it without becoming unduly fatigued. Nevertheless, the mere fact of doing so would cheapen an executive; it would make *him* (or her) the messenger. It therefore becomes necessary for him or her to ask a secretary or some other underling to dial the number.

In a robotized industry, there may well be a tendency, therefore, for managers and other executives to create a layer of human beings between themselves and the robots, in order to avoid dealing with machinery directly and thus preserve their status. This would, naturally, defeat much of the purpose of robotization.

Yet these psychological difficulties, though they may affect morale and increase tension, though they may produce frictions that may slow robotization and render it less effective, cannot possibly stop it. What's more, the difficulties may be ameliorated.

Managers can be introduced to robots before they are installed. They can be familiarized with robots slowly, patiently, and privately and in small groups. Education need not be too public; temporary failures or difficulties need not be made too embarrassing.

For lower-level employees, difficulties—psychological and physical—are more serious. With robots introduced into their midst, these employees may feel that high-tech advances in general make it easier for employers to oversee them, and so would fear and resent the "Big Brother is watching" possibility. They might fear that robotization would further erode their ability to bargain with employers on equal terms, and that they would lose all chance of control over their wages and working conditions. Yet even these fears are minor compared to the overriding terror inspired by robots, a terror that can be expressed in one word—unemployment.

If a robot on an assembly line, in a tailor shop, or anywhere, can do a particular job more efficiently, more tirelessly, more satisfactorily, and, eventually, far more cheaply, than three humans could possibly do, that is good for productivity. The three human beings, however, might then be out of work, and that is bad for humanity.

It might well be argued that the bad is bound to outweigh the good; that human suffering, a disrupted economy, and social unrest would be an impossibly high price to pay for a temporarily blacker tinge of ink in company ledgers.

It might even be argued that robotized industries would not even profit. There is the famous story of the auto manufacturer pointing to new machinery and saying to the auto labor leader, "Those machines don't want higher wages, pension funds, or fringe benefits." To which the labor leader replied, "They don't buy automobiles, either." And yet the tendency to reduce the human work force would be nearly irresistible. Industries, in periods of recession, might lay off employees in large numbers and later seize the opportunity to robotize. As the economy recovered, such robotization would then allow expansion of production without the need to rehire employees. Yet at no point would the industry, in our free-enterprise society, have done anything that could be considered unreasonable. It would have done what economic survival made necessary. All this is not lost

Woody Allen disguised himself as a robot-butler in order to avoid pursuers in the hostile, futuristic world to which he awakened in the 1973 film Sleeper.

on many employees, who now view the future with fear and insecurity. In particular, it is a matter of great concern for labor unions.

Some might expect that labor unions would campaign vigorously against computerization and, in particular, against the installation of robots. We might fear militant attempts to destroy robots that are installed and economic warfare that would disrupt our society. There were, after all, episodes during the early period of the Industrial Revolution in which fearful workingmen rioted and tried to destroy the new machinery. In England, these destroyers were called "Luddites," after their leader Ned Ludd. And the name has been given to extreme technophobes ever since.

So far, there seems no sign of a Luddite reaction to robots today. In the United States, unions have declined in strength due to the dwindling of traditional unionized industries such as steel, automobiles, and mining. Furthermore, the growing interconnection of the world economy makes it clearly impossible for the United States to remain unrobotized in a world that is becoming robotized. Even the most militant labor leaders see this. The unions are faced with either losing jobs to robots, or losing still more jobs as noncompetitive industries contract. Finally, unions have learned from history, and know that to attempt to dam (or even damn) technological change is useless; that it is more fruitful to direct it into useful and beneficial channels.

It might well be argued that history makes it plain that advancing technology is, in the long run, a job creator and not a job destroyer. The coming of the automobile put a number of blacksmiths and buggy manufacturers out of business and decreased the need for whips and hay. It created, however, a far greater number of automobile-related jobs and vastly expanded and broadened the need for gasoline, rubber, and highways.

In a more general way, the Industrial Revolution, despite the miseries of the early decades of the new factory system (low wages, long hours, bestial working conditions, and the heartless exploitation of women and children) eventually brought a relatively high standard of living to millions who would never have experienced it otherwise.

Unfortunately, the events of the early Industrial Revolution, two centuries ago, cannot be used as an accurate guide and precedent because the time scale is different. Initially, the Industrial Revolution was confined to Great Britain and spread relatively slowly to other nations. It took

George Lucas's famous robotic duo, C3P0 and R2D2, in Star Wars, 1977. Lucas had in mind the robot Maria from Metropolis, when describing C3P0 to illustrator Ralph McQuarrie, hence the Art Deco look. On the other hand, R2D2 was constructed from a metal vacuum cleaner.

perhaps half a century to reach high intensity in Great Britain, and at least that long in other nations it eventually affected. However difficult the period of transition, those difficulties were limited because the change took place slowly, by today's standards.

Nowadays, technological change takes place far more quickly and spreads across the face of the Earth with astonishing rapidity. The number of robots being used is increasing rapidly in many nations. The kind of changes that took fifty years in centuries past, will take ten years now. The problems that result will inundate us much more quickly and will require remedies that must be applied at once and resolutely.

For instance, all agree that to minimize unrest and insecurity among the labor force, it is unwise to present the introduction of robots as a fait accompli. To have employees feel that they do not know what changes are being planned, and what will face them on any given morning when they show up at work, will force them to expect the worst at all times and will shatter morale. To invite them, on the other hand, to participate, well in advance, in the decision making that goes into such changes, to allow them to feel that their interests and well-being are taken into account, would go far toward allaying their fears. It might even allow workers to welcome robots for the advantages they will bring.

Obviously, there must be job security. Insofar as is possible, it must be clear that there will not be wholesale discharges and that an employee replaced at one job will be shifted to another. If there *must* be an overall reduction in the work force, it should be carried through as far as possible by attrition. Employees who retire, take other jobs, or just quit, would simply not be replaced.

Reducing the work force by attrition does not help unemployment figures, even though it is less visibly painful than firing. Every time someone who might ordinarily be hired is not, unemployment goes up by one just as it does when an employee is fired. We will be left, then, one way or another, with an unemployment problem.

We might argue that this need not disturb us because the situation will be temporary and will be taken care of by the myriad of new job openings that a robotized society will make available. But surely matters will not be quite that simple. Though the new jobs will be greater in number than the old, perhaps far greater, the natures of those new jobs will differ. A person who has been tightening bolts on an assembly line cannot simply take over a new job as a robot repairman.

In fact, we can be certain that those employees replaced by robots will not qualify for the new jobs. These jobs will require considerable specialized knowledge and power of thought. Therefore, before changing from an old job to a new, an employee must acquire new specialized knowledge or skills, or both. The employee must also learn how to use the power of thought more intensely on the new job than had been necessary on the old. Yet if these adjustments are not made, new jobs will also be lost to robots. What will be required, then, is retraining and reeducation if the wholesale shifting of jobs that robotization will necessitate is to take place.

Clearly, this task cannot be left to the individual employee. Only the most gifted and ambitious could carry through such reeducation on his or her own, and it is entirely unlikely that someone sufficiently gifted and ambitious to do that would find himself or herself in the kind of limited work easily done by a robot.

Industries will have to organize classes and training programs, probably with financial support from the government, or the government will have to manage the programs directly. Such programs may not be completely successful. There are bound to be people who, because of age, temperament, lack of a proper educational foundation, or through the damage done to them by years at repetitive, undemanding jobs, will find such retraining difficult or impossible. Nevertheless, jobs, wherever possible, should be found for them. Welfare, or the equivalent, is always demoralizing and a last resort—a sure sign of a society's failure to function properly.

If all works well, the transition period, though painful and expensive, should not be long-lasting. One generation may be all that is required in any region that undergoes the robot revolution. It may be all that is required of the whole world, if the robot revolution occurs, as it just possibly may, on a planetwide basis.

What is needed, and what may come to pass, is a simultaneous and corresponding revolution in educational techniques and aims. People simply must be educated to fit into a robotized world (or, more generally, a computerized and automated world). And this world will be expanding rapidly into space, not merely to explore, but to settle and exploit, on a cushion of computers and robots.

Such an educational revolution is not utterly unprecedented. It happened once before. When the Industrial Revolution began, it meant a wholesale shift of labor from the home and the farm into the mills and factories. Such a change could not take place in isolation.

In the home and on the farm, formal education was scarcely needed. Children, apprentices, and hired hands could all simply do as they were told. They picked up all necessary skills by imitating their elders. Very little was required to make that possible—even literacy, the basic baggage of reading and writing, was superfluous. Nor was much in the way of innovation expected or even desired.

In the mills and factories, however, there were expensive new machines to run, and the pressures of periodic improvement. Word-of-mouth instruction was not enough, for there was too much to remember easily, and even minor

Astro-Boy and Dr. Edefan, the Director General of Science Ministry in Production Processes.

mistakes could be very damaging. It became necessary for workers to be able to read instructions, write reports, and perform calculations of some degree of sophistication. In short, they had to be educated in a new and more intense way. At the same time they were finally able to achieve the vote in the more enlightened societies, such as Great Britain and the United States, a privilege originally reserved for property owners. As Benjamin Disraeli said drily, "Let us educate our new masters!"

There was no way of producing large numbers of at least minimally educated employees without the government getting into the act. The nineteenth century, therefore, saw the rise of free public schools, supported and regulated by government bodies.

It was inevitable. One cannot have industrialization and widespread illiteracy at the same time, unless one is willing to have foreign nations of greater educational proficiency build factories and supply skilled workers—which is like humbly asking to be exploited and impoverished.

Public schools have never been totally efficient, and since World War II, when attempts were made to broaden and lengthen attendance, with governmental commitment declining and the teaching profession losing status, matters have been growing worse. The United States has millions of functional illiterates, people who cannot read or write well enough to work at anything but unskilled labor, who are nothing but animated back muscles and biceps. This weakens our industrial potential.

Given the earlier, imperfect educational revolution and today's declining rather than improving system, how can we now erect a second and more intense revolution upon the back of the first?

The chief problem of the first revolution was that it represented *mass* education. It had to. Before free public education, only the children of the well-to-do were educated, in relatively small classes or by private tutors. There are not enough tutors to go around if the education of the masses is aimed at, and small classes won't do. Futhermore, if we are to make sure that such mass education is reasonably uniform, there must be not only large classes but a curriculum that all teachers, sometimes statewide, sometimes nationwide, must slavishly follow and by which all students must slavishly learn.

Education is turned out in a manner that is precisely equivalent, therefore, to the assembly line, and with the same stultifying effect on the brain.

It is quite impossible that a mass curriculum, *any* mass curriculum, can satisfy any great number of students. Some will find the pace of study too fast and they will grow confused; others will find the pace of study too slow and they will grow bored; still others will not be interested in the subject matter and they will grow sullen. They become either too confused, bored, or sullen to learn.

However, we are entering the age of computers and that, in itself, creates a revolution. Computerization increases our ability to transmit and handle information. When computers are in the average home, when libraries are computerized and their contents available for consultation and facsimilization on home television screens, and when questions can be answered and instruction can be offered by carefully designed computer programs, schools will have a powerful ally. In the end, the tail will wag the dog, and schools will chiefly function to direct students on the best and most efficient way of achieving education via the computer.

Although schools will always have to handle those subjects that require human interaction—public speaking, nature studies in the field, laboratory courses in the sciences, and so on—with the computer we will effectively return to the days of one-to-one education. Every student will have a personal tutor, because such tutors will be available to everyone. Youngsters and, indeed, people of all ages, finding themselves able to learn at their own speed and in their own way, will devour learning and actually *enjoy* education. A new generation will arise that will by and large fit the technological aspect of the world in which it lives.

What's more, the educational revolution will have its pleasant surprises, as the earlier revolution did. In preliterate days, those few who could read, write, and do simple arithmetical calculation, such as clerics and merchants, were all too ready to believe that theirs was a rare and unusual talent; that the dull mass of humanity such as peasants, laborers, and even the lumpish aristocracy, simply lacked all mental capacity for literacy, except in a very few remarkable and exceptional cases. It was the coming of mass education that revealed literacy not as an unusual talent but as a skill that almost anyone, given the proper instruction and encouragement at an early age, could learn.

Nowadays, it is common for those who possess, or who imagine themselves to possess, creativity, ingenuity, or the

In 1922, the Italian futurist Enrico Prampolini idealized the machine in his work **The Broom**, *despite the tanks, planes, and machine guns of World War I.*

capacity for constructive thought, to believe that they have an unusual talent the general run of humanity does not and cannot possess. In all probability, this view is totally wrong. Given the proper kind of individualized education by a teaching computer, a surprisingly high percentage of people will surely turn out to possess creativity and ingenuity.

We can imagine, then, a high-tech society, filled with high-tech people engaged in creative labors, leaving to robots the dull and dangerous work that would harm the human mind or body.

To be sure, what we call "high-tech work" right now is not necessarily always high tech. There are a great many jobs in connection with the construction, management, and overseeing of robots and computers that can be as repetitious, boring, and unrewarding as anything on an assembly line or in the lower levels of office work.

Someone whose task might be to keep an eye on a serried rank of robots so that he (or she) might immediately observe any showing signs of being out of order, could scarcely find his task an improvement over what he was doing before. In fact, he might find it much worse, for he would be surrounded by fewer people, perhaps by none, so that the chance of social interaction would be diminished or even destroyed and the sense of separation and alienation greatly increased.

Similarly, a job involving the assembly of delicate components that are to be used in robots may involve very meticulous work and may, ultimately, make possible high-tech machines, but the work itself can be as repetitious and stultifying as adjusting a bumper on an automobile frame—and may be more poorly paid.

These are problems of transition, however. As robotization advances, robots will be able to report their own malfunctioning and probably correct minor errors themselves. As for the repetitive aspects of robot construction, that will eventually be left to robots, too.

In the end, there will be plenty of truly creative jobs to be done by humans, and plenty of creative humans to do those jobs.

There *are* dangers more dramatic than unemployment. Might not human beings be killed by robots?

Of course they might. Human beings have been killed by every tool and machine invented since the dawn of technology, even when those tools and machines were not primarily intended for killing. The notorious example of that

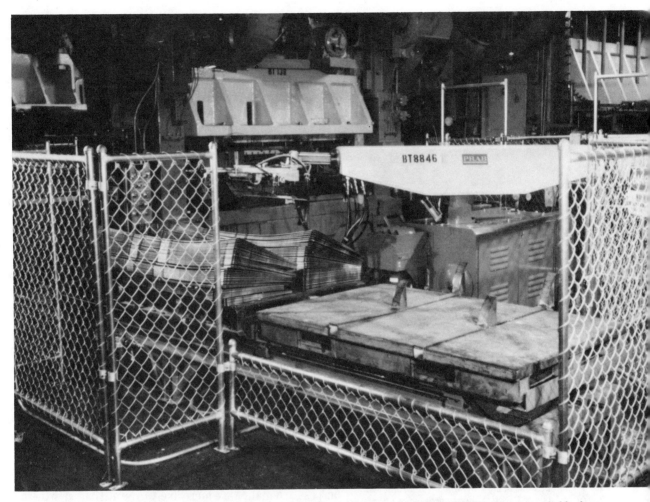

To prevent accidents, this robot is surrounded by fencing. After it removes oven liners from die cavities, it swings counterclockwise to stack them on pallets.

mass killer, the automobile, has already been mentioned.

But there is a difference, again. Robots aside, machines are recognized as inanimate and irresponsible. It is impossible, outside the realm of horror stories to suppose that there is purpose or malice in anything that an automobile or any other machine does. The responsibility is always that of the human running the machine, or that of the manufacturer of the machine, or that of the person who carelessly stepped in the way of the machine; it is never that of the machine itself. Only in the case of the robot is there a vague feeling that the machine might have had something to do with an accident. The robot, after all, is doing something so closely associated with the human that one can't help but wonder....

Robby the Robot was the star of the 1956 film **Forbidden Planet.** *Besides being chivalrous, Robby obeyed the Three Laws of Robotics—when ordered to shoot a human with a ray gun, the robot nearly blew a fuse while waiting for the insidious instruction to be cancelled.*

The first human being killed by a robot was a Kawasaki worker in Japan in July 1982. He attempted to repair a malfunctioning robot and neglected to cut off all power by opening the chain fence that enclosed it. He hopped over the fence instead and shut off the power manually. Somehow the power was inadvertently turned on again, and the robot, proceeding with its function, struck the man and killed him. The fault clearly lay with the worker's carelessness, but when the death was made public some months later, it proved a shocker.

The news reports, usually headed "Robot Kills Man," might have given some people the impression of a helpless human being pursued by a fiendlike mechanical monster with machine oil dribbling from the corner of its mouth and its eyes gleaming malevolently. Numerous reporters asked what had happened to the Laws of Robotics. It was explained that robots were not yet advanced enough to have the Three Laws built in, but that the chain fence, which had been ignored, was an external First Law and it was not the robot's fault if a human being did not use that fence.

Roboticists are well aware of the Three Laws of Robotics and while they know that these laws are derived from a series of science-fiction stories, they consider them a laudable safety goal. Marvin Minsky of MIT and Joseph Engelberger are two people who have spent a good deal of time considering methods of equipping robots with the equivalent of the Three Laws.

In fact, it is essential that the laws, or something like them, eventually come into operation. For as robots become more advanced and, possibly, more human in appearance, purpose and malice are more likely to be attributed to them, and *they* (not human beings or unfortunate circumstances) will be held responsible for accidents.

Nevertheless, the mere fact that robots are computerized machines means that highly sophisticated safeguards can be built into them. If robots can be designed to give the illusion of human ability, they can also be made to give the illusion of human carefulness, and the unsophisticated may be as ready to believe the latter as the former.

Yet, putting accidents to one side, is there not a far more overwhelming danger in robots, and in computers generally? As robots become more sophisticated and more capable, as cleverly manipulable hands and various senses and the capacity for something like reason are developed, might they not take over jobs that, right now, seem safely and forever human? Might it not be that human beings will have to be shifted from one job to another, always seeking something that robots cannot do, yet finding that robots inexorably follow them to higher and higher levels, until there is nothing at all left for human beings to do?

What would happen then?

One possibility in that case is that human beings might all live a life of idleness and luxury, with their wants and needs supplied by robots. In one sense, this would be a return to Eden, but one suspects that such idleness would have a softening effect—that our abilities would decay, that deprived of challenge we would simply die off.

Or, even less benignly, robots would early recognize us as unnecessary excrescences. Robots, which might have

Robby the Robot had several starring roles. Here "he" is in The Invisible Boy, *a 1957 film.*

become more capable than we, would "consider" us inferior beings. We might then be starved out, or killed off, by the robots, which would take over as *Homo superior.*

In short, might not our robotic adventure end in humanity becoming obsolete and extinct?

If one wishes to be cynical or, perhaps, simply rational, the proper answer might be "Why not?" If robots are eventually devised that are superior to human beings, with stronger bodies and more intelligent brains, and a better sense of social obligations, why shouldn't they replace us, just as mammals replaced less-intelligent reptiles as the dominant form of vertebrate land-life on earth?

One might even argue that all of evolution has proceeded by trial and error, and by the slow and inefficient mechanism of natural selection, only to evolve a species intelligent enough to *direct* evolution and create its own successor. The chain of life would then continue so that changes would take place in mere centuries that would earlier have taken eons—toward some goal we cannot guess. Indeed, if we indulge ourselves in unrestrained misanthropic musings, we might even conclude that it is not the coming of the displacing robot that we must fear, but the possibility that it might not come quickly enough.

The human record, after all, is a dismal one. Our treatment of one another, of other species, and of the very planet on which we live has been brutal in the extreme. We now have the power to destroy civilization, and even, perhaps, our planet's ability to support complex life forms. We can have no confidence, on the basis of history, that we will refrain from such suicidal behavior.

Perhaps we *should,* then, be replaced by thinking machines that might very well prove more rational and decent than we. And if we do so with resignation, robot-historians writing of us in the future might well say that nothing in the life of our species became us so well as our manner of leaving it.

But enough of such dyspeptic and unpleasant imaginings. The question, after all, is not whether robots, and computers, generally, should or should not overtake and replace us, but whether they will or will not do so.

It is not at all easy to say that something will, or will not happen, but there are logical reasons for suggesting that robots will *not* overtake human beings, let alone replace them. We may well destroy ourselves, but it is extremely unlikely that robots will save us the job.

For one thing, the human brain is not that easy to match, let alone surpass. The brain contains 10 billion neurons and ten times as many supporting cells. Each neuron is connected to anywhere from one hundred to one hundred thousand others. What's more, each neuron is not merely an on-off switch—that would, in itself, be enough to make the brain enormously complicated—but is an ultra-complex physical-chemical system that we are not even on the brink of understanding. The brain's total complication is almost beyond expression, let alone beyond comprehension.

An important difference between any computer (such as one controlling a robot) and the human brain is that the computer is completely defined. One knows exactly what a robot can do and just how it will go about doing it. On the other hand, one does not know precisely what a human brain can do—even its owner does not know—and one certainly does not know *how* it does it.

Thus, we know how a computer memory works, exactly what its contents are, and how it retrieves a particular item among those contents. We do *not* know how the memory of the human brain works, nor what its contents may be, nor how it retrieves a particular item.

With respect to the human brain, in fact, the whole, operation of memory and recall is an enormous puzzle. Someone who knows English well, for instance, knows at once that *claim* is an English word, and *clain* is not; that *career* is an English word and *creer* isn't. On the other hand, *careep* is not an English word, and *creep* is. But how are these distinctions made? Does a person somehow leaf through all the English words in his brain's dictionary and note that a particular letter combination is not included among them? Is it possible for a brain to do this in the split-second it takes to recognize that a letter combination does not form an English word? Is there an alternative? . . . No one knows.

Similarly, creative artists in many fields do things, almost without thought, that are incredibly difficult, considering that neither we nor they can really describe just how it is done. It can be something as seemingly prosaic as baseball: At the crack of a bat, an experienced outfielder will make an instantaneous estimate as the ball begins its flight. He turns and races to a particular place, lifts his gloved hand, and plucks the ball out of the air. No spectator can understand how he knew exactly where to run and when to reach for the ball, but the amazing thing is that the outfielder

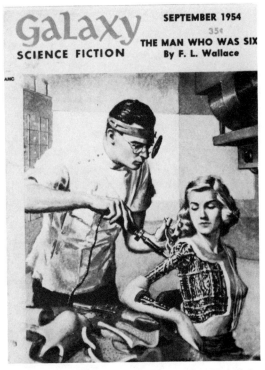

Science-fiction robots could be humanoid indeed. If, in 1954 this one was not outrageously expensive, the demand should have been high.

doesn't know either. He just does it.

Even people who are quite ordinary, who are not what the world would call "creative" or "talented," who are not even very bright, do many things every day—without any conscious effort—and do them by some means that neither they, nor anyone else, can explain.

Think of it. You, or almost anyone, can look at the letter *A* in its capital form, or as a small letter, or in italic, bold face, or any of a hundred styles of print; or as a handwritten capital or small letter in the separate handwritings of a thousand different people. In each case, you would recognize it almost at once and with no effort, as the letter *A*. You would probably be surprised if anyone told you that you were doing something remarkable, but it must be, for we can't, as yet, program a computer to do it.

You can recognize any of an indefinite number of voices, and do so at once even when it is distorted by the imperfections of a telephone or a recording device, and even, sometimes, when you have not heard it for a long time. The ability to do so doesn't astonish you—but we can't, as yet, program a computer with that ability.

What we *can* get a computer to do is, essentially, simple arithmetic. Any problem, however seemingly complex, that we can somehow break down into a well-defined series of arithmetical operations, we can program a computer to do. The computer can amaze us with its capabilities because it can perform these operations in billionths of a second, and can do so without any chance of making a mistake. The computer can't do anything we can't do, but it would take us billions of times longer to do it, and we would almost certainly make many mistakes in the process.

Surely, the reason that we do computer stuff so poorly is precisely because it is unimportant to us. The human brain is not designed to plod away at infantile calculations. These have only become important, superficially, as civilization has introduced taxation, commerce, business, and science. Even so, these remain unimportant in the context of what anyone would consider the major concerns of living. We have done as well at calculations as we have only because, over the last five thousand years, we have invented mechanical aids for the purpose, from the abacus and Arabic numerals, through logarithms and slide rules, to mechanical calculators and computers.

The business of the human brain, on the other hand, is and has always been, judgment and creative thought, the ability to come to a reasonable conclusion on the basis of insufficient evidence; the knack of being able to think philosophically, insightfully, fancifully, imaginatively; the ability to extract knowledge, beauty, excitement, and delight out of the world that surrounds us, and out of what we ourselves create.

Can we, perhaps, get the robot's computer to do what the human brain does, even though we can't reduce our human skills to specific arithmetical operations? Might we perhaps learn to mimic the human brain in simplified form at least, even if no more than a Tinkertoy construction might mimic a skyscraper? Might we then at least make a beginning in having a computer do what the brain does?

Or might we, perhaps, abandon attempts to fashion a computer's workings into a form of the brain, and merely devise a computer that can *learn* after the fashion of a human brain? Could the computer, if not we, ourselves, learn enough about the human brain to design a computer that would be closer than itself to the brain? Would this new computer, then, be a better and clearer learner and be able to devise a brain that was still closer to the human brain, and so on? In that case, might we not end up with a brainlike computer, even though we still didn't understand how the brain worked?

Even if any of this were possible, the chances are that we would not want to do it, except possibly on a very small scale on the off-chance that it would teach us something about the brain. To actually make a full-scale, brainlike computer would probably take far too much effort for any good it might do us.

Consider the analogous situation of machines that move. For a long time, we have had inanimate devices that could move on land. Until the early nineteenth century, they moved only if they were pushed or pulled by human beings or animals, but in recent times they could "move by themselves," thanks to the steam engine, and then to the internal-combustion engine. These devices, however, did not move as human beings move. They made use of the wheel and axle and rolled; they did not walk. Rolling is useful because it does not involve periodic lifting, whereas in walking, there is a lifting process at every step.

On the other hand, rolling requires a continuous, more or less flat and unobstructed course, so that roads must be built. The more advanced the vehicle, the more elaborate the roads, so that now we have paved, multilane super-

Science-fiction robots might be idealized and point the way to heaven, even if humanity is reluctant to go.

highways with elaborate cloverleaf exits. These highways are incredibly expensive to build and require constant effort to maintain. In walking, one steps over minor obstructions, of course, and roads need be little more than paths.

Why not, then, strike a happy compromise and build internal-combustion vehicles that walk rather than roll?

It is possible to build a walking machine. Yet it is done only rarely because a mechanical walker is so much more difficult to build than a mechanical roller. And a mechanical walker is so clumsy and so slow, in comparison to a roller moving on a reasonably smooth surface, that the walker would be useless for anything but the most specialized applications.

In the same way, even if a robot should be equipped with a computer equivalent to a simplified version of a human brain, it is very likely that it would take enormous effort and enormous time to design and build the robot, and that we would end up with a robot that was a very pale substitute for the human brains we produce by the billions in the ordinary way.

Might this not be merely unadventurous thinking? If a computer can be designed to design one better than itself, which then could design one still better, and so on, might the process not go out of control? Could we find ourselves not only with a human-level robot, but a super-human-level one, before we quite realized what was happening?

This is almost certainly not likely. The advance is sure to be sufficiently slow as to allow human beings to recognize the danger long before it arrives, and they would then "pull the plug." It is likely, in fact, that human beings are already so suspicious and fearful of robots that they will see danger where none exists, and are more likely to pull the plug unnecessarily rather than let themselves be caught napping.

No, if our technology is to bring about *Homo superior*, it will arise out of ourselves. With newfound techniques of genetic engineering, we may well learn how to improve our brain and increase its efficiency, even as we learn to increase the capabilities of robots.

It is extremely likely, under such circumstances, that robots and human beings would continue to advance along parallel paths. Robots would continue to do what they do so much better than we, while we continue to do what we do so much better than they. And both could get better and better. There will always be room for both of us, so that we will be symbiotic allies rather than competitive foes. And as allies,

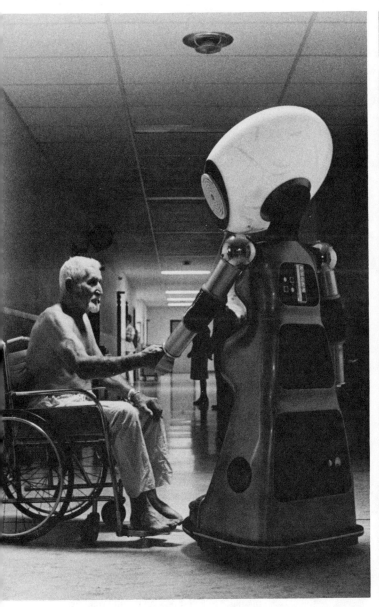

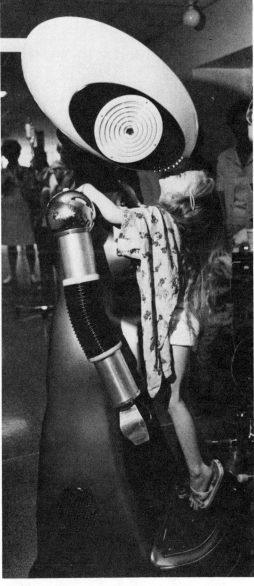

The entertainment robot SICO cheers the young and old in hospitals.

we will advance together with an ever-greater understanding of the behavior of the Universe and the wise use of its laws, than either could possibly manage alone.

What we need really fear is not that through fatuous overconfidence we will nurture a master and supplanter, but that through foolish suspicion we will fail to avail ourselves of an absolutely necessary helper and friend.

GLOSSARY

Accuracy   A measurement of the difference between the calculated point in space and the actual location reached by a robot arm.

Algorithm   A finite set of well-defined rules or procedures for solving a problem step by step.

Analog Computer   A computer operating on the principle of physical analogy, usually electrical, to solve problems. Variables of a problem are represented as continuous physical changes in voltage and current and are manipulated by the computer according to mathematical expressions of the analogy.

Batch Production   Refers to the lot size of identical parts produced in a factory. Batches range from three hundred to fifteen thousand parts.

Binary   A number system that has only two digits, 0 and 1.

Bit   An abbreviation for "binary digit" that is the smallest unit of data for a digital computer. A bit can be 1 or 0, the equivalent of yes or no, or on or off.

Byte   A string of eight bits equals one byte.

CAD/CAM   Computer-Aided Design/Computer-Aided Manufacture. The use of a computer to help design parts or complete products and to simulate performance tests without building a prototype. Manufacturing equipment shares the data base so that manufacturers can go from the design on the computer screen to the actual finished product.

Cartesian Coordinates   A set of three numbers defining a point in space based on three perpendicular axis, X, Y, and Z.

Chip   An integrated circuit.

Closed Loop   A control system in which output data is measured and fed back to the control for comparison with the input data, so that information flows back and forth.

CMOS   Complimentary Metal Oxide Semiconductor. A type of integrated circuit that has moderately

dense circuitry, moderate speed, and low power dissipation.

Controller   The device that regulates a robot arm's movement and position by comparing the difference between the actual and calculated values and sending the signals necessary to make them match as much as possible. The controller of the PUMA contains a microprocessor, servo boards, RAM EPROM, and the power supply.

Digital Computer   A computer that processes information represented by combinations of discrete data, compared to an analog computer, which processes continuous data.

Encoder   A type of transducer that converts information about the position of a joint into a signal that is fed back to the robot's controller.

End Effector   A gripper, hand, or tooling device mounted at the tip of a robot arm.

EPROM   Erasable Programmable Read-Only Memory (see ROM). A ROM that can be erased by exposure to ultraviolet light and reprogrammed electronically.

Gripper   A clamp at the tip of a robot arm used for grasping an object. A gripper is one type of end effector.

Hardware   The physical parts of a computer system, including printed circuit boards and wiring—in contrast to software, the programs and languages of a computer system.

Integrated Circuit   A solid-state microcircuit contained in a silicon chip.

K   An abbreviation for kilo, meaning 1,000. When used as a measure of a computer's memory capacity, K means 1024 bits, the product of 2 to the 10th power.

Mainframe Computer   The principal computer in a system of computers.

Mass Production   The production of identical parts in lot sizes of over ten thousand.

Master/Slave Manipulator   A type of teleoperated arm that is positioned by a human who controls it with a remotely located joy stick.

Microprocessor   A computer whose central processor functions are on one printed circuit board or chip.

MIG Welding   Metal Inert Gas Welding. A method of joining metal parts by passing current from a metal rod to the grounded parts. When an electric discharge melts the rod, a weld forms. A shielding gas prevents oxidation of the molten joint so that it retains its integrity. A type of arc welding.

Open Loop   A control system in which data flows unidirectionally, that is, only from the control to the mechanism but not from the mechanism back to the control.

Payload   The largest weight that an industrial robot can lift.

Piece Production   The production of identical parts in lot sizes of three hundred or less.

Pixel   From the words picture and element. A unit of a television camera image that is assigned a value of brightness and is digitized so that image data can be computer processed.

RAM   Random-Access Memory. A memory device that retrieves recently stored data in the same amount of time as it retrieves data that was stored earlier. It provides immediate access to any storage location point in the memory.

Real Time   Computer control performed in the actual time needed for a physical process, instead of a predetermined or preprocessed control response.

ROM   Read-Only Memory. A memory containing a fixed pattern of bits that are generally unalterable by the user. More permanent than a RAM, the data in this device is entered during manufacture and cannot be altered during the normal operation of the system. The information can be read, but not written, and it remains even if power is lost.

Repeatability   A measure of a robot arm's ability to achieve the same position. It specifies the extent that an arm's position will vary when aiming at the same point from cycle to cycle.

Servo Controlled   Controlled by a signal that is determined by the difference between a present position and a desired position. A feedback control system.

Software   The instructions of a computer system. Its programs and programming languages, as opposed to hardware—the physical components of a computer system.

Solid-State Camera   A television camera with a solid-state integrated circuit to convert light images into electronic signals.

Spot Welding   A method for joining two metal parts by using a welding gun to press the parts together and pass electric current through them. The metal melts at the spot where the gun's electrodes clamp the parts together.

Teleoperator   A master/slave-operated device that is manipulated remotely by a human.

Vidicon Camera   A television camera with a vacuum tube that converts incoming images into video signals.

Work Envelope   The space within reach of a robot arm.

SOURCE NOTES

1. *The Nevv World of Words: or a General English Dictionary*, 3rd ed., published by Edward Phillips, printed for N. Brook, at the Angel in Cornbil, near the Royall Exchange, 1671.

2. Noah Webster, *An American Dictionary of the English Language Usage*, vol. I. (New York: S. Converse, 1828).

3. Noah Webster, *An American Dictionary of the English Language*, revised and enlarged by Chancey A. Goodrich (Springfield, Massachusetts: George and Charles Merriam, 1850).

4. Noah Webster, *An American Dictionary of the English Language*, revised and edited by C. A. Goodrich and N. Porter (Springfield, Massachusetts: George and Charles Merriam, 1879).

5. *Webster's New International Dictionary of the English Language*, 2nd ed., unabridged, 1934.

6. As quoted in Barbara Krasnoff, *Robots: Reel to Reel* (New York: Arco Publishing, 1982), p. 99.

7. *Industrial Robots: A Summary and Forecast*, 2nd ed. Tech Tran Corp. (Naperville, Ill, March 1983), pp. 84–87.

8. *Industrial Robots: A Summary and Forecast*, 2nd ed. Tech Tran Corp. (Naperville, Ill, March 1983), p. 86.

9. *Industrial Robots: A Summary and Forecast*, 2nd ed. Tech Tran Corp. (Naperville, Ill, March 1983), pp. 84–87.

10. *Industrial Robots: A Summary and Forecast*, 2nd ed. Tech Tran Corp. (Naperville, Ill, March 1983), p. 161.

11. *Industrial Robots: A Summary and Forecast*, 2nd ed. Tech Tran Corp. (Naperville, Ill, March 1983), p. 161.

12. Mitchell I. Quain and James B. Townsend, *Factory Automation* (New York: Wertheim & Co., April 1981), p. 11.

13. From the speech "Energy and Productivity Opportunities for GE," Hotel Pierre, New York, December 9, 1980.

14. "Competitive Position of U.S. Producers of Robotics in Domestic and World Markets" (U.S. International Trade Commission report, December 1983).

15. *Computerized Manufacturing Automation: Employment, Education and the Workforce* (Office of Technology Assessment, April 1984).

16. *Robotics Age* (January-February, 1981). "An Interview with Joseph Engelberger," by Jerry W. Saveriano.

17. Interview with Walter Weisel, November 11, 1983.

18. "Complete Robots: U.S. Imports for Consumption, by Types, 1979–83," in *"Competitive Position of U.S. Producers of Robotics in Domestic and World Markets"* (International Trade Commission, December 1983), p. 33.

19. *Forbes* magazine, December 20, 1982.

20. From "The Race to the Automatic Factory," by Gene Bylinsky, *Fortune*, January 21, 1983.

21. "Flexible Systems Invade the Factory," by Paul Kinnucan, *High Technology* magazine, July 1983.

22. From "Design of a Multitask Exoskeletal Walking Device for Paraplegics," in *Biomechanics of Medical Devices*, Dhanjoo N. Ghista, ed. (New York and Basel: Marcel Dekker, 1980), pp. 569–639.

23. *New York Times*, August 26, 1982, p. D2.

24. From a speech by Sir Geoffrey Jefferson, Chair of Neurosurgery, Manchester University, in his Lister Oration, "The Mind of Mechanical Man," June 9, 1949.

25. Alan Turing, as quoted in the London *Times*, June 11, 1949.

26. René Descartes, *Discourse on Method* (New York: Penguin Books, 1966), Section 5, p. 82.

27. As reprinted in *Faster than Thought*, B. V. Bowden, ed. (London: Pitman and Sons, 1953), pp. 368–69.

28. Ibid., p. 369.

29. Ibid., p. 398.

30. Pamela McCorduck, *Machines Who Think* (San Francisco: W. H. Freeman, 1979), p. 61.

31. Alan Turing, "Computing Machinery and Intelligence," *Mind*, vol. LI, no. 235 (October 1950). An excerpt appears more recently in *The Mind's I*, Douglas R. Hofstadter and Daniel C. Dennett, eds. (New York: Basic Books, 1981).

MANUFACTURERS AND TRADE ASSOCIATIONS

INDUSTRIAL ROBOT MANUFACTURERS IN THE U.S.

Accumatic Machinery Corporation
3537 Hill Avenue
Toledo, OH 43607
(419) 893-2979

Advanced Robotics Corporation
777 Manor Park Drive
Columbus, OH 43228
(614) 870-7778

Ameco Corporation
P.O. Box 385
W158 N9335 NOR-X-WAY Avenue
Menomonee Falls, WI 53051
(414) 255-3910

American Robot Corporation
121 Industry Drive
Pittsburgh, PA 15275
(412) 787-3000

Anorad Corporation
110 Oser Avenue
Hauppauge, NY 11788
(516) 231-1990

ASEA Robotics, Inc.
Industrial Robot Division
4 New King Street
White Plains, NY 10604
(914) 428-6000

American Can Company
American Technologies Division
American Lane
Greenwich, CT 06830
(203) 552-2000

Automatix, Inc.
1000 Tech Park Drive
Billerica, MA 01821
(617) 667-7900

Binks Manufacturing Company
9201 West Belmont Avenue
Franklin Park, IL 60131
(312) 671-3000

Cincinnati Milacron
Industrial Robot Division
Lebanon, OH 45036
(513) 932-4400

Comet Welding Systems
900 Nicholas Boulevard
Elk Grove Village, IL 60007
(312) 956-0126

Control Automation, Inc.
Princeton-Windsor Industrial Park
P.O. Box 2304
Princeton, NJ 08540
(609) 799-6026

Cybotech Corporation
Division of Ransburg Corp.
P.O. Box 88514
Indianapolis, IN 46208
(317) 298-5890

Cyclomatic Industries, Inc.
8123 Miralani Drive
San Diego, CA 92126
(619) 578-8580

DeVilbiss Company
300 Phillops Avenue
Toledo, OH 43692
(419) 470-2353

Elicon
245 Viking Avenue
Brea, CA 92621
(714) 990-6647

Everett/Charles Automation Systems, Inc.
700 East Harrison Avenue
Pomona, CA 91767
(714) 621-9511

Expert Automation, Inc.
40675 Mound Road
Sterling Heights, MI 48078
(313) 977-0100

Fleximation Systems Corporation
5 Suburban Park Drive
Billerica, MA 01821
(617) 663-7000

Fared Robot Systems
3405 Avenue D.
Arlington, TX 76011
(817) 265-2283

Fibro, Inc.
Division of Laepple Group
5113 27th Avenue
East Rock Industrial Park
Rockford, IL 61109
(815) 229-1300

GCA Corporation
Industrial Systems Group
One Energy Center
Naperville, IL 60566
(312) 369-2110

General Electric Automation Systems
1285 Boston Avenue
Bridgeport, CT 06602
(203) 382-2876

GMF Robotics Corporation
5600 New King Street
Troy, MI 48098
(313) 641-4242

Graco Robotics, Inc.
12898 Westmore Avenue

Livonia, MI 48150
(313) 523-6300

Hitachi America Ltd.
50 Prospect Avenue
Tarrytown, NY 10591-4698
(914) 332-5800

Hobart Brothers Company
Hobart Square
Troy, OH 45373
(513) 339-6011

Intelledex, Inc.
33840 Eastgate Circle
Corvallis, OR 97333
(503) 758-4700

International Business Machines
Corporation
Advanced Manufacturing Systems
1000 N.W. 51st Street
Boca Raton, FL 33432
(305) 998-2000

International Robomation/Intelligence
2281 Las Palmas Drive
Carlsbad, CA 92008
(619) 438-4424

Mack Corporation
3695 East Industrial Drive
P.O. Box 1756
Flagstaff, AZ 86001
(602) 526-1120

Mobot Corporation
980 Buenos Avenue
San Diego, CA 92110
(619) 275-4300

MTS Systems Corporation
Box 24012
Minneapolis, MN 55424
(612) 937-4000

Pickomatic Systems
37950 Commerce
Sterling Heights, MI 48077
(313) 939-9320

Positech Corporation
Rush Lake Road
Laurens, IA 50554
(712) 845-4548

Prab Robots, Inc.
6007 Sprinkle Road
Kalamazoo, MI 49003
(616) 329-0835

Reis Machines
1150 Davis Road
Elgin, IL 60120
(312) 741-9500

Rimrock Corporation
1700 Rimrock Road
Columbus, OH 43219
(614) 471-5926

Rhino Robots, Inc.
2505 South Neil Street
Champaign, IL 61820
(217) 352-8485

Robogate Systems, Inc.
750 Stephenson Highway
Suite 30
Troy, MI 48084
(313) 583-9900

Seiko Instruments USA, Inc.
2990 West Lomita Boulevard
Torrance, CA 90505
(213) 530-8777

Sterling Detroit Company
261 East Goldengate Avenue
Detroit, MI 48203
(313) 366-3500

Thermwood Corporation
P.O. Box 436
Dale, IN 47523
(812) 937-4476

Unimation, Inc.
Shelter Rock Lane
Danbury, CT 06810
(203) 744-1800

United States Robots
650 Park Avenue
King of Prussia, PA 19406
(215) 768-9210

United Technologies
Automotive Group
5200 Auto Club Drive
Dearborn, MI 48126
(313) 593-9600

VSI Automation
165 Park Street
Troy, MI 48084
(313) 588-1255

Wear Control Technology, Inc.
4041 172nd Street
Flushing, NY 11358
(718) 762-4040

Westinghouse Electric Corporation
Industry Automation Division
400 High Tower Office Building
400 Media Drive
Pittsburgh, PA 15205
(412) 778-4300

233

INDUSTRIAL ROBOT CONSULTANTS

Productivity Systems, Inc.
1210 East Maple
Troy, MI 48083
(313) 583-6995

Robot Systems, Inc.
50 Technology Parkway
Technology Park Atlanta
Norcross, GA 30092
(404) 448-4133

ROBOTIC VISION SYSTEMS MANUFACTURERS IN THE U.S.

Cognex Corporation
1505 Commonwealth Avenue
Boston, MA 02135
(617) 254-1231

Control Automation, Inc.
Princeton-Windsor Industrial Park
P.O. Box 2304
Princeton, NJ 08540
(609) 799-6026

Diffracto Ltd.
P.O. Box 36716
Detroit, MI 48236
(313) 965-0410

Intran Corporation
670 North Commercial Street
P.O. Box 607
Manchester, NH 03105
(603) 669-6332

Machine Intelligence Corporation
330 Potrero Avenue
Sunnyvale, CA 94086
(408) 737-7960

Object Recognition Systems, Inc.
521 Fifth Avenue
New York, NY 10175
(212) 682-3535

Octek, Inc.
7 Corporate Place
South Bedford Street
Burlington, MA 01803
(617) 273-0851

Perceptron
23920 Freeway Park Drive
Farmington Hills, MI 48024
(313) 478-7710

Robotic Vision Systems, Inc.
425 Rabro Drive East
Hauppauge, NY 11788
(516) 273-9700

Vuebotics Corporation
6086 Corte del Cedro
Carlsbad, CA 92008
(619) 438-7994

PERSONAL, INSTRUCTIONAL, PROMOTIONAL, AND REMOTELY CONTROLLED ROBOTS

Androbot, Inc.
101 East Daggett Drive
San Jose, CA 95134
(408) 262-8676

Ametek-Straza
790 Greenfield Drive
P.O. Box 666
El Cajon, CA 92022
(619) 442-3451

Bell and Howell
Automated Systems Division
411 East Roosevelt Street
Zeeland, MI 49464
(616) 772-1000

Cybot Corporation
1-24 7-chome, Uehonmachi
Tennoji-ku, Osaka Japan
Tel: (06)779-1107

Feedback
620 Springfield Avenue
Berkeley Heights, NJ 07922
(201) 464-5181

GCAPaR Systems
3460 Lexington Avenue North
St. Paul, MN 55112
(612) 484-7261

Heathkit
Heath Company
Benton Harbor, MI 49022
(616) 982-3417

Hydro Products
P.O. Box 2528
San Diego, CA 92112
(619) 453-2345

International Robotics, Inc.
611 Broadway, Suite 422-B
New York, NY 10012
(212) 982-8001

Microbot, Inc.
453-H Ravendale Drive
Mountain View, CA 94043
(415) 968-8911

Mitsubishi Electric
Sales America, Inc.
3030 East Victoria Street
Rancho Domiugues, CA 90221
1-800-421-1132

M.T. Hikawa Co., Ltd.
49-2, Kinomoto, Miyoshi, Miyoshi-cho
Nishikamo-gun, Aichi Pref.
Japan
Tel:05613-4-1611

Distributed by:
Nissho Iwai American Corporation
1211 Avenue of the Americas
New York, NY 10036
(212) 704-6500

Namco Ltd.
Asahi Building
5-38-3, Kamata
Ota-ku
Tokyo 144
Japan
Tel:Tokyo 736-1211

Odetics, Inc.
1380 South Anaheim Boulevard
Anaheim, CA 92805
(714) 774-5000

Pedsco Canada Ltd.
180 Finchdene Square Unit 3
Scarborough, Ontario
Canada M1X 1A8
(416) 298-9989

RB Robot Corporation
14618 West 6th Avenue, Suite 201
Golden, CO 80401
(303) 279-5525

Rhino Robots, Inc.
2505 South Neil Street
Champaign, IL 61820
(217) 352-8485

Robotics International Corporation
2335 East High Street
Jackson, MI 49203
(517) 788-6840

ShowAmerica, Inc.
841 North Addison Avenue
Elmhurst, IL 60126
(312) 834-7500

Tasman Turtle
Distributed by:
Harvard Associates, Inc.
260 Beacon Street
Sommerville, MA 02143
(617) 492-0660

TeleOperator Systems Corporation
45 Knickerbocker Avenue
Bohemia, NY 11716
(516) 567-8787

INDUSTRIAL ROBOT ASSOCIATIONS

Robot Institute of America
One SME Drive
P.O. Box 930
Dearborn, MI 48128
(313) 271-7800

Robotics International of the Society of
Manufacturing Engineers
One SME Drive
P.O. Box 930
Dearborn, MI 48128
(313) 271-1500

Japan Industrial Robot Association
Kikai Shinto Kaikan Building
3-5-8 Shiba-koen Minato-ku
Tokyo 105 Japan

British Robot Association
International Fluidics Services Ltd.
35-39 High Street
Kempston, Bedford MK42 7BT England

Association Francaise de
Robotique Industriele
60 Allee de la Foret
92360 Meudon de la Foret France

Societa Italiana perla Robotics Industriale
Instituto di Elettrotechnica ed Elettronics
Politechnico di Milana
Piazza Leonardo da Vinci 32
20133 Milano Italy

Belgian Institute for Regulation
and Automation
ROBOTICA FN Industry
Rue de Page 69/75
B-1050 Bruxelles Belgium

Swedish Industrial Robot Association
Strogt. 19 S-114 85 Stockholm Sweden

ROBOT HOBBYIST ORGANIZATIONS

U.S. Robotics Foundation
1250 Oakmead Parkway, Suite 210
Sunnyvale, CA 94086
(408) 735-9622
Pres.: Mark Arc

Robotics Society of America
200 California Avenue, Suite 215
Palo Alto, CA 94306
(415) 326-6095
Exec. dir.: Walter Tunick

Robig Club
3205 Syndenham Street
Fairfax, VA 22031
(703) 573-6437
Dir.: Kent Myers
(Washington, DC, club)

Atlanta Computer Society's Robotics
Special Interest Group
4581 Lucerne Valley Road
Liburn, GA 03247
(404) 972-7082 Dir.: John W. Gutmann

Boston Computer Society's Robotics
Special Interest Group
164 Wilshire Drive
Sharon, MA 02067
(617) 784-6557
Chairman: Ted Blank

PUBLICATIONS

MAGAZINES

Robotics Age
Strand Building
174 Concord Street
Peterborough, NH 03458
(603) 924-7136
Publisher: Carl Helmers

Robotics Today
One SME Drive
Dearborn, MI 48128

Robotics World
Communication Channels, Inc.
6255 Barfield Road
Atlanta, GA 30328
Publisher: Walter Moore

FMS Magazine
IFS Publications Ltd.
35-39 High Street
Kempston, Bedford MK42 7BT
England
Deputy Editor: Anna Kochan

AI Magazine
American Association for
Artificial Intelligence
445 Burgess Drive
Menlo Park, CA 94025
(415) 328-3123

NEWSPAPERS AND NEWSLETTERS

Robot/X News
Robotics Publications, Inc.
P.O. Box 450
Mansfield, MA 02048
Editor: K. L. Stewart

Automation News
Grant Business Publications, Inc.
160 East 48th Street
New York, NY 10017
(212) 223-0232
Publisher: Gerald J. Giannone;
Editor: Robert Malone

Robot Insider
11 E. Adams Street, Suite 1400
Chicago, IL 60603
(312) 663-3500
Editor: Jack Thornton

Industrial Robotics International
Technical Insights, Inc.
158 Linwood Plaza
P.O. Box 1304
Fort Lee, NJ 07024
(201) 944-6204
Publisher: Kenneth Kovaly;
Editor: J. Robert Warren

Robomatix Reporter
EIC/Intelligence Publishing Division
48 West 38th Street
New York, NY 10018
(212) 944-8500

JOURNALS

*The International Journal of
Robotics Research*
MIT Press Journals
28 Carleton Street
Cambridge, MA 02142
(617) 253-2889
Editors: Mike Brady, Richard Paul

Artificial Intelligence
Elsevier North-Holland, Inc.
52 Vanderbilt Avenue
New York, NY 10017
(212) 916-1250

BIBLIOGRAPHY

Adams, Russ. "Multi-Purpose Mechanical Hand." *Robotics Age*, May/June 1983, pp. 19–22.

AFL-CIO, *The Future of Work*, Washington, D.C., AFL-CIO, 1983.

Albus, James S. *Brains, Behavior, & Robotics.* Peterborough, N.H.: McGraw-Hill, BYTE Books, 1981.

———. *Peoples' Capitalism: The Economics of the Robot Revolution.* Kensington, Md.: New World Books, 1976.

Alexander, Tom. "Practical Uses for a 'Useless' Science." *Fortune*, 31 May 1982, p. 139.

"The American Machinist Award: Joseph F. Engelberger," *American Machinist*, December 1982, pp. 68–75.

Amram, Fred M. "Robotics: The Human Touch." *Robotics Today*, April 1982, p. 28.

Argote, Linda, Goodman, Paul S., and Schkade, David. "The Human Side of Robotics: How Workers React to a Robot." *Sloan Management Review*, Spring 1983.

Aron, Paul H. "Robotics in Japan: Past, Present, Future." In *Robots VI Conference Proceedings*. Dearborn, Mich.: Society of Manufacturing Engineers, 1982.

———. "Testimony before the Subcommittee on Investigations and Oversight of the Committee on Science and Technology, U.S. House of Representatives." 97th Cong. 2nd sess., 2 June 1982.

Artley, John W. "Robot Vision—The Future Is in Sight." *Robotics World*, February 1983.

Asada, Hari, Kanade, T., and Takeyama, I. "Control of a Direct-Drive Arm." *Transaction of the American Society of Mechanical Engineers*, September 1983, pp. 136–42.

Ayres, Robert U., and Miller, Steven M. "Industrial Robots on the Line." *Technology Review*, May/June 1982, pp. 35–47.

———. *Robotics: Applications & Social Implications.* Cambridge, Mass.: Harper & Row, Ballinger Publishing, 1983.

Bailey, J. Ronald. "Product Design for Robotic Assembly." *Conference Proceedings of the 13th International Symposium on Industrial Robots and Robots 7*, 1983, pp. 11-44–11-57.

Bender, Eric. "Home Robots: Fad or Future?" *ISO World*, 13 June 1983, p. 26.

Bortz, Fred. "Herbert Simon Talks About Building Brighter 'Beasties.'" *Carnegie-Mellon Magazine*, Spring 1983, pp. 14–19.

Bowden, B. V. *Faster Than Thought.* London: Sir Isaac Pitman, 1953.

Bradt, L. Jack. "The Automated Factory: Myth or Reality?" *Engineering: Cornell Quarterly*, vol. 17, no. 3 (Winter 1982-83).

Broad, William J. "Building a Robot: The Crash Course." *New York Times*, 3 May 1983, p. C1.

———. "Further Adventures of Hero, the Android." *New York Times*, 10 May 1983, p. C1.

———. "U.S. Factories Reach into the Future." *New York Times*, 13 March 1984, p. C1.

Brown, Paul B. "Business Goes to College." *Forbes*, 11 October 1982, p. 196.

Byrne, John A. "Whose Robots are Winning?" *Forbes*, 14 March 1983, pp. 154–58.

Bylinsky, Gene. "Those Smart Young Robots on the Production Line." *Fortune*, 17 December 1979, pp. 90–96.

———. "And Now, Chips That Can See." *Fortune*, 10 August 1981, pp. 161–64.

———. "The Race to the Automatic Factory." *Fortune*, 12 February 1983, p. 52.

Capek, Karel. *R.U.R.*, trans. by P. Selver. New York: Washington Square Press, 1973.

Caporali, M., and Shahinpoor, M. "Design and Construction of a Five-Fingered Robotic Hand." *Robotics Age*, February 1984, pp. 14–20.

Chamot, Dennis, and Baggett, Joan M., eds., *Silicon, Satellites and Robots*, Washington, D.C.: AFL-CIO, 1979.

Cichowicz, Ron. "Robots: Who Wants Them and Why?" *Carnegie-Mellon Magazine*, Winter 1984, pp. 11–19.

Cohen, John. *Human Robots in Myth and Science.* New York & South Brunswick, N.J.: A. S. Barnes, 1967.

Conigliaro, Laura. Robotics Newsletters: 23 April 1980, 10 November 1980, 25 March 1981, 5 May 1981, 28 October 1981, 25 January 1982, 4 May 1982, 22 September 1982. New York: Bache Halsey Stuart Shields.

———. "Trends in the Robotics Industry." In *Robots VI Conference Proceedings*, Dearborn: Mich.: Society of Manufacturing Engineers, 1982.

———. *Robotics Newsletter*, 13 December 1982. New York: Prudential-Bache Securities.

———. *Computer Integrated Manufacturing Newsletters*: 8 March 1983 and 3 June 1983. New York: Prudential-Bache Securities.

Cyert, Richard M. "Making a Case for Unmanned Factories." *New York Times*, 15 July 1984, p. F4.

"The Dance of the Androbots." *Newsweek*, 17 January 1983, p. 43.

Davis, Bob. "Robot Hands: Research Tries to Simulate Human Motion." *Wall Street Journal*, 6 April 1984, p. 31.

Dizard, John W. "Giant Footsteps at Unimation's Back." *Fortune*, 17 May 1982, pp. 94–99.

Donlon, Thomas G. "Robot Explosion: Competition Is Growing Even Faster Than the Field Itself." *Barron's*, 5 April 1982, p. 8.

Edelhart, Mike. "Robots: Fantasies and Realities." *Omni*, April 1983.

Engelberger, Joseph F. *Robotics in Practice: Management and Applications of Industrial Robots.* London: Kogan Page, 1981.

Enomoto, Katsuo, and Sento, Hiroshi. "Hitachi Industrial Robots." *Hitachi Review*, vol. 30 (1981), no. 4, pp. 205–10.

Feigenbaum, Edward A., and Feldman, Julian, eds., *Computers and Thought.* New York: McGraw-Hill, 1963.

Feigenbaum, Edward A., and McCorduck, Pamela. *The Fifth Generation.* Menlo Park, Calif.: Addison-Wesley, 1983.

Fine, Jean. "Sophisticated Automation to Robotry." New York: Gruntal, 1980.

Fleck, Glen., ed., *A Computer Perspective.* Cambridge, Mass.: Harvard University Press, 1973.

Froehlich, Leopold. "Robots to the Rescue?" *Datamation*, January 1981, p. 85.

Geduld, Harry M., and Gottesman, Ronald., eds., *Robots, Robots, Robots.* Boston: Little, Brown, New York Graphic Society, 1978.

George, Alexander. "Philosophy and the Birth of Computer Science." *Robotics Age*, January/February 1983, pp. 26–31.

Gevarter, William B. *An Overview of Artificial Intelligence and Robotics*, National Bureau of Standards Report NBSIR 82-2479, Washington, D.C.: U.S. Department of Commerce, 1982.

Harkins, William E. *Karel Capek.* New York: Columbia University Press, 1962.

Harris, Ross J. "An A-Mazing Logo Experiment." *Hands On!*, vol. 6, no. 2, pp. 12–14.

Hayes, B. D., and Blaesi, LaVon. "Training a New Generation of Robotics Personnel." *Robotics World*, April 1983, p. 15.

Hero. "The New Wave of Personal Robots" and "January Robomate of the Month." *Computers & Electronics*, January 1983, pp. 37 and 46.

Hill, John W. "Introducing the Mini Mover 5." *Robotics Age*, Summer 1980, pp. 18-25.

Hill, John W., and Smith, Clement M. "The Microbot Teachmover." *Robotics Today*, July/August 1982.

Hillis, William Daniel. "Active Touch Sensing." MIT Artificial Intelligence Lab Memo 629, April 1981.

Hilts, Philip J. "The Dean of Artificial Intelligence." *Psychology Today*, January 1983, pp. 28-33.

Hirose, Shigeo, and Umetani, Yoji. "Kinematic Control of Active Cord Mechanism with Tactile Sensors." 2nd World Congress on Theory of Machines and Mechanisms, Warsaw, Poland, 1976, pp. 241-252.

——. "The Kinematics and Control of a Soft Gripper for the Handling of Living or Fragile Objects." In *Proceedings*, 2nd World Congress on Theory of Machines and Mechanisms, 1979, pp. 1175-78. Published by American Association for Mechanical Engineers.

——. "The Basic Motion Regulation System for a Quadruped Walking Vehicle." Presented at the Design Engineering Technical Conference, Beverly Hills, 1980.

Hirose, Shigeo, Oda, Shunta, and Umetani, Yoji. "An Active Cord Mechanism with Oblique Swivel Joints and Its Control." In Preprints of 4th World Congress of the International Federation Symposium on the Theory and Practice of Robots and Manipulators, Warsaw, Poland, 1981, pp. 395-407.

Hodges, Andrew. *Alan Turing: The Enigma*. New York: Simon & Schuster, 1983.

Hofstadter, Douglas R., and Dennett, Daniel C., eds., *The Mind's I: Fantasies and Reflections on Self and Soul*. New York: Bantam Books, 1981.

Hogan, Mike. "Meet Rosie the Robotic Riveter." *California Business*, May 1982, p. 88.

Holland, S. W., Rossol, L., and Ward, M. R. "Consight-I: A Vision-Controlled Robot System for Transferring Parts from Belt Conveyors." In *Computer Vision and Sensor-Based Robots*, George G. Dodd and Lothar Rossol, eds. New York: Plenum Publishing, 1979.

Hollerbach, John M. "Workshop on the Design and Control of Dexterous Hands." MIT Artificial Intelligence Lab Memo 661, April 1982.

Holusha, John. "The Robot Makers Stub Their Toes." *New York Times*, 4 March 1984, p. F4.

"Home Robots Are Coming." *Business Week*, 13 December, 1982, p. 62.

Hunt, V. Daniel. *Industrial Robotics Handbook*. New York: Industrial Press, 1983.

Hymowitz, Carol. "Manufacturers Press Automating to Survive, but Results are Mixed." *Wall Street Journal*, 11 April 1983, p. 1.

Industrial Robots: A Summary and Forecast, 2nd ed. Naperville, Ill.: Tech Tran Corporation, 1983.

Ingrassia, Paul, and Darlin, Damon. "Cincinnati Milacron, Mainly a Metal-Bender, Now is a Robot Maker." *Wall Street Journal*, 7 April 1983, p. 1.

Jablonowski, Joseph. "Robots that Assemble." *American Machinist*, November 1981, pp. 175-90.

——. "Just How Many Robots Are Out There?" *American Machinist*, December 1981, pp. 121-22.

——. "Robots: Looking Over the Specifications." *American Machinist*, May 1982, p. 163.

Japan External Trade Organization. "Japanese Industrial Robots" and "Era of Flexible Manufacturing System Arrives." *Japan Industrial & Technological Bulletin*, no. 12, 1982, pp. 1-27.

Japan External Trade Organization. *Industrial Robots*, no. 32, Tokyo, 1981.

Jones, Reginald H. "Energy and Productivity: Opportunities for General Electric." Presentation to financial community representives, Hotel Pierre, New York, 9 December 1980.

Kindel, Stephen, and Brady, Rosemary. "Creative Chaos." *Forbes*, 20 December 1982, pp. 136-43.

Kinnucan, Paul. "How Smart Robots are Becoming Smarter." *High Technology*, September/October 1981, pp. 32-40.

——. "Flexible Systems Invade the Factory." *High Technology*, July 1983, p. 32.

Klein, Charles A., Oson, Karl W., and Pugh, Dennis R. "Use of Force Sensors for Locomotion of a Legged Vehicle Over Irregular Terrain." *International Journal of Robotics Research*, vol. 2, no. 2 (Summer 1983), pp. 3-17.

Krasnoff, Barbara. *Robots: Reel to Real*. New York: Arco Publishing, 1982.

Laskin, Daniel. "Machines that Mock Men." *GEO*, May 1981, pp. 124-44.

Logsdon, Tom., *The Robot Revolution*. New York: Simon & Schuster, 1984.

Lohr, Steve. "The Japanese Challenge." *New York Times Magazine*, 8 July 1984, p. 18.

Lozano-Perez, Tomas. "Robot Programming." MIT Artificial Intelligence Lab Memo 698a, December 1982.

Luria, Daniel. "UAW: We Need Technology." *Tooling and Production*, February 1982, pp. 106-108.

Lustgarten, Eli S. "Robotics and Factory Automation." New York: Paine Webber Mitchell Hutchins, 15 December 1981.

——. "Robotics 1982: Intense Competition Pervades a Weak Market." New York: Paine Webber Mitchell Hutchins, 24 March 1982.

——. "Machine Tool Industry: Is There Life After Detroit?" New York: Paine Webber Mitchell Hutchins, 6 December 1982.

Machine Vision Systems: A Summary and Forecast. Naperville, Ill.: Tech Tran Corporation, 1983.

Macri, Gennaro C., and Calengor, Charles S. "Robots Combine Speed and Accuracy in Dimensional Checks of Automotive Bodies." *Robotics Today*, Summer 1980, pp. 16-19.

Malone, Robert. *The Robot Book*. New York: Harcourt Brace Jovanovich, 1978.

Marcus, Steven J. "Robots' Future Taking Shape." *New York Times*, 18 August 1983, p. D2.

——. "Seeing Robots as Machines." *New York Times*, 7 April 1983, p. D2.

McCarthy, John, Minsky, Marvin L., Rochester, Nathaniel, and Shannon, Claude E. "A Proposal for the Dartmouth Summer Research Project on Artificial Intelligence." Rockefeller Foundation Archives, August 1955.

McCorduck, Pamela. *Machines Who Think*. San Francisco: W. H. Freeman, 1979.

McDermott, Jeanne. "Robots Are Playing New Roles as They Take a Hand in Our Affairs." *Smithsonian*, November 1983, pp. 60-69.

McGlone, Stephen A., Jr. "Army Manufacturing Technology Efforts Using Industrial Robots." U.S. Army Manufacturing Technology Division, 17 April 1983.

Meintel, Alfred J., Jr., and Larson, Ronald L. "NASA Research in Teleoperation and Robotics." Presented at the Society of Photo-Optical Instrumentation Engineers Conference, San Diego, 23 August 1982.

Minsky, Marvin L. "K-Lines: A Theory of Memory." MIT Artificial Intelligence Lab Memo 516, June 1979.

——. "Jokes and the Logic of the Cognitive Unconscious." MIT Artificial Intelligence Lab Memo 603, November 1980.

———. "Why People Think Computers Can't." *Technology Review,* November/December 1983, pp. 65–81.

Minksy, Marvin L. and Papert, Seymour. *Perceptrons.* Cambridge, Mass.: MIT Press, 1969.

Moravec, Hans P. "The CMU Rover." *Proceedings of the National Conference of Artificial Intelligence,* August 1982, pp. 377–80.

Parrett, Tom. "The Rise of the Robot." *Science Digest,* April 1983, p. 68.

Parsons, H. McIlvaine, and Kearsley, Greg P. "Robotics and Human Factors: Current Status and Future Prospects." *Human Factors,* vol. 24, no. 5, October 1982.

Philips, Leonard A. "The Robot Man." *Technology Review,* May/June 1982, p. 37.

Poggio, Tomaso. "Vision by Man and Machine." *Scientific American,* April 1984, pp. 106–16.

———. "Marr's Approach to Vision." MIT Artificial Intelligence Lab Memo 645, August 1981.

Pollack, Andrew. "Getting Robots to Walk." *New York Times,* 26 August 1982, p. D2.

———. "Selling Artificial Intelligence." *New York Times,* 13 September 1982, p. D1.

"The Push for Dominance in Robotics Gains Momentum." *Business Week,* 14 December 1981, p. 71.

Quain, Mitchell I., and Townsend, James B. *Factory Automation.* New York: Wertheim, 1981.

Raibert, Marc H., and Sutherland, Ivan E. "Machines that Walk." *Scientific American,* January 1983, pp. 44–53.

Raphael, Bertram. *The Thinking Computer: Mind Inside Matter.* San Francisco: W. H. Freeman, 1976.

"Recession Even Hits Robots." *New York Times,* 12 January 1983, p. D1.

Reichardt, Jasia. *Robots: Facts, Fiction and Prediction.* New York: Penguin Books, 1978.

Robot Institute of America. *Worldwide Robotics Survey and Directory.* Dearborn, Mich.: Robot Institute of America, 1982.

———. *Worldwide Robotics Survey and Directory.* Dearborn, Mich.: Robot Institute of America, 1983.

"The Robot Revolution." *Time,* 8 December 1980, p. 72.

"The Robots are Coming and They're Bringing a New Industrial Revolution." *Barron's,* 11 April 1983, p. 8.

"Rolls-Royce Target: Batches of One." *FMS Magazine,* January 1983, pp. 90–94.

Rosen, Charles A., and Gleason, G. J. "Evaluating Vision System Performance." *Robotics Today,* Fall 1981.

Rossol, Lothar. "Technological Barriers in Robotics: A Perspective from Industry." Presented at the 1st International Symposium of Robotics Research, Bretton Woods, New Hampshire, August 1983.

Rovetta, Alberto. "A New Robot with Voice, Hearing, Vision, Touch, Grasping, Controlled by One Microprocessor, with Mechanical and Electronic Integrated Design." In *Conference Proceedings of the 13th International Symposium on Industrial Robots and Robots 7.* Dearborn, Mich.: Society of Manufacturing Engineers. 1983, pp. 3-57-3-67.

Ruby, Daniel J. "Computerized Personal Robots." *Popular Science,* May 1983, p. 98.

"Russian Robots Run to Catch Up." *Business Week,* 17 August 1981, p. 120.

Sabliere, Jean. *De L'Automatie à L'Automation.* Paris: Gauthier-Villars, 1966.

Saveriano, Jerry W. "An Interview with Joseph Engelberger." *Robotics Age,* January/February 1981, pp. 10–23.

"SCAMP is Unveiled." *FMS* Magazine, January 1983, pp. 76–79.

Seireg, Ali, and Grundman, Jack G. "Design of a Multitask Exoskeletal Walking Device." In *Biomechanics of Medical Devices,* Dhanjoo N. Ghista, ed. New York: Marcel Dekker, 1980.

Sheridan, Thomas B. "Supervisory Control of Remote Manipulators, Vehicles and Dynamic Processes: Experiments in Command and Display Aiding." MIT Man-Machine System Laboratory Report, 1983.

Silk, Leonard. "Strange New Robotic World." *New York Times,* 4 May 1983, p. D2.

Simpson, J.A., Hocken, R. J., and Albus, J.A. "The Automated Manufacturing Research Facility of the National Bureau of Standards." *Journal of Manufacturing Systems,* vol. 1, no. 1, pp. 17–32.

Smith, Donald N., and Wilson, Richard C. *Industrial Robots: A Delphi Forecast of Markets and Technology.* Dearborn, Mich.: Society of Manufacturing Engineers, 1982.

Society of Manufacturing Engineers. *Conference Proceedings of the 12th International Symposium on Industrial Robots and Robots 6,* Dearborn, Michigan, 1982.

———. *Conference Proceeding of the 13th International Symposium on Industrial Robots and Robots 7,* Dearborn, Michigan, 1983.

Stockton, William. "Creating Computers that Think." *New York Times Magazine,* 7 December 1980, p. 20

Stokes, Henry Scott. "Japan's Love Affair with the Robot." *New York Times Magazine,* 10 January 1982, p. 24.

Susnjara, Ken., *A Manager's Guide to Industrial Robots.* Shaker Heights, Oh.: Corinthian Press, 1982.

Swaine, Michael. "Hobby Robotics." *InfoWorld,* 8 November 1982, p. 25.

———. "How to Talk to a Robot in the Year of Robot Debutantes." *InfoWorld,* vol. 5, no. 5. (1982), p. 24.

Tanner, William R. "Can I Use a Robot?" *Robotics Today,* Spring 1980, p. 43.

"Teaching the Turtle New Tricks. *Time,* 11 October 1982, p. 66.

Tesar, Delbert. "Trip Report: Visits to Major Research Centers in Robotics in Europe and Russia." Mimeographed. Gainesville: University of Florida, 1981.

Thurow, Lester C. "The Case for Industrial Policies." Cambridge, Mass.: MIT Sloan School of Management, 1983.

———. "Losing the Economic Race." *New York Review of Books,* 27 September 1984, pp. 24–31.

Turing, Alan M. "Computing Machinery and Intelligence." *Mind* LIX (1950) 236: 420–60.

U.S. Congress, House and Senate, Subcommittee on Monetary Fiscal Policy of the Joint Economic Committee. *Robotics and the Economy,* A Staff Study. 97th Cong., 2nd sess., 26 March 1982.

U.S. Congress, House and Senate, Subcommittee on Economic Goals and Intergovernmental Policy of the Joint Economic Committee. *The Impact of Robotics on Employment.* 98th Cong., 1st sess., 18 March 1983.

U.S. Congress, Office of Technology Assessment. *Exploratory Workshop on the Social Impacts of Robotics.* July 1981.

U.S. Congress, Office of Technology Assessment. *Computerized Manufacturing Automation: Employment, Education, and the Workplace.* April 1984.

U.S. Congress, Senate, Subcommittee on Science, Technology, and Space of the Committee on Commerce, Science, and Transportation. *Role of Technology in Promoting Industrial Competitiveness.* Hearing on S. 428, S. 632, and S. 1286, 98th Cong., 1st sess., 21 and 23 June 1983.

U.S. International Trade Commission. *Competitive Position of U.S. Producers of Robotics in Domestic and World Markets.* Report on Investigation no. 332-155, Under Section 332(b) of the Tariff Act of 1930, USITC Publication 1475, December 1983.

Villers, Phillipe. "One Vision System Handles Parts Assembly and Weld Seam Tracking." *Sensor Review,* July 1982, p. 122-25.

Waldrop, M. Mitchell. "Artificial Intelligence (I): Into the World." *Science,* 24 February 1984, pp. 802-5.

———. "The Necessity of Knowledge." *Science,* 23 March 1984, pp. 1279-82.

Wellborn, Stanley N. "Machines that Think." *U.S. News and World Report,* 5 December 1983, pp. 59-62.

Wilford, John Noble. "Shuttle's Robotic Arm Hoists Dummy Spacecraft." *New York Times,* 2 September 1983, p. D20.

———. "Shuttle Set for New Effort to Capture Ailing Satellite." *New York Times,* 10 April 1984, p. C1.

———. "Shuttle's Robotic Arm Snares Errant Satellite." *New York Times,* 11 April 1984, p. A1.

Williams, Gurney. "Heath's Hero." *Omni,* January 1983, p. 32.

Winston, Patrick. *Artificial Intelligence.* Cambridge, Mass.: MIT Press, 1984.

Yates, David. "Let Your Robot Do the Walking." *Science Digest,* May 1983, p. 31.

INDEX

We wish to thank the following people and organizations.
Credits are listed by page (top to bottom on pages with more than one photo from different sources).
Credits for color photographs from the inserts are at the end of this section.

BLACK-AND-WHITE PHOTOGRAPHS AND ILLUSTRATIONS

1 Photo courtesy of Photo-Hachette
2 Photo courtesy of the Chapter House of S. Niccolo, Treviso.
3 Photo courtesy of American Heritage
4 Photo courtesy of Photo-Hachette
5 Used by permission of The Bettmann Archive
6 Photo courtesy of Musée Conservatoire Arts et Letiers
7 Used by permission of Granger
8 Used by permission of The MIT Museum./ Reprinted by permission. Copyright © 1962 by International Business Machines Corporation
9 Used by permission of The MIT Museum./Reprinted by permission. Copyright © 1985 by International Business Machines Corporation
10 Used by permission of Harvard University; Cruft Photo Lab
11 Used by permission of Harvard University; Cruft Photo Lab
12 Used by permission of Harvard University; Cruft Photo Lab
13 Photo courtesy of N.Y. Public Library Picture Collection
14 Used by permission of The MIT Museum
15 Photo courtesy of the National Museum of History and Technology
16 Reprinted by permission. Copyright © 1985 by International Business Machines Corporation
17 Reprinted by permission. Copyright © 1985 by International Business Machines Corporation
18 Used by permission of The Bettmann Archive
19 Used by permission of The Franklin Institute
20 Photo courtesy of N.Y. Public Library Picture Collection
21 Used by permission of International Robotics
22 Used by permission of SRI International
23 Photo courtesy of N.Y. Public Library Picture Collection
24 Photo courtesy of N.Y. Public Library Picture Collection
25 Used by permission of Robotics Today
26 Used by permission of Robotics Today
27 Used by permission of George Devol./Bernie Powell
29 Photo from the MOMA Film Stills Archive
31 Used by permission of The Henry Ford Museum
33 Used by permission of The Hughes Aircraft Company
34 Used by permission of The Hughes Aircraft Company
37 Used by permission of Robotics Today
39 Used by permission of General Motors
41 Used by permission of General Motors
43 Used by permission of Prab Robots, Inc.
45 Used by permission of RB Robot Corp., Golden, Colorado. Copyright © 1983 by RB Robot Corporation
47 Photograph of Joe Engelberger copyright © 1982 by McGraw-Hill, Inc. All rights reserved. Used by permission of American Machinist
49 Used by permission of Texas Instruments
50 Used by permission of Nordson Corporation, Amherst, Ohio
51 Used by permission of Expert Automation
52 Used by permission of Expert Automation
53 Photograph copyright © 1982 Advanced Robotics Corporation. All rights reserved. Used by permission of

Lord, Sullivan & Yoder Advertising. Cyror is a registered trademark of Advanced Robotics Corporation
55 Used by permission of U.S. Army
56 Used by permission of Prab Robots, Inc.
59 Used by permission of Binks Manufacturing Company
61 Used by permission of ASEA, Inc.
63 Used by permission of Chrysler Corp.
65 Used by permission of Control Automation (both photos)
67 Used by permission of GCA Corporation, PaR Systems
68 Used by permission of General Dynamics
69 Used by permission of Ametek, Straza Division./ "Grips" Underwater Manipulator System photograph copyright © 1983 by Brett Kraft. All rights reserved. Used by permission of Kraft Ocean Systems, Inc.
71 Used by permission of Chrysler Corp.
73 Used by permission of American Robot
74 Used by permission of American Robot
80 Used by permission of Unimation
81 Used by permission of Unimation
82 Used by permission of Unimation
86 Used by permission of Unimation
87 Used by permission of Unimation
92 Used by permission of Unimation
95 Used by permission of RB Robot Corp., Golden, Colorado. Copyright © 1983 by RB Robot Corporation
97 Used by permission of Heath Company, Benton Harbor, Michigan
99 Used by permission of Tomy Corporation. Omnibot is made and sold by Tomy Corporation
101 "Hero in the Halls of Congress" photograph copyright © 1982 by Gustavo Rincon. All rights reserved. Used by permission of Gustavo Rincon
103 Photograph copyright © 1983 by Roger Ressmeyer. All rights reserved. Used by permission of Roger Ressmeyer./Wheeler Pictures
105 Photograph copyright © 1985 by Harvard Associates Inc. All rights reserved. Used by permission of Harvard Associates, Inc., 260 Beacon Street, Somerville, Massachusetts 02143
107 Photograph copyright.© 1984 by Mark Wexler. All rights reserved. Used by permission of Mark Wexler./ Wheeler Pictures
109 Used by permission of Paul M. Starnes, DeKalb Area Technical School
110 "Turtle making a drawing, Documenta, Kassel, West Germany, 1977. © 1977 by Becky Cohen. All rights reserved. Used by permission of Becky Cohen.
111 Scorpion photograph copyright © 1984 by Rhino Robots, Inc. All rights reserved. Used by permission of Rhino Robots, Inc.
112 Rhino Rite attachment photograph copyright © 1984 by Rhino Robots, Inc. All rights reserved. Used by permission of Rhino Robots, Inc.
113 Used by permission of AP./Wide World Photos
115 Used by permission of ShowAmerica, Inc. "QUADRACON" and "PEEPER" are trademarks and their likenesses are copyrighted 1979 and 1984 by ShowAmerica, Inc., Elmhurst, Illinois, USA
116 Used by permission of AP./Wide World Photos
117 Used by permission of ShowAmerica, Inc. "QUADRACON" and "PEEPER" are trademarks and

their likenesses are copyrighted 1979 and 1984 by ShowAmerica, Inc., Elmhurst, Illinois, USA
118 Used by permission of U.S. Navy, Naval Sea Systems, SEA-90M3, Washington, D.C.
119 "Robot Redford at Work" photograph by Craig Fitch, copyright © 1983 by Superior Robotics of America. All rights reserved. Used by permission of Superior Robots of America
120 Used by permission of International Robotics, Inc.
121 Used by permission of AP./Wide World Photo
122 Used by permission of AP./Wide World Photo
123 Used by permission of General Electric Company
125 Photograph copyright © 1985 by IFS Publications. All rights reserved. Used by permission of IFS Publications, Ltd.
134 Used by permission of AP./Wide World Photo
142 Reprinted by permission. Copyright © 1985 by International Business Machines Corporation
144 Used by permission of General Electric Company
145 Used by permission of General Electric Company
147 Used by permission of General Electric Company
149 Used by permission of Hitachi America, Ltd., Industrial Components Sales and Service Division
151 Used by permission of Renault USA, Inc.
153 Used by permission of Expert Automation
154 Used by permission of Fiat Auto S.p.A.
155 Photograph copyright © 1985 by IFS Publications. All rights reserved. Used by permission of IFS Publications, Ltd.
156 Photograph copyright © 1985 by W. B. Heginbotham. All rights reserved. Used by permission of Professor W. B. Heginbotham, O.B.E. D.S.C., Nottingham, England
157 Photograph copyright © 1985 by IFS Publications. All rights reserved. Used by permission of IFS Publications, Ltd.
158 Photograph copyright © 1985 by W. B. Heginbotham. All rights reserved. Used by permission of Professor W. B. Heginbotham, O.B.E. D.S.C. Nottingham, England
159 Used by permission of General Electric Company
160 Used by permission of GMF Robotics
161 Used by permission of GMF Robotics
163 Photograph copyright © 1985 by IFS Publications. All rights reserved. Used by permission of IFS Publications, Ltd.
164 Photograph copyright © by IFS Publications. All rights reserved. Used by permission of IFS Publications, Ltd.
165 Reprinted by permission from Robotics Age, Inc., 174 Concord Street, Peterborough, New Hampshire
167 Used by permission of AP./Wide World Photos
169 Cognex Eye copyright © 1985 by Cognex Corp. All rights reserved. Used by permission of Judy Cobb.
175 Used by permission of General Motors./Used by permission of General Motors
179 Used by permission of Hitachi, Ltd. Mechanical Engineering Research Lab
181 Used by permission of Professor Ali Seireg. Walking machine developed at the University of Wisconsin— Madison under the supervision of Professor Ali Seireg (both photographs)
183 Used by permission of AP./Wide World Photos
184 Used by permission of Odetics, Inc.

185 Used by permission of Odetics, Inc.
187 Reprinted by permission from Robotics Age, Inc.,
174 Concord Street, Peterborough, New Hampshire (all
six photos)
189 Photo of the robot designed by Prof. Hirose. Copyright
© 1985 by Shigeo Hirose. All rights reserved. Used by
permission of Shigeo Hirose.
191 Photos of the robots designed by Prof. Hirose.
Copyright © 1985 by Shigeo Hirose. All rights reserved.
Used by permission of Shigeo Hirose (both photos).
192 Photo of the robot designed by Prof. Hirose. Copyright
© 1985 by Shigeo Hirose. All rights reserved. Used by
permission of Shigeo Hirose.
193 Photo courtesy of NASA
195 Used by permission of Ivan Sutherland
197 Photo courtesy of NASA
199 Used by permission of The MIT Museum
201 Photo courtesy of N.Y. Public Library Picture
Collection
202 Photo from MOMA Film Stills Archive
203 Photo from MOMA Film Stills Archive. Courtesy of
MGM./Used by permission of International Robotics
205 Photo from MOMA Film Stills Archive. Copyright ©
1960 by Allied Artists
206 Photo from MOMA Film Stills Archive. Courtesy of
Republic Pictures
207 Copyright © 1984 by Robert Ramer. Used by
permission of the artist
208 Photo from Smithsonian Library. Courtesy of MGM
209 Photo from MOMA Film Stills Archive. Courtesy of
MGM
210 Photo from MOMA Film Stills Archive. Courtesy of
Universal
211 Photo from MOMA Film Stills Archive. Courtesy of
Universal
213 Photo from MOMA Film Stills Archive. Copyright ©
1973 by United Artists Corporation
215 Photograph copyright © Lucasfilm, Ltd. (LFL) 1977.
All rights reserved. Courtesy of Lucasfilm, Ltd.
217 Astro Boy copyright © 1985 Tezuka Productions. All
rights reserved. Used by permission of Tezuka
Productions
219 Photo from N.Y. Public Library Picture Collection
220 Copyright © 1984 by Robert Ramer. Used by
permission of the artist (both illustrations)
221 Used by permission of Prab Robots, Inc.
222 Photo from MOMA Film Stills Archive. Courtesy of
MGM/Loew's Incorporated
223 Photo from MOMA Film Stills Archive. Copyright ©
1957 by Loew's Incorporated
225 Photo from N.Y. Public Library Picture Collection
227 Photo from N.Y. Public Library Picture Collection
229 Used by permission of International Robotics (both
photos)

COLOR PHOTOGRAPHS

INSERT A follows page 54

1 Used by permission of Unimation
2 Used by permission of Thermwood
3 Used by permission of Prab Robots, Inc./Used by
permission of Cincinnati Milacron
4 Used by permission of GMF Robotics./Used by
permission of Unimation
5 Used by permission of Prab Robots, Inc.
6 Used by permission of Prab Robots, Inc.
7 Used by permission of General Electric Company./
Used by permission of GMF Robotics
8 Used by permission of General Electric Company (both
photos)
9 Used by permission of General Electric Company
10 Used by permission of General Motors./Used by
permission of Los Alamos National Laboratory
11 Used by permission of Unimation./Used by permission
of Tetra Tech Hydro Products
12 Photograph copyright © by Dan McCoy. All rights
reserved. Used by permission of Dan McCoy

INSERT B follows page 118

1 Used by permission of Heath Company, Benton Harbor,
Michigan
2 Photograph copyright © 1984 by Mark Wexler. All
rights reserved. Used by permission of Mark Wexler./
Wheeler Pictures
3 Photograph copyright © 1984 by Mark Wexler. All
rights reserved. Used by permission of Mark Wexler./
Wheeler Pictures
4 Photograph copyright © 1983 by Roger Ressmeyer. All

rights reserved. Used by permission of Roger
Ressmeyer./Wheeler Pictures
5 Photograph copyright © 1983 by Roger Ressmeyer. All
rights reserved. Used by permission of Roger
Ressmeyer./Wheeler Pictures
6 Photograph copyright © 1985 by George Fischer. All
rights reserved. Used by permission of George Fischer
7 Used by permission of Renault USA, Inc.
8 Used by permission of Renault USA, Inc.
9 Used by permission of Renault USA, Inc.
10 Used by permission of Comau
11 Used by permission of GMF Robotics
12 Used by permission of GMF Robotics

INSERT C follows page 182

1 Used by permission of General Electric Company
2 Photograph copyright © 1984 by Mark Wexler. All
rights reserved. Used by permission of Mark Wexler./
Wheeler Pictures
3 Used by permission of Odetics, Inc. (both photos)
4 Photo courtesy of NASA
5 Photo courtesy of NASA
6-7 Photo of the robot designed by Prof. Hirose. Copyright
© 1985 by Shigeo Hirose. All rights reserved. Used by
permission of Shigeo Hirose.
8 "The Clock Man" copyright © 1978 by Walter Einsel.
All rights reserved. Used by permission of Walter Einsel.
9 Astro Boy copyright © Tezuka Productions. All rights
reserved. Used by permission of Tezuka Productions
10 Copyright © 1985 Tezuka Productions. All rights
reserved. Used by permission of Tezuka Productions
11 Copyright © 1985 by Tezuka Productions. All rights
reserved. Used by permission of Tezuka Productions
12 Used by permission of Toby Buonagurio, Gallery Yves
Arman, New York City